Standard Usage

of hers

... the pertinent sections of chapter 8 to understand and correct your errors.

Spelling

Make a study of your habitual spelling errors. Though overrated as a public measure of educated intelligence, correct spelling should not be underrated in importance. It is in fact because of this public misperception that correct spelling is especially to be observed.

Punctuation

Give close attention to the not-so-little matters of punctuation. Be aware that punctuation clarifies sentence structure and therefore requires some grammatical knowledge. For a review of grammatical principles and forms, see Appendix A, **Basic Sentence Analysis,** and Appendix B, **Glossary of Grammatical Terms.**

Grammar

Observe accurate grammatical usage in order to give maximum impact to your ideas and spare your reader annoying distractions.

Standard Form

Conform to professional standards for academic writing. Refer to chapter 9 for guidelines and examples.

Format and Layout

Show respect for your written assignment by making sure it meets specifications concerning manuscript form.

MLA Documentation

Accept your responsibility to identify your sources accurately and honestly. Use consistently your instructor's requested style of documentation.

A Comparison of Styles

MLA
CMS
APA
CBE
    Author–Year
    Numerical Coding
       Alphabetical
       Consecutive

Online and Electronic Sources

COLLEGE
Writing

Ronald Horton

BJU PRESS

GREENVILLE, SOUTH CAROLINA

Note:
The fact that materials produced by other publishers may be referred to in this volume does not constitute an endorsement by Bob Jones University Press of the content or theological position of materials produced by such publishers. The position of Bob Jones University Press, and of the University itself, is well known. Any references and ancillary materials are listed as an aid to the student or the teacher and in an attempt to maintain the accepted academic standards of the publishing industry.

College Writing

Ronald Horton, Ph.D.
Professor of English, Bob Jones University

Produced in cooperation with the Department of English in the Division of English Language and Literature of the College of Arts and Science, Bob Jones University.

Portions of this book were published previously in *Sentence Review* (© 1998, 2000 Bob Jones University Press) and *Companion to College English,* Second Edition (© 2000 Bob Jones University Press).

Project Manager: Richard Ayers
Compositor: Szymon Kryston
Designer: Wendy Searles

Cover (background): PhotoDisc, Inc.

ISBN 1-57924-810-1

15 14 13 12 11 10 9 8 7 6 5 4 3 2 1

How forcible are right words!

JOB 6:25

Contents

PREFACE

Though this book is the labor of less than a year, it is in very real ways the product of forty years of teaching the elements of writing. Thanks are in order to the thousands of students whose improvement in writing has been a personal challenge for them and this teacher alike. Thanks are also due to the colleagues who have toiled with me in this long effort through the years and whose experience plays into what is offered here in countless ways. Special thanks are in order for the discerning, diligent work of the book's project director, Steven Skaggs, and project editor, Rebecca Moore, who determined to help me bring the book to birth during Bob Jones University's seventy-fifth year. And I am grateful as well to Don Congdon for providing this text's information regarding online and electronic sources.

A famous poet once told the story of a venerable old oak who was verbally assailed by a "bragging briar," spinning off Jotham's fable in Judges 9:8–15. The jeering, eloquent briar, who was supported by the oak, denounced the oak to the husbandman in most contemptuous terms, insisting on its total worthlessness. The old oak huffed and sputtered, trying to get his thoughts in order and find words for them. Before he could do so, the husbandman returned with his axe and cut down the tree. When winter came, the briar, who had been supported by the tree, also came to dismal ruin.

The moral of Edmund Spenser's fable is the age-old tragedy of inarticulate wisdom. The fool is ready to utter his falsehood and has the skills to do so persuasively. The wise are unable or unready to counter with the truth. It is to the enablement of articulate wisdom that the present work is prayerfully dedicated.

INTRODUCTION

Written assignments were once a major component of almost all college courses. The weekly or biweekly essay vitalized the learning process. Carefully read, returned, and discussed with the student, it brought together the best thinking of the student and his instructor. It drove student progress not only in course knowledge but also in general intellectual skills. A lengthy course paper was the capstone of the student's learning experience.

Though the written component of college courses is neither so large nor so universal as it once was, it has by no means disappeared, and for good reason. Prospective employers and directors of graduate admissions still consider a portfolio of well-written papers strong evidence to supplement transcript data and practical experience. Copies of graded and critiqued papers may in fact be a required part of application materials. It is well known that academic writing develops skills that benefit business and the professions and that a well-written paper can certify intellectual maturity and competence.

Though we cannot reasonably hope to restore the essay and the documented paper to the place they once held in higher education, we can try to make the written assignment more manageable, for student and instructor alike. Such is the aim, at least, of *College Writing*. Like other guidebooks, it shows both the general route ("The Writer's Path") and major points of interest and concern ("The Writer's Reference"). Perhaps it may even, here and there, spark some enthusiasm for the journey.

Part

ONE

The
Writer's
Path

Chapter 1

Commit

The urge to express an opinion is a deeply human trait. Most of us are ready on an instant to give our views on a subject of interest, especially if it is tied to a deep conviction. But this urge to persuade is not so compelling when we are asked to argue our view in a formal public setting.

One such setting is the college written assignment. Who would want to display his reasoning to an eager critic, stuffed with facts and bristling with standards and rules? Who would not prefer to keep his views to himself under such conditions?

Yes, the need to submit a paper for critical review can be daunting, especially when the paper is a major course requirement. Tensions rise when personal stakes are high. No doubt the best antidote for such anxiety is to be well informed and to have had previous success. But in the meantime anxiety can be made to work for you if it is tempered by faith. In fact, God often builds our faith through facing us with the unknown. Responding to a writing assignment is a venture into the unknown, all the more so when the process of writing is not a skill established by long habit. It is an act of faith, for it requires you to believe that your efforts can unite with God's to produce a fully formed, satisfactory document.

Responding to a writing assignment is also an act of obedience, for faith involves obedience. Your instructor draws his authority from God, and a proper response to any class assignment is one that receives it as a divine command. The assignment itself may be open to question, as are all things human, but the need to perform it conscientiously is not. You should apply yourself to your instructor's requirements with the same seriousness with which you try to carry out all the commands of God.

Commit the task to God and commit yourself to the task. Receiving and obeying instructions is part of the fabric of life. Believing that there is divine purpose in far more odious challenges than writing a paper will strengthen the spirit and sweeten the labor. Give yourself generously and wholeheartedly to the work. God will see to it that your invested time and effort are not lost. Like that bread "cast upon the waters," it will return to you in good time (Eccles. 11:1).

Chapter 2

Conceptualize

One need not be drawn into New Age mental imaging to recognize the importance of visualizing a task one intends to do. The prudent man of Scripture does just that, sizing up his project, weighing its possibilities and perils, and calculating the cost.

So it is that what you write can hardly become better than your preconception of it—what an Elizabethan writer called the author's "fore-conceit." It is here that student writing often starts to go wrong. The writing begins too soon when it lacks the front-end thinking necessary to a precise formulation of the task. The student writer does not know where he is going, exactly, but he is on his way. An experienced writer knows he must allow his idea time to mature into a fully formed conceptualization if a lucid, coherent essay is to result.

Taking time to think about what you are going to write is especially important when the writing takes you into unfamiliar territory. In academic writing a student is being apprenticed to procedures that are broadly applicable in life but are specifically applicable only to the professions. He is showing he can work independently in a predetermined subject area and write up his findings in keeping with the standards of scholarship and his chosen profession. His task is more challenging than ordinary writing because it is not yet natural to him, being restricted by a formal discipline whose concepts and terminologies are still unfamiliar to him. He confronts a twofold challenge.

He must, like all writers, strive to be convincing and clear. But he must also, meanwhile, adapt to a quasi-professional situation with customs and standards and idioms he has not yet fully learned. Like David, asked to fight Goliath in the armor of Saul, he may be inclined to say, "I cannot go with these; for I have not proved them." In extreme cases, he may decide to "put them off him" and do the job his own way—with less success, of course, than David.

Understanding the task—getting well in mind the nature and responsibilities of academic writing—is the first requirement of front-end thinking for a college written assignment, and it is to this concern that we now turn.

CONTEXT

The author of a well-regarded book on style, John Trimble, makes this key observation: "The thinking process of a skilled writer is directly determined by how he conceives the writing situation" (*Writing with Style: Conversations on the Art of Writing,* 1975, p. 16). Trimble compares growing up in writing to becoming an adult in normal life. The threshold of maturity is the same in both: the emerging of "social sensitivity." The novice writer, like a child, becomes aware of a world of people beyond himself and sees the importance of their needs and interests. He gets centered outside himself.

This decentering, as Trimble says, is a "dawning realization," but it is also a willed action. It must be, for college writing requires subjection to a highly specific and potentially demanding set of reader expectations. The writing situation you must conceptualize is predetermined and **prescriptive.**

Is the paper to be a personal essay? a report using sources? a documented argument? Is it limited to five hundred words? Is it a ten-page paper requiring an annotated bibliography? If it requires a title page, is there a form for it? If it requires an outline, does the outline use sentence or topic headings? Does it require references to four sources excluding the textbook? Are at least two of these sources to be books published within the last ten years? Should the documentation style be that of the *Chicago Manual of Style* (CMS), the American Psychological Association (APA), the Council of Biology Editors (CBE), or the Modern Language Association (MLA), or does your choice of style not matter so long as you use it consistently?

Specifications such as these are under the jurisdiction of your instructor. They may be many or few, detailed or general, strictly to be observed or somewhat flexible. But they are to be taken seriously. They are designed to support course objectives, acquainting you with academic and professional standards, involving you more deeply with course content, and developing mature mental discipline. Take care to understand what is expected of you, and follow the instructions precisely.

The context of your assigned writing then is narrowly course related, reflecting the learning objectives, and sometimes even personal preferences, of the instructor. It is also prescriptive in a more general sense. College writing is convention bound. It calls for plain, forthright, well-ordered expression, not fancy, wordy, laborious prose. It also observes the standards of educated usage in grammar, punctuation, and mechanics, features explained in Part 2. These conventions are to some extent arbitrary and artificial; but, like social manners, they are no less important for being so, and most have logic behind them. The reader of your paper will expect, then, writing that is direct and correct. You will not want to disappoint him.

An area of special concern in conventional expectations is the use of sources. Professional standards and personal honesty require your acknowledging all personal help and fully disclosing all indebtedness to authored material for borrowed ideas and words. Carelessness here can be severely damaging to a course grade and even to academic standing. This requirement is explained in Part 2.

The context of college writing is then firmly prescriptive. It asks you to conform diligently and in good humor to a set of expectations that were established long before you began college work and will exist long after you have finished. Your writing therefore will be somewhat constrained by background considerations foreign to your customary style. But fortunately the situation is also **personal.** It asks you to speak in your own voice, to be yourself, in conversation with another person, a reader who is not yourself.

The need to be yourself may seem so obvious as to be hardly worth mentioning. But false writer identities can cause problems that ripple through the entire writing process. It is true that each of us has multiple versions of himself that come into play in different situations. Yet within these diverse facets of a personality is a single voice that is recognizably and genuinely ours. Whether we give a report for a class, read Scripture in a church service, enjoy a telephone conversation with a friend, or advise a younger sibling, we are easily known. Our variations of manner are not role-playing. Within them we are still ourselves.

Which of these personal manners is appropriate for our college writing? Certainly not a false manner. You do not become an instant world authority when you research a subject for two hours, or even two days. You do not become a prophet-sage by meditating on a universal human problem for thirty minutes. You are not a professional scholar, social critic, preacher, celebrity intellectual, or candidate for election. You do not write with the assurance of one who has lived fifty years in the world and seen life from many angles or with the emotional eagerness and urgency of a zealot.

Most of us have grown up in a sermon culture that encourages strong moral convictions and ready proclamation of the truth. The desire to correct, admonish, and exhort is bred into us. If we are not careful, this desire will cause us to misconceive our writing situation and will take over our writing project. Our tone will become aggressively self-assured and our style tense and pontifical. As a result we will seem false to ourselves and foolish to our reader.

This impulse toward a false manner is abetted by a sense of insecurity. The college writer, especially the beginning writer, is a novice, both with respect to his subject area and with regard to his ability to write about it in a standard way. To compensate for his inexperience, he may try to dress up his style in ways that are unnatural to him, using big words imprecisely and complicating his sentence structure beyond his skill. He is not himself, and he knows it. For him, writing becomes a painfully awkward exercise in role-playing. It shows in strained effects of style that fake the competence he lacks. False mannerisms are hard to control when one is thrust on stage.

Also, the beginner may come to realize that it is actually easier with a little practice to write obscurely in a fancy way than to write simply and clearly. Such writing also can fill space when one's ideas are imperfectly formed and unready for public exposure. Stilted expression serves the purpose of vague thought better than clear, direct expression. Oscar Wilde said it wryly: "If you write intelligibly, you run the risk of being found out."

So, be yourself; but "which self?" is still the question. Here is where you need to stop and sketch in your mind the full writing situation. It contains, as it were, a speaker and a responding audience. Who is this audience, and what sort of speaker does it want and expect? What kind is suitable to the occasion? For the situation is not only personal but **public.**

The audience, of course, is your instructor, but he will not read your paper as if it were written to himself. He will regard himself as proxy for a wider audience of persons interested in your subject. Your paper is being, as it were, filtered through him on its way to this phantom audience of readers. Create a mental image of a representative member of this audience as your real reader. Give him a face and a personality and an interest level just adequate to prompt a glance at what you have done. Your challenge then will be to write in such a way as to hold his interest and leave him benefited by what he has read.

You will accept your role as this reader's servant, a conduit of useful information on a subject of value and interest. Your proposed reader has something to gain, you believe, by accepting your conclusion, and so you will support your thesis solidly and argue it vigorously, underscoring your key points. This reader is willing to listen, willing to be convinced, but no pushover. Imagine in him your own agreeable but critical self.

COST

In college writing, as in business, "costing a job" is crucial to succeeding in it. Accurate cost assessment is necessary to cost containment, which in turn determines profit. But whereas a contractor is free to turn down a job that exceeds his resources, a student must trim the job according to his cost analysis. He must suit the assigned task to his available time, knowledge, materials, and maturity. Ordinarily he will be allowed some flexibility. He will be given a range of subject options. He can narrow a subject—take a slice of it—to create a manageable topic. He can choose from a prescribed group or category of subjects. He can limit his claim to match the scope of his research (see below). Since he knows the assignment deadline weeks in advance, he can begin early to get at least the preliminaries done. But there is nothing more important to the success of a college paper than taking stock of assets and cutting the job down to manageable size.

Obviously the starting point is to know fully the mind of your instructor concerning the nature and size of your task. Pay close attention to oral and written instructions. Be willing to ask for clarification. You will want to be clear about all the particulars of the assignment that will make demands on your time and resources and affect the payoff. How long must the paper be—500 words? 1500 words? 5000 words? This is always the first question asked, and it is important since it has a bearing on the time allotted to the task and the thoroughness expected by your instructor. But it by no means tells the whole story. A short paper can take longer to do well than a long one. In how much depth must the paper treat its subject? Is it to be heavily informational? Is it a documented paper requiring investigation of sources? Must the subject be extensively researched? Is it a comprehensive survey, or may it focus narrowly on a small consideration? May it do either? How much range of choice and freedom of approach is allowable in the selection of subject? How important is creative, original thought—the writer's own thinking about the subject—or may the paper be largely derivative (with proper acknowledgment of indebtedness, of course)? How formally is the material to be presented? Is a certain format specified? Are you to use a particular documentation style?

The answers to these questions will indicate your cost in time and concentrated effort. Estimate your time in hours and budget for it. It is better to distribute the total over a length of days for two reasons. First, beginning early will allow you a safety margin to increase your time investment if you have underestimated the time or to cut back on what you had intended to do. If you discover the demands of the task exceeding the time available, rethink the scope of your undertaking; distinguish between the inflexible, preset requirements (length, subject area, library support, etc.) and the variables (extent of subject, number of sources, etc.) and determine what can be trimmed without loss. A high-quality focused effort may succeed better than a mediocre expansive one. Second, it will allow time for your ideas to coalesce and mature in the background of your thinking. Our sense of what we are doing or need to be doing has a strange way of taking shape over time. In all creativity the elements of design fall into harmonious, fully formed order only gradually, through an emergent process that cannot be hurried.

Cost assessment in writing as in business improves with experience. Inexperienced writers worry about generating enough content to meet the minimum length of the assigned paper and may compensate in either or both of two ways. They may widen their subject beyond reasonable limits. The result is writer's block and procrastination, superficial or quirky treatment of the subject, and often late submission of a roughly written and poorly proofread paper. If, on the other hand, these writers discover that their content is too small for their purpose, they may try to stretch it by dragging in irrelevancies or by recycling relevancies so that the same idea reappears in different verbal guise. Either way, the result is a loose, verbose effect, easily recognized and universally condemned as padding. Accurate cost estimation together with serious disciplined commitment skirts these dangers.

CONTENT

From cost assessment should come a projection of the breadth and depth of the paper's content. Plan to generate more than enough idea content and factual material to meet the minimum requirement of your envisioned paper. If you stop below the minimum level, you will be forcing connections and stretching ideas to fill space, trying to work as much mileage as possible out of what you have collected. That is not the kind of economy that your instructor admires! If you stop at the minimum level, you will draw on all that you have dredged up in your investigation, first-, second-, and third-rate, and perhaps worse, piecing together a patchwork of uneven, ill-assembled, loosely relevant information. How much better it is to continue your gathering until you have the luxury of selecting only the best from your heap of ideas and facts, those items that carry the most logical and persuasive weight and that fit together most naturally. A filmmaker shoots much more film than he will actually use. In his editing, he will keep only the very best and most useful of his materials and leave the rest (some quite good) on the cutting-room floor.

Your instructions will indicate whether your paper is intended to be heavily informational, the result of research, or whether it is meant to be personal-analytical, mostly from your own head. But in almost all academic writing there is the assumption that the bulk of the content will consist of factual specifics, either the product of research or the details of analysis. A common failing in student writing is due to the opposite assumption: that space-filling generalization, if accurate and eloquent, can constitute the bulk of the paper's substance. The right to deliver a generalization must be earned with evidence and analysis. Concrete substance will be needed as ballast for your high-soaring observations.

Most good papers written in college will be mindful of sources, regardless of how little the papers may be required to draw from them. You need as early as possible to have a general sense of how much research content your paper's topic requires so that you can budget time for gathering it. Whether your paper is to be broadly grounded in research, studded with quotations and specific references to sources, or is to be mostly spun out of your own thinking with perhaps a quotation to start the introduction or a factual reference here or there to anchor a generalization, gauging the amount of derivative content is important to your estimate of the total job.

As mentioned above, you should allow for a search long enough to let you accumulate several times the amount of source material your paper will have space for. You want to be in the position of being able to select from your pile of notes only those quotations and factual references most supportive of your purpose. You want your citations to underpin and ornament your argument, not weigh it down. Make a generous allowance for the gathering of necessary source materials. Whether substantive or mainly decorative, references to sources, when managed well, indicate academic competence and maturity.

The best papers written for college also show the imprint of an individual mind. As indicated, they are both public—conscious of a larger audience—and personal. An ordinary, acceptable informational paper will present the facts of research, packaged sensibly, tagging on the obvious conclusion, with little sense of a processing mind—little analysis, little interpretation, little sense of a question raised and answered, a problem posed and solved, a curiosity aroused and satisfied. The best papers take the reader on a journey the writer has traveled, giving a sense of unfolding realization, of progressive discovery. The writer has thought his way along his reader's path and has smoothed it for him. (This can be done, by the way, without reliance on personal references, without the pronouns *I* and *you*.) There is a vibrant persuasive thrust, even in what could otherwise seem the most pedestrian matter-of-fact explanation. As a narrative of your (and your reader's) mental journey, your account of a potentially dull subject can have a human side. It can bear the stamp of your personality. It can vitalize your discussion and make your subject appear interesting and important to your reader.

How is this done? It is not done by adopting a casual familiarity of manner that assumes a preexisting relationship between writer and reader that does not exist and reveals the writer more than what he is writing about. It emerges through a strictly coherent line of thought in which thoughts succeed each other with intellectual pressure and precision and with no waste motion. The reader senses an energetic mind, pressing ahead, steering, staging, ramifying, pausing in places to consolidate before renewing its forward motion. Transitional words, phrases, sentences, and even short paragraphs signpost the thought path and provide resting points for him, keeping him mindful of his guide. The reader feels he is following a track well laid out by someone who keeps him in mind. He senses a living, breathing person behind the ideas being delivered to him. Raw content has been collected and processed in an individual way and with the intention of engaging other minds. It is this sense of a participating author that helps to enliven the work of the best writers of history and science, for example, and to keep them well represented on best-seller lists. The writer's own mind appears inextricably involved with his accumulated content.

So you need to budget time for reflective thinking. Your concepts need time to solidify, sharpen, and harmonize. Your creative processes need time to work upon the inert mass of ideas and facts you have assembled. Imagination must come into play along with logical analysis and synthesis. Solutions to questions of adding and curtailing, of joining and segmenting, do not always come on demand and are not always worked out consciously. It takes time to make a body of content your own.

CLAIM

Content, like everything else in a piece of writing, is subservient to the writer's purpose. Something is to be achieved in the thinking of a reader. His thinking is to be corrected or confirmed or otherwise vitalized on some point of importance to the writer. This point will be the writer's thesis.

You may wonder why the thesis, which is the conclusion of a paper and the outgrowth of the thinking that has gone into the paper, should be considered a preconception. Why should formulation of the thesis belong to the preliminaries, the conceptualizing stage?

Preconceiving the thesis is important for the same reason that preformulating a hypothesis is important in scientific investigation. Every investigative effort needs the kind of direction that a hypothetical pre-stated conclusion can provide. Whatever your writing task, research or otherwise, your mental universe of possibilities concerning your subject needs a center in the form of an assertion. The point you think you will be proving should be available to you from the beginning in a trial form.

The thesis at this juncture is, again, highly tentative. It originates with a question that you expect your research and reflection to answer and a guess at the answer—an educated guess, of course. Throughout the later stages of your thinking and collecting of materials, your thesis is subject to change and refinement. For now, it needs to be out there, in front of you. Eventually it will amount to more than something proposed. You will commit to it. It will become a claim, a claim *about* your subject. Having only a subject or a topic is not having enough.

Making a claim is what good papers do and what poor papers do not do. This is an exaggeration but only a slight one. The author of a textbook on critical thinking and arguing observes that "perhaps the most common mistake of speakers and writers is to fail to make clear their conclusions" (James Herrick, *Critical Thinking: The Analysis of Arguments,* 1991, p. 273). He could just as well have put it "fail to make a definite claim." A well-formed claim, or thesis, gives shape to the writing process and strong alignment of parts to the product of that process, the fully formed paper. Without it the writer is contending for he knows not what—if, indeed, he is contending at all.

In forming your preliminary or tentative thesis, be sure that it makes a substantial claim. A workable thesis is not a known fact or a mere truism, something already known or believed by your reader. As a claim it must require proving. A debate is not possible on an issue on which both sides agree. A trial does not materialize when plaintiff and defendant have composed their differences. A teaching session is pointless when the learner already understands what is being taught.

A workable thesis then is **controversial**—better yet, provocative. To be certain your thesis is controversial, try to write an opposing assertion—an anti-thesis—that your argument will require your reader to reject. If you cannot produce an assertion that conflicts credibly with your thesis, then your thesis is not sufficiently controversial to amount to a meaningful claim.

If your tentative thesis passes the test of controversiality, test it for verifiability. Take your anti-thesis as your claim and back it with the strongest reasons and evidence you can generate against your thesis. Construct a counterargument that contains the proofs that your intended argument will need to defeat. Then, having considered the strength of your counterargument, determine whether your tentative thesis is maintainable. If the counterargument is the stronger of the two, your thesis is not sufficiently **verifiable** to amount to a successful claim.

If your thesis survives the test of verifiability, check its form. A useful thesis statement is assertive, not timid. "It seems as if" or "It would be true that" or "It appears to me that" is not the way to begin an arguable proposition. Though your thesis is tentative—subject to modification and even rejection during the remainder of the writing process—it needs to be asserted clearly and forthrightly. Even if only a guess, it can and should be expressed as a strongly **declarative** guess.

A workable thesis statement is also **single** and **simple.** Avoid a "double-barreled" thesis, which combines two statements into one:

> The animal-rights movement is an offshoot of Darwinism, and its position downgrades human life.

Likewise, avoid compound subjects and predicates in a thesis statement.

> *The animal-rights movement and environmentalism* downgrade human life.

> The animal-rights movement *is an offshoot of Darwinism and downgrades human life.*

Compound structure in a thesis statement produces a double focus in a paper. Two arguments, though perhaps related, get coupled together in parallel formation, weakening unity. If the compound elements are more than two, the focus will be multiple.

Frequently the compound elements can be reordered so as to provide a single focus, as in the two examples below.

> The animal-rights movement, an offshoot of Darwinism, downgrades human life.

> Darwinism has produced advocacy movements that downgrade human life.

Notice how unity and clarity increase when the lesser elements are precisely subordinated to the greater.

Avoid decorative elements in your thesis statement.

> Darwinism has spawned advocacy movements that drag down humanity to the level of the merest gnat.

Keep it plain and concise, free of emotive and figurative expression. Adapted for incorporation into your paper, your thesis statement may take on emotional coloration, particularly when reasserted at the end; but for now you need a working thesis that shows with the greatest clarity and accuracy what is contained in your claim.

It is uncanny how often problems in a paper can be traced to flaws in the content and even form of the thesis statement. As a rule, your paper will be no more clear, coherent, and convincing than the statement it purports to prove. Water cannot flow higher than its source. Put your best thought into staking out your claim.

Collect

If your topic requires documented support, you are now ready to lay out a task of reading and proceed with it. Consult your instructor for the best sources for your topic. He may point you to an authoritative book or a key article. He may recommend your textbook—suggestions for further reading, a selected bibliography, chapter notes—as a good place to start. He also can acquaint you with the standard reference tools in your discipline. Be cost conscious. Utilize the near at hand before pursuing what will require more time and effort.

To expand your list of possible sources, you will probably go first to the college library. If the library contains specialized annotated bibliographies in the area of your subject, they can shorten and sharpen your search. Then you will check the online catalog of the library to add recent titles not appearing in the bibliographies you have scanned. Consult the library staff for helpful search methods if these are unfamiliar to you. Once you have been directed to the area in the stacks primarily concerned with your subject, take a few minutes to browse in that area for books of value that may have escaped your online catalog search.

While searching the online library catalog for books, do not neglect the periodical bibliographies that cover journals in your field. Notice in their listings promising titles of articles from journals carried by the library and add the article information to your reading list.

Think always in terms of keeping your search within practical limits, restricting your sources to those that you can determine are directly valuable. Before checking out a book from the library, glance at its table of contents to get a sense of its scope and focus. Scan its index for words and phrases that link with your topic and look up the passages to which they refer. Size up its usefulness on the spot. If it has little value for your study or if its useful passages can be easily photocopied or written on cards, finish with it there and return it to its shelf. It will mean one less book to carry home—to weigh on your back and on your mind. A tall stack of books can be more a hindrance than a help, causing mind block and ultimately a paper that is only a patchwork of quotations. Also a book returned to the shelf will remain available to another researcher to discover and find useful.

The Internet, used discriminately, can be useful in your search. It is becoming increasingly important as a quick, practical source for factual content of all kinds. There are pitfalls, however, to Internet research. Internet information is notoriously uneven in authority and value. Therefore, corroboration from other informational sources is often wise. Keep in touch with your instructor concerning what is admissible and useful from the Internet and what is not and also concerning how to document the content you use.

Be sure not to undervalue and overlook encyclopedias, almanacs, yearbooks, statistical compilations, and other fact books, as well as biographical reference works. These contain a wealth of concrete detail on a vast range of subjects especially useful in lighter essays to introduce a point or pin down an observation. (Journalists, for example, rely on factual data from the *Congressional Record* and the governmental *Statistical Abstract* to start their discussions of issues.) A scholarly encyclopedia article may be a good place to introduce yourself to a subject in which you are interested but about which you have little previous knowledge.

If your paper will incorporate a large amount of source material, you should first quickly survey the articles and books you have accumulated and target what seems of genuine value, if you have not already done so. Then read thoughtfully the promising materials and write on separate cards, one idea per card, the passages of possible use to you. Include all bibliographical information necessary to identify and locate the cited content. Summarize or paraphrase unless direct quotation would add authority or special zest to the point you are supporting. Be sure to set off in quotation marks all verbatim quotation and thoroughly change the wording of whatever is not thus set off. Carelessness at this stage can result in plagiarism in the final paper.

NOTE CARDS

If your paper will use more than just a few sources, you will find it efficient to record the bibliographical facts of each source on a small (3" × 5") file card. As you continue to find sources and fill out cards for them, you can add the titles to your stack without disturbing alphabetical order. This method will enable you to find a source in your collection quickly at any time. It will also provide for rapid compiling of the final reference list for inclusion in your paper. There will be room on the card also for indicating promising pages and sections for later note taking. Be sure to record accurate, complete information so that you will not need to return to the source once you have finished note taking.

Scruton, Roger
Modern Philosophy: An Introduction and Survey
New York: Penguin, 1994

See esp. pp. 232-33, 299-301

Experienced researchers know the advantage of using cards (normally 4" × 6") for note taking. If each card is limited to a single idea, the cards can be shuffled and reshuffled as ideas are chosen and discarded, sequenced and resequenced, in the process of arriving at the final selection and final order. Notes on cards allow flexibility during note taking and efficiency in drafting the preliminary version, when they can be clipped to the manuscript at the points where they apply, expediting the writing.

A note card includes, besides the note itself, a shortened reference to the source and the location of the passage. The author's last name is sufficient unless you have two or more works by the same author or two authors by the same name, in which cases you will add the title of the work or author's first name for clarification. If the note extends beyond one page, indicate the page break by a slash mark so that you will know exactly the page on which a particular portion you decide to use is found.

Also a note card normally contains a "slug," a word or phrase describing its content. Placed in an upper corner, it enables rapid sorting of materials. When slugs are keyed to headings of a tentative outline, they can indicate by the thickness of the note cards whether research is adequate for particular parts of the paper.

Animals and humans
Animals are separated from humans by an unbridgeable gap. "Animals
have beliefs and desires; but their beliefs and desires concern present
objects: perceived dangers, immediate needs, and so on." In this re-
spect and in many others (Scruton lists seven) in which animals "fail
to match our mental repertoire, / there is the thing which, according
to some philosophers, explains them all: namely, the fact that animals
lack speech." This "systematic divide" between human and animal has
been rightly recognized since ancient times.
Scruton, pp. 300-301

Use cards also to record your own observations as they occur to you during the content-collecting phase. Ideas and facts can be more easily sorted and arranged in order of use on cards than when written in random order on sheets of paper. The latter method, however, may be entirely adequate for short papers that depend little on sources.

The collecting of content may seem a dreadful drudgery, but it need not be so. If you have a curiosity about your subject, the collection process can be fascinating. It can give pleasure as you see your tentative thesis becoming confirmed by the support you unearth and your total concept rounding into shape. It can open new vistas on your subject, new paths to explore, and also introduce bordering subjects for future investigation. Some of the most valuable insights and pieces of information come through serendipity—that is, through incidental encounter while one is in pursuit of something else. Indeed the collection of content can become the most enjoyable and most rewarding part of all. But this process must begin early and be pursued vigorously. Content needs time to be collected and also to be absorbed.

Chapter 4

Configure

Sizing and shaping the collected material in support of your claim can be the most frustrating part of the writing endeavor. There is indeed an intuitive force that must come into play. From mysterious processes of the mind must emerge a sense of how those separate scraps of data can synthesize into a unified scheme. Patience is required. Belief that a matured shape will emerge is an exercise of faith. But "faith without works is dead," say the Scriptures, and so you will proceed to do what you can do.

What you can do begins with a hard look at your claim, hereafter referred to as the thesis. Its status up to now has been only tentative. It was an important guide to you during your collection of material. But you know more about your subject now than you did when you framed it. In the light of your improved knowledge, is the thesis, as presently stated, maintainable? If so, is it phrased in the most precise way?

Revisiting your thesis is pivotal at this point. All that comes later will flow from it. Your revised thesis will contain the seeds of success or failure of the final paper. Not only will it be an outgrowth of all the decisions made earlier concerning its subject and purpose and content. It also will picture the relationships of its parts. It will be both a consequence of the thinking that went before and a cause of the thinking thereafter. It will lay down a track for the reasoning to follow.

Let us suppose that the following is a tentative thesis you are preparing to use.

The animal-rights movement, an offshoot of Darwinism, downgrades human life.

The word *offshoot* strikes you as too indicative of a direct connection between the animal-rights movement and Darwinism when all you mean to suggest is that the movement has developed naturally from conditions created by Darwinism. You do not want to burden yourself with proving that animal rights are inherent in Darwinism, though in fact they may be. All you need to prove is a general causal connection between Darwinian theory and the advocacy movement.

Also, you hesitate over the verb *downgrades,* and with good reason. The verb in a thesis statement is the core of the assertion and needs to be precise. *Downgrade* is a relatively recent word (first recorded in 1930) and is still more common in informal than formal writing, though that alone would not rule it out. It does imply conscious agency, a purposed reduction in status, which you do not need to prove. The synonym *debases* is momentarily tempting but implies a lowering in substance as well as status. So also does *degrades.* All three are more aggressive verbs than you need and would raise the stakes of your argument. They would commit you to a more subjective and demanding critique of the animal-rights movement than you need to undertake. The words are arguably accurate but are not expedient to your purpose.

What this concern for tone exemplifies is an important principle of style, one that should affect all your writing but especially govern the thesis statement. Do not choose a word more vibrant and bold than your meaning requires. It is better to understate slightly your thesis idea than to overstate it. Moderation with precision will enhance credibility.

You eventually arrive at language that best states your thesis idea.

The animal-rights movement, a product of Darwinism, devalues human life.

The scrutinizing of your original thesis has yielded dividends. By revising its language, you have clarified and reduced the extent of your claim. You have made it more manageable, easing your burden of proof.

Let us see now what the very form of your revised thesis statement can do for the shape of your paper. Notice that its syntax suggests the relative importance of its ideas. This scaling of importance by the syntax will influence the allotment of space for the ideas of the paper. It would be poor distribution of space to give equal treatment to Darwinism and the animal-rights movement. The argument would weaken in focus and thrust. Instead, the syntax itself will keep reminding you as you compose the paper that the greater part of your discussion belongs to the idea that appears in the predicate, the devaluing of human life.

The syntax suggests a certain order for the ideas it contains. Subordinating animal rights to Darwinism in an appositive phrase indicates that Darwinism is a background idea. Placing the devaluing of human life in the predicate indicates that it is your foreground idea. The background idea, the derivation from Darwinism, will be treated first so that it can supply an explanatory, enriching context for the foreground idea, the devaluing of human life. The syntax also implies that these ideas relate as cause and effect, that the derivation from Darwinism has something to do with the devaluing of human life. The form of the thesis statement thus depicts the logical scheme of the paper and prefigures the order in which its ideas will be treated. Getting the thesis right is the first, and most important, step in configuring your content.

When you are satisfied that your thesis statement is accurate and precise, you are ready to derive your organization from it. The structure of your paper will be a projection of your expanded thesis. Expand your thesis in this manner. Earlier you wrote an anti-thesis to test the controversiality of your thesis. State the anti-thesis in a *whereas* clause and place it at the front of the present thesis statement. Join them with a *nevertheless* expression. Let us continue with the example thesis.

> *Whereas* its avowed purpose is to extend moral status and legal protection to all conscious life, *it is nevertheless true that* the animal-rights movement, a product of Darwinism, devalues human life.

To finish expanding the thesis statement, you now consider what facts and inferences led you to the conclusion that became your revised thesis. You will form this material into distinct reasons supporting your thesis. Then you will incorporate these supporting reasons into a *because* clause and add this clause to the end of your revised thesis statement. If the supporting reasons are numerous, you display them in tabular form.

Whereas its avowed purpose is to extend legal protection and moral status to all conscious life, *it is nevertheless true that* the animal-rights movement, a product of Darwinism, devalues human life

because

1. it levels animals legally upward but humans morally downward;
2. it would prevent the common uses of animals in ordinary human life;
3. it materializes human nature, denying the soul;
4. it would burden society with legal restrictions and litigation;
5. it would prevent the use of animals in research for expanding knowledge and improving human life;
6. it challenges the centrality of man in his social world.

Your six reasons impress you as a mixed bag. You want two or three major supporting points to develop, not six. You also want tight connections among them. They need to be a cohesive set.

Having expanded your thesis, you are now at the second major step in configuring a paper. The expanded thesis presents you with final decisions about the content and shape of its support. It is time to select and arrange the points confirming the thesis. After studying the series of supporting reasons, letting your mind play over their relationships, you may notice that three of the reasons state specific concrete harms. Animals would no longer be available for food, clothing, and work, historically part of normal life. Second, extending rights to animals would create endless legal difficulties. Third, animals would no longer be available for research important to advances in knowledge and to improvements in the quality of human life. The other three reasons state broader theoretical objections: that the concept of animal rights costs man his distinctness, denying spirituality, weakening moral responsibility, and challenging his right to be central in his society.

With this distinction in mind, you divide the original six reasons into two sets and give each set a heading.

Set A

1. It would lower the quality of human life as we know it.
    a. It would prevent the common uses of animals in ordinary human life.
    b. It would burden society with legal restrictions and litigation.
    c. It would prevent the use of animals in research for expanding knowledge and improving human life.

Set B

2. It rejects a religious view of man important to the social order.
    a. It levels animals legally upward but humans morally downward.
    b. It materializes human nature, denying the soul.
    c. It challenges the centrality of man in his social world.

Now your attention must turn to the arrangement of ideas in the newly created sets or subsections. There are two major methods of sequencing ideas. In parallel or coordinate order, the ideas are roughly of the same kind and importance, and their positions in the sequence are not fixed but variable. Their order is determined by considerations external to the ideas themselves. Should the most important idea be put last? the most interesting idea first? the weakest idea in the middle? On the other hand, in logical order the sequence is predetermined by the nature of the ideas themselves. The ideas are chained in logical necessity, each idea building upon the preceding and extending an emergent line of thought. The sequence of units is fixed rather than variable, cumulative rather than merely additive.

The ideas in subsection 1, which lists harms, are logically parallel. Their order is variable and therefore will be determined by considerations external to them: by sequencing principles such as general-to-specific, increasing importance, obvious-to-less-obvious, emphasis, interest, and the like. To say that the ideas do not require a certain logical order is not to say that there may not be a preferred order or a natural arrangement that suits your purposes best.

Reasons *a* and *c* pair together as consequences of animal-rights legislation that militate against normal human life and human betterment. They should probably be placed together. Reason *b* is different. It pertains to the inevitable legal tangles and constraints in the wake of animal-rights legislation. Reason *a* is more general than *b* and *c* and, following the principle of general-to-specific, should probably appear first. The outgrowth of these reflections is the following arrangement, which takes the reader from the general to the specific and allows the supporting reasons with affinities to stay together.

1. It would lower the quality of human life as we know it.
   a. It would prevent the common uses of animals in ordinary human life.
   c. It would prevent the use of animals in research for expanding knowledge and improving human life.
   b. It would burden society with legal restrictions and litigation.

Since the order proceeds from the most to the least obvious, you suppose it to be also an order of ascending interest.

The ideas in subsection 2 are not of the kind that can be variable in their order. The ideas relate to one another not as independent equals but as dependent unequals. Their order is logically determined, established by the progress of thought. Of the three, the most rudimentary objection against animal rights is reason *b,* which underlies all other objections. Reason *a* shows the effect of reason *b* on human moral character and behavior, with implications for human relationships. These implications are targeted in reason *c,* according to which man becomes simply another competing species and human society simply one life community among many. The most logically coherent order would allow *a* to draw from *b* and allow *c* to draw from both *a* and *b.* The series then would build cumulatively to reason *c,* which concludes the argument in a striking way. The result would look like this.

2. It rejects a religious view of man important to the social order.
   b. It materializes human nature, excluding the soul.
   a. It levels animals legally upward but humans morally downward.
   c. It challenges the centrality of man in his social world.

Your sense of the logical fitness of this arrangement is confirmed when you notice that the ideas now follow the order in which they appear in heading 2: from religious to moral to social. All that remains is to change the alphabetical notation of the series.

Now you are ready to display the supporting reasons and standardize them as an outline under the thesis statement.

Thesis statement: *Whereas* its avowed purpose is to extend moral status and legal protection to all conscious life, *it is nevertheless true that* the animal-rights movement, a product of Darwinism, devalues human life.

I. The animal-rights movement would lower the quality of human life as we know it.
   A. It would prevent the common uses of animals in ordinary human life.
   B. It would prevent the use of animals in research for expanding knowledge and improving human life.
   C. It would burden society with legal restrictions and litigation.
II. The animal-rights movement rejects a religious view of man important to the social order.
   A. It materializes human nature, denying the soul.
   B. It levels animals legally upward but humans morally downward.
   C. It challenges the centrality of man in his social world.

Your ongoing effort in configuring the paper is proving its value. A full, coherent treatment of your subject is before you in outline form.

Now that you are in a position to see the extent of what your thesis and outline entail, you notice that there is a great deal of necessary subject matter here for a paper of medium length. You in fact have some hesitation about whether you can do justice to this plan within time and page limits. So you return to the practical question of cost and take final stock of your ability to meet the demands of the undertaking as projected.

Let us say that, although the points under heading II interest you more than those under heading I, they are less easily supportable. You realize that developing them would extend your writing effort beyond available time and allowable length or force you into superficiality. So you decide to limit your paper to the first set of points, modifying the present thesis, replacing its core with heading I, raising the subpoints of heading I to main points, and adding new subpoints. You also decide to drop the Darwinian phrase from the present thesis statement because the Darwinian background is no longer integral to your plan. You also can see now that "the quality of" is an unnecessary idea, and you eliminate it from your thesis. The result is as follows.

> Thesis statement: *Whereas* its avowed purpose is to extend moral status and legal protection to all conscious life, *it is nevertheless true that* the animal-rights movement would lower human life as we know it.

I. It would prevent the common uses of animals in ordinary human life.
   A. Animals would no longer be available to sustain life in undeveloped societies.
      1. Animals would be unavailable for food and clothing.
      2. Animals would be unavailable for protection and work.
   B. Animals would no longer be available to enhance life in developed societies.
      1. Meatless menus would make life less pleasant for many and would have a profound effect on cattle growers and the food industry.
      2. Dogs would no longer be available for police work and guard duty and for serving the physically disabled.
      3. Animals would be unavailable for spectator enjoyment.
      4. Animals would be unavailable for companionship as pets.
II. It would prevent the use of animals in research for expanding knowledge and improving human life.
   A. It would end medical experimentation with animals.
      1. Animals would be unavailable for trial surgery.
      2. Animals would be unavailable for testing drugs.
      3. Animals would be unavailable for genetic experimentation.
   B. It would end behavior studies with animals that simulate human behavior.
III. It would burden society with legal restrictions and litigation.
   A. It would raise questions of legal standing in plaintiff representation.
   B. It would endlessly extend the scope of civil and criminal litigation.
   C. It would trivialize and cripple the judicial process.

You may notice that the *whereas* part of the thesis statement is not represented in the outline. The reason for the omission is that it is context for the argument, not part of the argument itself. In a short essay it likely would be treated in an introductory paragraph. If doing justice to it should require more space than is available in a beginning paragraph of reasonable length, explanatory content can be reserved for paragraph two or, if necessary, extended into additional subsequent paragraphs. Fortunately so, for setting the background of this thesis will likely require several paragraphs.

A unit of content represented neither in the outline nor in the thesis but required in a fully formed argument is the rebuttal of anticipated objections. In our discussion earlier of a verifiable claim, it was suggested that you test your thesis against the strongest reasons you can find that oppose it to see whether it is sustainable against reasonable objections. Return now to this counterargument and take note of any opposing reasons that are not disposed of by your main argument. Address these objections in a section immediately before your conclusion.

For example, you might want to respond to charges of insensitivity to the plight of animals with a qualification of your position, a concession that distinguishes precisely what your argument is opposing from what it is not opposing. You might, that is, suggest that animal advocacy would be reasonable were its goal to change from animal rights to animal welfare ("Of course, the animal-rights cause must not be confused with the very legitimate concern for animal welfare"). A careful argument is conscious of resistance to its claim and shows patience in responding to the opposing arguments. It also is prepared to qualify its claim with appropriate concessions. Doing so clarifies the position being argued and renders it less vulnerable to objections. In fact, the final version of your outline might very well incorporate headings for background and concession paragraphs into its system of points.

In the next unit you will see how to paragraph from the outline. For now, you have arrived at a workable shape from which to compose. You have taken the time to configure your content into a form that is easily perceptible to you and that will be readily perceptible to your reader.

Chapter 5

Compose

If you have given due attention to collecting and configuring the content, the present stage, composing, should be the easiest of the entire writing process. Now, with your thesis and outline before you, renew your sense of what you mean to prove. Make any final adjustments concerning scope and shape, proportion and sequence, modifying the plan as required or desired. With the scheme fully in mind and solidified, you can move forward with full confidence and focus.

Put your note cards or slips in the order of presumed use. Make an alphabetical list of your sources, including full bibliographical information. That information must be at hand for documenting quotations and other indebtedness.

Remind yourself of what constitutes a strong middle paragraph (see below) and mark off the paragraph divisions on your outline. These are subject to change, as indeed are all decisions prior to the final draft. They amount to predictions concerning how the content will break. Paragraphs are logical units but also units of convenience for the reader.

Consecutive paragraphs need not conform to consecutive parallel points of your outline. For example, whereas one paragraph may be devoted entirely to a major heading and its subpoints, the next paragraph, because of the larger content of the next major heading, may be able to treat only the major heading and its first subpoint in order to keep the paragraph at reasonable length. The following paragraph then might develop the next subpoint or subpoints.

Avoid writing paragraphs of extreme length or of extreme brevity. Long paragraphs put high demands on the reader's memory. A complex development of thought in a paragraph of fifteen or more sentences can become a long blur without the resting points provided by paragraph breaks. Paragraphs of less than five sentences, on the other hand, obscure the overarching structure. They show the pieces without clarity of scheme. Both megaparagraphs and microparagraphs weaken emphasis. Since the beginning and end positions in paragraphs are the places of greatest emphasis, long paragraphs diminish emphasis by providing too few emphatic positions; short paragraphs, by providing too many.

Well-developed paragraphs in college papers normally average eight to ten sentences. But be prepared to vary paragraph length as the size of your thought units dictates. Also be aware that a two- or three-sentence paragraph can be useful in longer papers for a terse summing up and for a major transition between sections, though its length is too short for well-formed paragraphs in the sections themselves.

Standard paragraphs in informational writing normally begin with a governing sentence analogous to the thesis statement that governs the whole. This sentence, known as the topic sentence, controls the content of the paragraph just as the thesis statement controls the content of the entire piece. The topic sentence is supported by the remainder of its paragraph just as it participates itself in the system of points supporting the thesis statement. All content in a paragraph should be tested against the scope of the topic sentence just as all content in the total work should be tested for relevancy against the scope of the thesis statement.

The organization of the typical informational paragraph is divergent, with the topic sentence in first position and the supporting sentences following. The scheme extends treelike: first the trunk and then the branches. Paragraphs in essay writing, however, normally move toward their topic sentence, reflecting the natural progress of thought to a conclusion. The first sentence is less an indicator of the content than a bridge from the preceding paragraph or series of paragraphs to the new content. Their organization is convergent. Whereas readers of informational writing (news writing, for example) ordinarily key on the first sentence of a paragraph, readers of essays (editorial and feature writing, for example) expect to be somewhat suspended until the end or near the end. The structure of an essay paragraph, like that of the entire essay, is like a river system, moving toward a point of destination. Academic writing favors divergent paragraph structure.

With these paradigms in mind and with the paragraph breaks marked on your outline, take a final look at your outline. If its headings are phrases, turn them into sentences. You will adapt them for the first sentences of your paragraphs (or the first and second sentences of paragraphs that span more than one level of the outline). Make sure the sentence headings have strong predication. If, for example, the heading is "Guide dogs for the blind" and you expand it to "The loss of guide dogs for the blind is another possible consequence of animal-rights legislation," you do not have a strongly assertive sentence for launching a point. Good structural sentences say something *about* the topic they are introducing rather than just announce it as the next subject to be treated. Instead, write something like "Animal-rights legislation may leave guide dogs unavailable for the blind." Though the two statements say almost the same thing, the latter is more forceful.

Structure each paragraph unit with the same care with which you framed the entire paper. Know exactly what you are putting into every paragraph. Grasp each of its ideas, connect it to the other ideas in the paragraph, and follow through. Leave no loose ends, no ideas dangling. Bind the content into a rounded whole that fulfills the promise of the topic sentence. Include more than just general statements. Generalization alone is not enough. It must be substantiated and illustrated with concrete details and examples. These keep your writing from being superficial.

Smoothly integrate source material. Incorporate short quotations into the syntax of your own sentences, being careful to position the quotation marks so that they differentiate clearly and honestly between what are your words and the words of your source. Insert at the end of each reference, quoted or not, all necessary bibliographical

INTEGRATING QUOTATIONS

Insert grammatically incomplete quotations into your text so that they blend with your sentence structure. Compare the following introductions of a quotation—the first, weak; the second, stronger.

> Tom Regan states, "A growing consensus that many nonhuman animals have a mind that, in Charles Darwin's words, differs from the human 'in degree and not in kind.' "

> Tom Regan finds "a growing consensus that many nonhuman animals have a mind that, in Charles Darwin's words, differs from the human 'in degree and not in kind.' "

information that identifies its source. You may wish to take the time now to put the information in its final form, saving a step later. Be satisfied before you leave the paragraph that it occupies its place well in the scheme of the outline and clearly announces its location. If it lacks full development, take the time now to fill it out with enough solid relevant content. If it lacks connectivity with the surrounding elements of the outline, add clear locational markers—transitional expressions, demonstrative pronouns, and the like—to make more obvious its place in the larger scheme. These will receive more attention below.

MISCONDUCT IN THE USE OF SOURCES

A writer's obligation in the use of sources consists of (1) accurate representation of the ideas and words of his source, whether in the editing of quoted text or in paraphrasing, and (2) accurate representation of his own ideas and words and organization in distinction from those of his source.

Whereas misrepresentation of both kinds is serious, the second kind is gravely serious. In the academic world it may cost the student a passing grade in a course or even be grounds for dismissal. In a published document it can render a professional writer liable for damages and destroy his reputation. It amounts to a misappropriation of intellectual property and a breach of faith with the reader.

You **plagiarize** when you bring into your paper ideas or words or organization or closely followed sentence structure that you have drawn from a source and allow them to appear as your own. Even unintentional plagiarism is regarded as gross negligence and carries a presumption of dishonesty. Intentional plagiarism is theft and fraud.

The rule is as follows. All content taken from a source that is not general knowledge must be identified by note. All directly quoted elements of whatever length, even phrasal, must be identified by quotation marks or (if longer than, say, five lines) by block indentation in addition to being identified by note.

Exact demarcation of borrowed material is essential. Indebtedness to a source must not be blurred by (1) failure to indicate by a signaling phrase where borrowing of ideas begins or (2) incomplete paraphrase that incorporates fragments of the original wording without quotation marks or (3) semidirect quotation that substitutes synonyms at near intervals to justify the withholding of quotation marks. Integrity in the use of sources requires accurate, clear boundaries between what is and what is not the writer's own work.

Consider how ideas and language might be drawn from the following passages in *Modern Philosophy* by Roger Scruton. "Animals have beliefs and desires; but their beliefs and desires concern present objects: perceived dangers, immediate needs, and so on" (p. 300). "Underlying all those, and many other, ways in which animals fail to match our mental repertoire, there is the thing which, according to some philosophers, explains them all: namely, the fact that animals lack speech" (pp. 300–301).

1. "Underlying all those, and many other, ways in which animals fail to match our mental repertoire, there is the thing which . . . explains them all: namely, the fact that animals lack speech" (Scruton 300–301).

Here editing misrepresents Scruton, expressing as Scruton's own view the view he ascribes to "some philosophers."

2. Animals have beliefs and desires; but their beliefs and desires concern present objects.

This is flagrant plagiarism, using the ideas and words of a source without crediting the source.

3. Animals have beliefs and desires; but their beliefs and desires concern present objects (Scruton 301).

This also is flagrant plagiarism, noting the source but failing to identify verbatim quotation with quotation marks.

4. It is true that an animal can possess beliefs and desires, but these pertain only to its immediate concerns (Scruton 301).

This also is plagiarism. It is the same sentence with substitutions and adjustments.

5. Animals have no beliefs other than about "present objects" and no languages for expressing their limited beliefs (Scruton 300–301).

This is not plagiarism. It is satisfactory paraphrase with the source identified and the quoted part indicated by quotation marks. Notice that the word *beliefs* is not set off in quotation marks. Unlike the expression *present objects,* which bears the stamp of the author's mind, *beliefs* is basic language integral to the subject and almost inescapable in the context. Also the omission of *desires* and other content does not misrepresent the source. The writer has selected only what pertains to his purpose while taking care not to distort the thought of his source.

6. These differences, according to a noted conservative philosopher, are profound. Animals can choose only what they desire, lack self-consciousness, show no moral sense in their relations, have no aesthetic sense, lack a human range of emotions, and, of course, have no capacity for speech. There is, then "some kind of systematic divide" that separates us from the animals (Scruton 299–301).

This summary of the section in which the passages from Scruton occur is not plagiarism. But note carefully that without the signaling phrase "according to a noted conservative philosopher," the paragraph would be deceptive. The reader would not be aware that the indebtedness to the source extends beyond the directly quoted portion.

Plagiarism is easy to fall into through carelessness but also easy to avoid. During note taking, exercise care so that each piece of verbatim quotation no matter how small is set off exactly in quotation marks and that all writing not so marked is entirely your own. After you have read a passage you want to use without quoting, set the book or article aside and write its ideas in your own words. Then check what you have written against the text of the source to make sure that verbatim elements have not been retained. If they appear, either set them in quotation marks or paraphrase the verbatim or near-verbatim parts more thoroughly to eliminate the problem.

Experienced writers often save the writing of their introductory as well as concluding paragraphs until after they have finished the rest, and with good reason. The beginning and concluding paragraphs exist to frame the main content, and this special function gives them their specialized forms. Make these paragraphs mirror images of each other. Sheridan Baker in a groundbreaking book on writing, *The Practical Stylist,* described their shapes respectively as those of a funnel and an inverted funnel. In a sequel, *The Complete Stylist,* Baker compared the beginning, middle, and end of an essay to a keyhole. The first paragraph begins wide, reflectively, and narrows to the thesis statement. The last paragraph begins narrow with a thesis restatement and widens out from it reflectively. The first paragraph engages reader interest and supplies useful context for the thesis, leading into it. The last paragraph takes the proven thesis as its starting point and reflects on its ramifications.

A common problem with beginning and ending paragraphs that incorporate the thesis statement, even when the student has their forms down clearly in his mind, is knowing what to do with the rest of the paragraph, the part before the thesis statement and after the thesis restatement. Beginning paragraphs all too often simply mark time until the obligatory two or three sentences of empty generalization are offered up to the assignment and the time arrives, mercifully, to state the thesis. Concluding paragraphs can be equally lame. After the thesis restatement of even a very short paper, the writer can think of little other to do than to repeat the empty generalizations of his beginning paragraph or to summarize his points with the same language the reader has encountered only several paragraphs before.

Introductory Paragraphs

Notice the difference between an introductory paragraph that fills the obligatory space before the thesis statement with verbose, empty generalization (the first paragraph below) and one that provides useful context and staging for the thesis (the second).

For thousands of years man has lived with animals on planet earth. Man has assumed he is naturally and properly the ruler of the other animal species. He has considered animal life to be subservient to and supportive of his own life. He has incorporated animals into his diet, not regarding them as fellow citizens of his world. He has regarded working animals as available for duties but not deserving of rights. Lately certain groups have challenged this traditional way of thinking. They believe that animals should be protected from man's exploitation. This belief has become a cause they press fervently under the banner of animal rights. Their cause, however, should be opposed. If allowed to succeed, it would lower the quality of human life while not raising animal life at all.

In the last quarter of the twentieth century, the question of human moral responsibility to animals came to the forefront of social thought. In fact, a commitment to animal rights, so called, has become common among social progressives. Its popularity is evident in the trendiness of vegetarianism, almost a religious creed for some celebrity circles and intellectual elites. The avowed purpose of animal rights as a movement is to extend human ethical status to at least higher-level animal life, to bring animals within the human ethical community. Its effect, however, would be quite otherwise. While failing to elevate animal life meaningfully, it would lower human life as we know it.

Good beginnings and endings are usually concrete, not a cycling or recycling of mind-deadening generalizations. Your paper, to adapt T. S. Eliot, needs to begin and end with a bang, not with a whimper. The introductory paragraph can provide factual context for your thesis to render it more intelligible to your reader. If your thesis concerns a contested issue, the first paragraph can situate it in the context of the controversy. It can lay out other useful background—the essentials of an incident or situation or a thumbnail sketch of a life. Or it can raise or reinforce a receptive mindset with an anecdote. Experienced writers like to reserve from their collected data a striking fact or catchy detail that can springboard their line of thought at the beginning or clinch it at the end. Make functional use of these framing paragraphs rather than merely affixing something fore and aft out of deference to what is expected.

As you push toward the end, especially if you have labored long among scraps and scribblings, ill-assorted sheets and slips of paper, and discarded versions of a plan in the process of bringing your paper to birth, you will find it positively exhilarating to leave these fragments in your wake, dispatching them to the trash (which, however, you will not dispose of until your paper has been returned, lest something valuable be irretrievably lost) as the fully realized form materializes. You will find the pace of your progress increasing and the mental anxiety easing as you near your goal and it comes ever more clearly into view.

CONCLUDING PARAGRAPHS

Notice the difference between a concluding paragraph that follows the thesis restatement with a mechanical summary of points, though well stated (the first paragraph below), and one that goes beyond mere summary to add a final interesting implication or twist (the second).

> On the other hand, there should be no doubt that the agenda of animal-rightists is adverse to human interests. It would prevent the common uses of animals in both undeveloped and developed societies. It would make animals unavailable for medical and psychological research. And it would burden society with unsustainable legal restrictions and litigation. A sensitive and realistic care for animal welfare will accomplish the legitimate concerns of animal-rightism while leaving society the better rather than the worse for it.

> But clearly, to yield to the demands of animal-rightists would be greatly adverse to human interests. The impact would be felt

not only in highly developed societies but also and even more seriously in the disadvantaged regions of the world. Broadly, to implement animal rights would be to invite social anarchy. Perhaps such an outcome is not disagreeable to some animal-rights theorists, whose affluent lifestyle would protect them against the worst consequences of their positions. Most certainly, however, their ethical stance challenges and subverts in fundamental ways society as we know it today.

Chapter 6

Critique

Professional writers are fond of saying that they are really not so much writers as they are rewriters. One well-known novelist has remarked that his first draft is only a track for his actual writing, which begins with his second draft. Ernest Hemingway said he wrote the ending of *A Farewell to Arms* thirty-nine times simply "to get the words right." We are not professional writers, but we can benefit by such examples, for they point to an important truth. The labor a writer expends on what follows his first draft is very nearly as important as the labor that preceded it. This is the phase of critique.

By critique is meant the self-critical activity known as revision. The writer places himself in a readerly mode and reexamines what he might be tempted to call a finished product. What is before him is his first effort toward actualizing his preconception of what he was assigned to write. He has filled out the sections and subsections of his outline, packing each with solid, relevant content. The outline's sentence headings connect with one another and with the thesis and are inserted prominently in the text. All of the steps so far have been done well. Or have they?

Now it is time to reverse the direction of your earlier conceptualizing, your *pre-viewing* of what you intended to do, and to *re-view* what you have done, examining the full text from the vantage point of the conclusion. Read with detachment the entire paper in the light of what your thesis restatement claims to have been proved. Then ask yourself whether the path to that conclusion is as smooth and compelling for an uninformed, unconvinced reader as it seemed to you to be when you were writing. Will your line of thought as expressed hold an uncommitted, easily distracted attention?

Then on to specifics. Does the total structure appear an integrated, functioning whole? Is there *unity?* Check the overall proportions. Is the structure top-heavy with introduction or bottom-heavy with conclusion? It has been said that the shape of student compositions is too often like that of the paper wasp, with large head and abdomen joined tenuously to a small middle. Rather they should emulate the rounded shape of the wood tick, its beginning and end blending smoothly with the middle, forming a unified, integrated whole.

Does every part pull its own weight? Or do you meet the same idea, or even statement, inserted more than once when once is enough? It may be that you introduced it earlier than you needed it and then found it necessary to return to it when it was important in your developing thought. As a rule, incorporate ideas and facts no earlier than they come directly into play in your ongoing argument, leaving what is marginally relevant at the present point in your paper for a later section where it serves your purpose more precisely. In this way you will eliminate redundancy and provide for *economy.* An efficient conduct of thought is a mark of writer maturity.

Economy has to do also with the frugal use of language. Learn to admire a simple, direct style. There is no absolute law that with words fewer is better. Amplification of ideas by repetition and illustration and spacing may ease the reader's task. The most important kind of economy is economy of the reader's effort. And yet, as noted historian and essayist Jacques Barzun has remarked, "Everybody likes the other fellow's prose *plain*" (*Simple and Direct: A Rhetoric for Writers,* p. 12, emphasis author's). And again, "Ideas will best slide into a reader's mind when the word noise is least" (p. 20). There is surprising power in terse expression freighted with thought.

Beyond unity and economy, is there forward movement? Is there a smooth lateral progression across the sections of your structure? Has your design work carried your paper beyond logical architecture to *fluidity?* Whereas the sentence headings beginning your paragraphs should map the terrain of your argument, keeping your reader located within your scheme of thought, continuity of sentence to sentence draws him along the path. In critique you not only consider total design but also scan the path for obstructions. Full critique reveals gaps and lurches and loose-endedness in the path of thought and smoothes the path as needed.

This is not to say that the reader's pace need be constant. His progress need not be a death march, nor should it be. A river does not always flow at the same speed or with uniform breadth and depth. Its current slows, quickens, hesitates, eddies even, from time to time, always returning to its main flow, moving on toward its end point. The pace may need some varying. The path needs signposts, and these may take a little time to read. Ideas need weighting, spacing, and staging according to their importance and their difficulty. Suiting pace to density—slowing as necessary to avoid memory overload—aids rather than hinders continuity. It also makes the reading more pleasant. Mature writing has both logical coherence and verbal cohesion.

Learn then the use of transitional expressions to strengthen clarity and continuity. Transitions can be word length *(furthermore, certainly, indeed, nevertheless, finally)* or phrasal *(on the other hand, as a rule, in that regard, aside from these concerns, to be sure).* They can be sentence length. "Surely the cause is not so simple as that." "What then should be done?" "Now, what should one make of that?" (Do not forget the usefulness of questions.) Transitions can be legitimate sentence fragments. "Well, certainly." "But to continue." "Now, on to specifics." "To summarize." (Use fragments, however, with care and by permission of your instructor.)

Transitions can provide the reader with helpful resting points. "Let us see where this leads us." "His whole point seems to be the following." "Now, what does all this add up to?" They can set the stage for major ideas or developments in a line of thought. "We come finally to the real cause of the problem." "The next disadvantage is the most serious of all." "We are now prepared to understand the full implications of this principle." You do not waste a sentence when you use it to highlight an important division of thought.

Expressions such as these are known by the term *metadiscourse,* writing about writing. They pertain not to the subject of the writing but to the act of writing about it. Their use can be overdone so that the effect is laborious, stilted pomposity, on the one hand, or annoying, chatty familiarity on the other. But handled well, metadiscourse can ease the reader's passage through the compartments of thought.

Incorporate parallelism where sentences, paragraphs, or longer sections contain ideas capable of serial alignment. Be sure to use similar language and syntax for the parallel items, whether phrases or sentences. A series of parallel points in an outline can be revealed as a set when they appear in parallel form as the topic sentences in a string of paragraphs. When you use parallelism within a sentence or paragraph or larger unit, you set up a rhythm of expectation in the mind of your reader that holds him to your line of thought, keeps him located in your series of points, and helps the continuity of the total reading experience. Parallelism also can help you elaborate complex ideas in manageable syntax and avoid sentence sprawl—a point that should be evident from the preceding sentence. By boosting arrangement, it serves clarity and emphasis of thought while promoting flow.

Less conspicuous but no less valuable promoters of cohesion are the repetition of key words and pronoun reference. Never hesitate to keep the same term for an idea that runs like a thread through your paper. If it appears at the end of a paragraph introducing it, let it reappear at the beginning of the next paragraph and in prominent positions in later paragraphs. The urge to vary expressions of a key idea for stylistic reasons is a misguided one and needs to be suppressed. Instead use demonstrative pronouns and pronominal adjectives—*this, that, these, those*—to avoid monotonous reiteration of terms. Be sure to provide these demonstratives with nouns to point to or modify so as not to weaken cohesion by vague reference *this*'s and *that*'s.

Unity, economy, fluidity—these concerns will be foremost in your thinking as you *re-view* your paper and revise it. Any lack of them will become evident as you stand back from your work and try to experience it in the mindset of a reader who does not know all you do about your subject and your view of it. What you discover in critique may require a thorough rewrite or a light touching up of potential trouble spots. Probably it will require something in between. But revision can and should be a pleasure if the earlier stages of the writing process have been well attended to.

When you are satisfied with your revising and have typed the final copy for submission, your work is not over. The checking step remains. This is important housekeeping work that is part of professionalism. The time you spend in this final, often neglected step is potentially more consequential than any comparable amount of time you have devoted to your paper up to this point. Teachers can be arbitrary and severe (and justifiably so) in the penalties they assign such matters as misspellings, grammatical errors, and departures from required form. Only a little impatient neglect of *proofreading* can wipe out the gains of many hours of conscientious, well-directed effort that have gone before. Retained glaring errors also communicate disrespect for the reader you are trying to convince and persuade.

Familiarize yourself with the content of Part Two (The Writer's Reference) and read your paper more than once aloud, scrutinizing it sentence by sentence, word by word. Check your quotations against their sources to make sure they are accurate in content and distinguished from your own writing by quotation marks and notation. Extend your scrutiny to the bibliography or works-cited page and all other pages appended to the main text. The twenty minutes or so you give to this function can yield huge dividends. With the advent of the word processor, even last-minute changes have become so simple as to remove any justification for dispensing with them. Even so, most teachers do not object to an occasional neatly written insertion or correction on the final copy itself.

Before leaving the subject of revision, let us address a question often asked. When should revision start? Should you let the work settle for a while before returning to it? Or should you revise quickly after your first draft while the particulars of the writing are still alive in your mind? Writers advise both. When you revise immediately after the first composing, you still have access to the flow of ideas and words from which you have drawn and which may soon slip from your memory. Surface improvements may be easier at this point than later. On the other hand, setting the writing aside and letting it cool in the mind will provide the distance that can help you grasp and polish the thought line and general shape.

The mature writer shines in self-critique. He knows the tremendous jump in quality that occurs between the first and subsequent drafts of a piece of writing. Self-critique, in writing as in other areas of life, is an act of humility. It is also an act of high self-interest.

Chapter 7

Consider

When your paper is returned, it may have critical notations from your instructor. Since his response to your work is an especially valuable part of this experience, you may wish to have him elaborate on his comments, either in conference or with additional comments on the paper, if his notes were few. In any case, look hard again at your paper. Adopt a positive frame of mind so that the learning benefits of your writing assignment can continue.

Teachers regard students' responses to written assignments as indications of personal character. Accepting a writing assignment with eagerness and seriousness of purpose, approaching it in a focused, systematic manner, and performing it with diligence and attention to instructions reveal personal maturity. These qualities, of course, bespeak maturity not just in the performing of a college writing assignment; they characterize a mature response to any complex and demanding task.

But it is as great a test of character to accept the criticism of your instructor with good humor and keenness to learn. A humble, eager spirit will enable you to ponder indicated weaknesses and try to learn from them. A proud, touchy spirit will cause you to recoil from and dispute indicated weaknesses, especially if they are penalized, effectively shutting off the benefits of experienced professional criticism. Character comes into play mightily when the criticism is severe. The ability to accept adverse criticism and learn from it, even when it appears ill founded (and, you may darkly suspect, ill purposed), is an evidence of an educable mind and—need it be said?—of mature moral character.

Whether or not a revision is requested, do a thorough correction and, if necessary, a rewrite. Word processors make the mechanics of clearing a text of errors and problem places relatively simple. (Consult Part Two for help in understanding your errors and for guidance in correcting them.) Do not be satisfied until you have made the changes that bring the paper to an approved finished form, a version as good as you can make it. The final printout of the perfected version will be to you a benchmark in your academic progress and intellectual growth.

Your instructor will want to hear that you have acted on his comments and produced an improved version. Give him a printed copy of this version along with a copy of the marked and returned version. He will take note of your extra effort and will share your pleasure in a job well done. Then file both versions in a portfolio of materials you will find useful later when applying for advanced study or for a competitive position.

A sample paper, "The Animal Rights Movement: Some Serious Implications," follows. It is the result of closely following The Writer's Path.

The Animal Rights Movement:

Some Serious Implications

by

Teresa Henderson

Ph 300 Introduction to Philosophy

Dr. Ronald Horton

November 19, 2002

Outline

Thesis statement: *Whereas* its avowed purpose is to extend moral status and legal protection to all conscious life, it is nevertheless true that the animal-rights movement would lower human life as we know it.

I. It would prevent the common uses of animals in ordinary human life.
   A. Animals would no longer be available to sustain life in undeveloped societies.
      1. Animals would be unavailable for food and clothing.
      2. Animals would be unavailable for protection and work.
   B. Animals would no longer be available to enhance life in developed societies.
      1. Meatless menus would make life less pleasant for many and would have a profound effect on cattle growers and the food industry.
      2. Dogs would no longer be available for police work and guard duty and for serving the physically disabled.
      3. Animals would be unavailable for spectator enjoyment.
      4. Animals would be unavailable for companionship as pets.

II. It would prevent the use of animals in research for expanding knowledge and improving human life.

    A. It would end medical experimentation with animals.

        1. Animals would be unavailable for trial surgery.

        2. Animals would be unavailable for testing drugs.

        3. Animals would be unavailable for genetic experimentation.

    B. It would end behavior studies with animals that simulate human behavior.

III. It would burden society with legal restrictions and litigation.

    A. It would raise questions of legal standing in plaintiff representation.

    B. It would endlessly extend the scope of civil and criminal litigation.

    C. It would trivialize and cripple the judicial process.

The Animal Rights Movement: Some Serious Implications

In the last quarter of the twentieth century, the question of human moral responsibility to animals came to the forefront of social thought. In fact, a commitment to animal rights, so called, has become common among social progressives. Its popularity is evident in the trendiness of vegetarianism, almost a religious creed for some celebrity circles and intellectual elites. The avowed purpose of animal rights as a movement is to extend human ethical status to at least higher-level animal life, to bring animals within the human ethical community. Its effect, however, would be quite otherwise. While failing to elevate animal life meaningfully, it would lower human life as we know it.

Basic to the issue of animal rights is the question of animal consciousness—whether animals are capable of thinking and choosing, of feeling pain and happiness. At one end of the spectrum is the view of the French philosopher René Descartes (1596-1650), who proposed that animals do not think or even feel. When one hears an animal cry out in "pain," he is merely hearing the cry of "damaged machinery" (Christian 496). At the other end of the spectrum is the position of ethicists Tom Regan and Peter Singer. Regan and Singer recognize no essential difference between human and animal consciousness that would warrant ethical distinctions. Regan finds a "growing consensus that many nonhuman animals have a mind that, in Charles Darwin's

words, differs from the human 'in degree and not in kind'"
("Animal" 27). It is a trend he supports and a view with which
he strongly agrees.

For Regan and Singer and other animal-rightists, it
follows that if animals possess something very much like human
consciousness—can think and feel and will as humans do—and if
there exists no immaterial soul in humans to raise them above
animals, then there can be no reasonable basis for humans'
claiming a superior ethical status for themselves. There is no
rational justification for not including at least higher-level
animals with humans as equal members of the moral community. In
Animal Liberation Singer puts this position quite bluntly:

> Racists violate the principle of equality by giving
> greater weight to the interests of members of their
> own race when there is a clash between their
> interests and the interests of those of another race.
> Sexists violate the principle of equality by favoring
> the interests of their own sex. Similarly speciesists
> allow the interests of their own species to override
> the greater interests of members of other species.
> The pattern is identical in each case. (9)

For the materialist Singer, since animal consciousness differs
from human only in degree, justice as fairness requires a moral
status and legal standing for animals equal to that accorded
human beings.

Animal-rights advocates reject the human use of animals
for any purpose. Their view stems from Immanuel Kant's ethical

imperative, second formulation, according to which one is to "so act as to treat humanity whether in thine own person or that of any other, in every case as an end withal, never as a means only" (qtd. in Jones 78-79). Their position extends to animals a moral maxim intended by Kant only for "humanity." Said Kant, "We have no duties to animals, only duties involving them; and all those duties involving them turn out to be only 'indirect duties to Mankind'" (Regan 27). An animal, then, like a human, according to animal-rightists, should be treated as an end and never only as a means to an end. Animals do not exist for human benefit of any kind. To subject them to experimentation or subdue them for purposes of work or recreation is an ethical violation that should be actionable in law.

Nonsense, says philosopher Roger Scruton. Rationality and self-consciousness are "an enormous gulf in the world of organisms: the gulf between us and the rest." To propose otherwise is to invite moral confusion and disserve both ourselves and the animals we desire to benefit. "We have capacities that we do not attribute to animals, and which utterly transform all the ways in which we superficially resemble them" (223). Animals have no beliefs other than about "present objects" and no languages for expressing their limited beliefs (300-01). Animals do what they do by a determining instinct, not by rational deliberation and choice.

> Animals have desires, but they do not "make up their minds" to act. When they act out of desire, the desire is sufficient cause of their action. If they

4

hesitate, it is because some other desire has
intervened and plunged them into conflict. Persons do
not only have desires; they also have intentions.
That is, they make decisions, form plans of action,
and carry them out. I can intend to do what I do not
want to do; I can also want to do what I do not
intend. (246)

Animals then have no capacity for moral deliberation or
for acting other than as they do by nature. The difference
between them and ourselves is profound. "There is no
exaggeration to say that we inhabit another *world* [emphasis
Scruton's] from the world of animals and are to a certain extent
freed from their servitude to present desire" (223-24). Our
freedom as humans from the tyranny of present desire, our
ability to choose against it, makes us morally responsible for
our behavior. It is foolish and ungenerous to lay upon animals
our burden of moral capacity and moral responsibility.

Scruton asks us to consider what might be our response to
the work of a fox in our chicken yard.

When you discover the violated chicken-run and the
headless corpses, you are naturally distressed. But
are you also *resentful* of the fox [emphasis
Scruton's]? Do you wish him to stand trial, to be
judged, to suffer condign punishment? Surely not. You
may stay up all night with a shotgun . . . but your
purpose is not to punish the fox; it is simply to be
rid of him. He did what he did by instinct, and

> without *mens rea* [guilty intent]. He had no duty to
> respect your chickens, nor did they have a right to
> life and limb that could be enforced against him.
> Animals have neither duties nor rights, and it is not
> merely sentimental, but absurd, to treat them as
> though such moral ideas applied to them. If you try
> to apply such ideas to animals, the result is not
> merely confusion, but a radical failure to relate to
> them at all. You will achieve nothing that you want,
> and nothing that they want either. (232-33)

Animal behavior, Scruton thus contends, does not fit into our moral categories. To try to force it into such categories is absurdly futile and will even keep us from connecting with animal life in meaningful ways.

It should be clear, then, that, apart from the laudable aim of stopping human cruelty to animals, giving them moral status would not improve their lot, for moral status confers on its subjects not only legal protection but also moral responsibility. We are now prepared to understand the ways in which broadening the human moral community to include animals would be seriously disadvantageous to man.

Most obviously the goals of the animal-rights movement would prevent the timeless uses of domesticated animals in ordinary human life. The brunt would be felt especially by undeveloped societies that depend upon animals for work and for food and clothing. Oxen and donkeys would no longer pull plows and sleds and thresh grain. Trained dogs would no longer gather herds and protect them from predators. Nor would seal and walrus be available to the frugal Inuit, for whom virtually every part of the carcass has its practical use. Cattle could not be kept for food or sheep sheared for their wool. Horses and mules and camels could not be harnessed or mounted and ridden. The position of animal-rightists implemented to the fullest would be disastrous to the bare-subsistence economies that still determine normal life in much of the inhabited world.

Less drastically but still quite noticeably, animal rights would diminish human life in more advanced societies as well. Consumers and food producers and distributors, not to mention cattle growers, would have to adjust radically to the effects of meatless menus. Dogs would be unavailable for police work and guard duty. They could no longer be trained to assist the paraplegic and guide the blind. For less necessary uses their absence would also be felt. As hunters' companions dogs would no longer point and retrieve and assist in the chase. Spectators would miss the opportunity to be entertained by animals in circuses (no doubt the least regrettable of the deprivations) and taught about them through their simulated worlds in aquariums and zoos. Millions of animal lovers would feel a keen personal loss in being deprived of the companionship of their pets. This loss would not be in all cases trivial, for animal companions can serve emotional needs. Extended-care facilities are beginning to recognize the therapeutic value of roaming felines for minds dulled by disease and depression. It is difficult to see how animal rights would not be perceived by the public as an example of coldness to human needs. It is hard to imagine that the concept would be tolerated in a popular society once its implications were understood.

More narrowly, animal rights would inhibit efforts of science to improve human life. Animals would no longer be available for experimentation. Medical science relies upon animal subjects for testing surgical procedures, medicines, vaccines, and gene therapies. New pharmaceutical products normally must be tested extensively with animals before trials with human volunteers can begin. Animal ethicists insist that animals be excluded from medical experimentation on the basis of the Nuremberg Code of Ethics developed for the trials of Nazis accused of medical crimes, which states,

> The voluntary consent of the human subjects is absolutely essential. This means that the people involved should have legal capacity to give consent; should be so situated as to be able to exercise free power of choice . . . ; and should have sufficient knowledge and comprehension of the elements of the subject matter involved as to enable him to make an understanding and enlightened decision.

The volunteer must be made to understand the "nature, duration, and purpose" of the procedure and "all inconveniences and hazards reasonably to be expected." The investigator must be able to guarantee and certify the "quality" of the person's consent (<u>Columbia</u> 50). This standard of consent is important protection for human subjects of research. But it obviously

8

excludes the use of animals, for which it was never intended. Spokespersons for medical science contend that the loss of animal subjects would bring their research to a halt.

Still more narrowly but no less importantly, applying human ethical standards to animals and giving them legal backing would burden society with impossible regulatory constraints and endless litigation. In civil cases there would be the problem of legal standing in client representation. Who could speak for an animal plaintiff in a civil suit? Who could bring charges in his behalf? If he were a defendant in a criminal trial, could he be judged mentally competent to stand trial? Who could enter a plea for him, guilty or not guilty? (He could only stand mute!) Obviously the law would have to be mightily adjusted to provide quasi-human judicial remedies for animal grievances beyond those already covering overt animal cruelty or negligence.

Still greater would be the social impact of enforcement. Indeed, the consequences can hardly be imagined. Stray animals presumably could no longer be euthanized, or neutered and spayed, or vaccinated for rabies against their will. Nor could herds exposed to mad cow or foot-and-mouth disease be destroyed. Marauding packs of dogs would have to be confined for psychological examination and kept for rehabilitation before being probationed back to the streets from which they came or to the wild. And how could a judge or jury adjudicate a civil case in which animals were *both* plaintiff and defendant?[1] Obviously, the effect of animal-rights legislation would be to make a mockery of the judicial process and enforcement. It would trivialize and defeat not only the institutions of justice but also the moral conceptions on which these institutions are universally based. Neither humans nor animals would gain.

A moderate alternative to animal rights is animal welfare. This ethical view provides for the humane treatment of animals while permitting the use of animals for human betterment. Animal-welfarists have no objection to the killing of animals for food or clothing or other human needs. They do object to killing for sport. They believe that the darker side of human nature is at work in one who gets an adrenaline rush from seeing a life end in pain. Animal-welfarists require that the use of animals be carried out humanely, involving the least possible amount of animal pain. They find it revolting, for example, to traffic in dog fur from China, where life, both animal and human, has been cheap and little account taken of suffering (MSNBC). Animal-welfarists join with animal-rights advocates in decrying the cramped conditions in "animal factories," where animals are bred and fed for human consumption.[2] They uphold human life as hierarchically more valuable than animal life, yet insist that with that superiority comes a responsibility to care for animals and not abuse them.

The concern of animal-welfarists for the kind treatment of animals is by no means inharmonious with Scripture. The noted biblical scholar Handley Moule is eloquent on what is all too often a contrast between divine and human regard for God's lesser creatures.

> Human mistreatment of animals is as painful a
> phenomenon of the world as can be named, next under
> the tremendous phenomenon of the cruelty of man upon
> man. And "the silence of God" seems, as a rule, to be
> unbroken over this sad scene. But here, through that
> silence, comes the Son of God, knowing all things
> that lie in the infinite heart of the Father, with
> whom He is one. And He says that no sufferings of the
> animal world are taken as nothing by the Eternal;
> "not one is forgotten before God" [Luke 12:6]. The
> poor tortured dog, the worn-out horse, the mistreated
> bird—eternal eyes are upon them all. The universe
> will surely hear further of it, for the supreme King
> remembers and takes note. Woe to the will that thinks
> scorn of the sufferings of the animal, whether the
> conditions of cruelty be savage or civilized, half-
> bestial or cloaked with a scientific plea. "Not one
> of them is forgotten before God." (193-94)

Surely to hold that the premises and agenda of animal-rights
activism are absurdly misconceived and hostile to civil values
is not to deny that a compassionate caring regard for animals
should be expected of civilized persons, not to speak of
Christians. In fact, such a humane care for animal suffering is
necessary for any rejection of animal rights to have persuasive
moral weight.

But clearly, to yield to the demands of animal-rightists
would be greatly adverse to human interests. The impact would be

felt not only in highly developed societies but also and even
more seriously in the disadvantaged regions of the world.
Broadly, to implement animal rights would be to invite social
anarchy. Perhaps such an outcome is not disagreeable to some
animal-rights theorists, whose affluent lifestyle would protect
them against the worst consequences of their positions. Most
certainly, however, their ethical stance challenges and subverts
in fundamental ways society as we know it today.

12

Notes

[1] For a straight-faced account of a hypothetical civil case brought against the wolf by the three little pigs with proper court decorum, procedural technicalities, and formal citations of evidence, precedent, and points of law, see *Wolf v. Pig* (Eagan, MN: West Group, 1999).

[2] For an exposé, with copious photographic documentation, of what both animal-rightists and animal-welfarists consider scandalous mistreatment of animals being raised for food, see Jim Mason and Peter Singer, *Animal Factories* (New York: Crown, 1980).

Bibliography

Christian, James. <u>An Introduction to the Art of Wondering</u>. Fort
  Worth: Harcourt, 1998.

<u>The Columbia University College of Physicians and Surgeons</u>
  <u>Complete Home Medical Guide</u>. Ed. Donald F. Tapley, et al.
  Rev. ed. New York: Crown, 1989.

Jones, W. T. <u>Kant and the Nineteenth Century</u>. 2nd ed., rev.
  <u>History of Western Philosophy</u> 4. New York: Harcourt, 1975.

Mason, Jim, and Peter Singer. <u>Animal Factories</u>. New York: Crown,
  1980.

Moule, Handley C. G. <u>Thoughts for Sundays</u>. Chattanooga, TN: AMG,
  1997. Rpt. Of <u>Thoughts for the Sundays of the Year</u>. 1907.
  <u>From Sunday to Sunday</u>. 1903. <u>The Sacred Seasons</u>. 1907.

MSNBC. "Investigation: Victims of Fashion? The Global Trade of
  Dog and Cat Fur." <i>MSNBC.com</i>. 15 Dec. 2001. www.msnbc.com/
  news/223630.asp (17 Jan. 2002).

Regan, Tom. "Animal Rights and Welfare." <u>The Encyclopedia of</u>
  <u>Philosophy: Supplement</u>. Ed. Donald A. Borchert. New York:
  Simon, 1996.

---, and Peter Singer, eds. <u>Animal Rights and Human Obligations</u>.
  Englewood Cliffs, NJ: Prentice-Hall, 1976.

Scruton, Roger. <u>Modern Philosophy: An Introduction and Survey</u>.
  New York: Penguin, 1994.

Singer, Peter. <u>Animal Liberation</u>. New York: Random, 1990.

<u>Wolf v. Pig</u>. Eagan, MN: West Group, 1999.

Part

TWO

The
Writer's
Reference

Chapter 8

Standard Usage

In the remainder of this book, you will be given the standards that your instructors will apply to your written work. These standards are widely approved in the academic and publishing worlds and also in business and the professions.

Observing these standards is expected of college graduates. The ability to understand and practice them marks the truly educated person. Your instructor therefore feels a duty to you to acquaint you with these standards and hold you accountable for meeting them. He also, as an educated person, feels a responsibility to the standards themselves. Though some of these standards of correctness admittedly are arbitrary, most have experience and intelligent purpose behind them. Taking them seriously is an indication of mature social awareness and respect for cultural institutions.

Christians conscious of the importance of their witness to the world have an additional reason to take standards of correctness seriously. It is a contradiction to stress correctness of spiritual beliefs and yet be willing to be incorrect in matters that give stature to those beliefs. It is also poor judgment to be willing to allow oneself behaviors that limit the scope of one's witness to only the uneducated. God expects us to learn all we can to facilitate our gospel witness and to put into practice what we have learned. Not to take seriously standards of correctness in writing and speech is not to be taken seriously by those who value such correctness. And those who value such correctness are as much in need of the gospel of Christ as those who do not.

Finally, it is important that a Christian always, as much as possible, be aligned with what is considered proper and right. The mature believer of Scripture is careful to "walk circumspectly," to "approve things that are excellent," and to "give none offense." He avoids slovenliness in all areas of his life. He tries to live blamelessly, above reproach, "redeeming the time, because the days are evil." Knowing and observing the best in practical conduct is important equipment for life and has the approval and favor of God, who wills that we "adorn the doctrine of Christ in all things."

Scripture tells us we are to "despise not the day of small things." Though matters of spelling, punctuation, and grammar may seem "small things," they are in fact large things in the college classroom and in much of the public world. Certainly as required standards, they also loom large in the view of God.

The units of this section are indexed for easy reference. Some require an elementary grasp of sentence structure. You may review grammatical concepts and terms in Appendices A and B.

SPELLING

Of all usage standards, correctness of spelling is the most dispro-
portionately valued in the public mind. For some readers it is an
indicator of a writer's intelligence. This perception is grossly inac-
curate and unfair. Still, because the perception exists, it is
irresponsible not to check your spelling meticulously. Misspellings
in print can be greatly distracting to readers and keep your writing from being taken as seriously as you would wish.

Spelling Rules

 Five rules are often helpful in common spelling situations.
Three of the rules refer to the adding of suffixes.

1. Words ending in a final silent *-e* drop the *-e* before suffixes be-   1
   ginning with a vowel and retain it before suffixes beginning with
   a consonant.

excitable	virtuous	hating	rarity
excitement	virtueless	hateful	rarely

   Notice the exceptions *truly, argument,* and *judgment.*

2. Single-syllable words, or words stressed on the last syllable, that   2
   end with a consonant preceded by a single vowel double the consonant before suffixes beginning with a vowel.

napped	referral	fatty	regrettable
occurring	thinner	remittance	controlled

3. Words ending in *-y* preceded by a consonant change the *-y* to *-i-*   3
   before all suffixes except those beginning with *-i-*.

godliness	friendliest	icily	livelihood
happier	magnificent	remedial	embodiment

The fourth rule pertains to the spelling of words containing *-ie-* or *-ei-*.

4. In syllables pronounced with an *ee* sound, *-i-* precedes *-e-* except   4
when following *c-*. After *c-* the order is reversed: *-e-* precedes *-i-*.
When the sound is other than *ee,* the vowel order is *-ei-*.

chief	belief	achieve	relieve
ceiling	deceive	receipt	conceit
eight	weigh	sleigh	sleight

The few exceptions are almost all spelled with *-ei-*.

either	seize	weird	caffeine
neither	leisure	protein	codeine

Notice also these exceptions: *species, financier, sieve.*

5. A fifth rule advises concerning words formed from parts with the   5
same consonants at the joining points. Usually both consonants
are retained.

posttraumatic	coolly	misstate	unnecessary
granddaughter	intentionally	misspelling	innumerable

However, if the first part of such a word ends in a double consonant,
the consonants are not tripled *(shrilly)*.

Problem Spellings

sp
1b   Learning the correct and complete pronunciations of words   1
can improve spelling.

environment	mathematics	length	quantity
government	athletics	strength	mischievous

Making accurate distinctions between similar-sounding words can   2
eliminate some common misspellings.

principle	affect	accept	moral
principal	effect	except	morale

The spelling of certain suffix pairs *(-ence, -ance; -ent, -ant; -ible,*   3
-able; -er, -or) follows no pattern and must be memorized.

resistance	independent	convertible	supervisor
existence	defendant	comfortable	engraver

When forming adverbs from nouns, begin with the adjective suffix   4
-*al* and follow it with the adverb suffix -*ly* to form the suffix -*ally*.
When forming an adverb from an adjective ending in -*ic,* add the
entire -*ally.*

incidentally	accidentally	occasionally	formally
historically	basically	heroically	caustically

The exception is *publicly.*

Only three words end in -*ceed: exceed, proceed, succeed.* Only one   5
word ends in -*sede: supersede.* The rest end in -*cede: precede, re-
cede, concede, intercede, accede,* and so on.

Give special attention to the correct pronunciation and spelling of   6
religious words.

pastoral	altar	Christian	sacrilegious

SOME COMMONLY MISSPELLED WORDS

Avoiding misspelling may seem like an unnecessary bother, important only to picky academics. But in the real world correct
spelling does count. It counts academically: most teachers, not
just in English, penalize grades because of incorrect spelling. It
counts vocationally too. It tells your readers what you really
think of them and your job. In Charleston, South Carolina, a sec-
retary who was given the task of reviewing job applications
pouring in from scores of prospective employees was told to
throw out every letter and résumé having even one misspelling—no matter how impressive the applicant's credentials.
Spelling thus may become a crucial part of the selection process
in business. Correct spelling also counts in your testimony. Even
when you write to friends or relatives who cannot spell well
themselves, they will often recognize the errors you make.
Careless spelling in prayer letters, church bulletins, posters, and
signs reflects negatively upon your Christian testimony and upon
your Savior.

If you are like most students, even those who consider themselves poor spellers, you misspell only a handful of words, three
or four dozen perhaps. By careful attention to especially trou-
blesome ones, you eliminate ninety-five percent of your spelling
problem. Usually just a tiny section of a word causes the problem—a single syllable, at most two or three letters. Knowing

word parts, learning the basic spelling rules, giving attention to correct pronunciation, keeping a list of your special problem words, proofreading your writing aloud by pronouncing deliberately the actual letters used, not those you had intended to use— all these are practical ways of improving spelling.

Although learning to spell the words below will not solve all your spelling problems—everybody has to look up the unusual ones—it is a useful list of words commonly misspelled, some confused with their sound-alikes, some misspelled because of faulty definition or pronunciation, others simply inscribed inaccurately in the public mind.

absence

accept   (a verb meaning "to agree to" or "to receive"; do not confuse with *except,* a verb meaning "to exclude" or a preposition meaning "with the exclusion of")

accommodate

accompanying

achievement

across

advice   (a noun; do not confuse with *advise,* a verb)

affect   (a verb meaning "to influence"; do not confuse with *effect,* a verb meaning "to bring into being, accomplish" or a noun meaning "result")

aisle   (cf. *isle*)

all right   (never *alright*)

already   (an adverb meaning "before or by a specified time"; do not confuse with *all ready,* "completely prepared")

altar   (a noun meaning "place of sacrifice"; do not confuse with *alter,* a verb meaning "to change")

altogether   (an adverb meaning "entirely"; do not confuse with *all together,* "in a group" or "unified")

among

anoint

argument

athlete

a while   ("a period of time"; do not confuse with *awhile,* an adverb meaning "for a period of time")

believe

breathe

Britain

calendar

cannot   (always written as one word, not two)

category

cavalry   (note pronunciation; do not confuse with *Calvary*)

Christian

cite   (a verb meaning "refer to"; do not confuse with *site,* a noun meaning "location")

clothes   (cf. *cloths*)

coming

compliment   ("to express esteem"; do not confuse with *complement,* "to complete or supply the deficiencies of")

conscious   (an adjective meaning "aware"; do not confuse with *conscience,* a noun meaning "the faculty that forces one's recognition of the goodness or evil of one's actions")

consistent

council   (a noun meaning "a group of advisors"; do not confuse with *counsel,* a noun meaning in a nonlegal sense "advice" or a verb meaning "advise")

criticism

definitely

dependent

describe   (also *description*)

desperate

destruction

dilemma

dining

disastrous

drowned   (note pronunciation—one syllable)

entrance

environment

equipped

escape

exaggerate

excel

exercise

existence

forth   (cf. *fourth*)

forty

further   (also *furthermore*)

genius
government
grammar
grievous   (note pronunciation—two syllables)

hindrance   (note pronunciation—two syllables)
hundred   (note pronunciation)
hypocrisy

independent
interest
interpretation   (note pronunciation)
interrupt
irrelevant   (note pronunciation)
its   (a possessive pronoun; do not confuse with *it's,* the contraction of *it is*)

led   (the past-tense and past-participle form of the verb *lead;* do not confuse with the noun *lead,* pronounced like *led,* which refers to a soft metal)
literature   (note pronunciation)
lonely
lose   (a verb meaning "to fail to keep"; do not confuse with *loose,* either a verb meaning "to untie" or "to detach" or an adjective meaning "not tight")

maintenance   (note pronunciation)
marriage
mathematics
meant
medieval
millennium
miniature
mischievous   (note pronunciation—three syllables)
moral   (cf. *morale*)

ninety
noticeable

occasion
occurred   (also *occurrence*)
opportunity
optimism

paid (the past-tense and past-participle form of *pay,* "to remunerate, give in return for"; do not confuse with *payed,* the past-tense and past-participle form of *pay,* "to slacken and allow to run out," as a rope)

parallel

passed (the past-tense and past-participle form of the verb *pass;* do not confuse with *past,* noun, adjective, adverb, preposition)

pastoral (note pronunciation)

persevere (note pronunciation)

personal (do not confuse with *personnel*)

piece (cf. *peace*)

possess

precede (cf. *proceed*)

predominant (do not confuse with the verb *predominate*)

prejudice

prescription

prevalent

principle (a noun meaning "fundamental law, rule, idea, component"; do not confuse with *principal,* an adjective meaning "chief" or a noun meaning "chief person," such as "chief teacher" of a school, "chief contestant" in sports competition, "chief participant" in a crime)

privilege

profession

pursue

quantity

quite (cf. *quiet*)

receive

referred (also *preferred*)

repentance

repetition

roommate

sacrilegious (note pronunciation)

seize

sense

separate

shepherd

shining

siege

significant

similar (note pronunciation)

sophomore (note pronunciation)

sponsor

stationary   (an adjective meaning "unmoving"; do not confuse with *stationery,* a noun meaning "writing paper")
strength
studying
subtle
surprise

temperament   (note pronunciation)
temperature   (note pronunciation)
than   (a conjunction used in comparison; do not confuse with *then,* an adverb meaning "afterward")
their   (the plural possessive pronoun; do not confuse with *there,* an adverb or expletive, or *they're,* the contraction of *they are*)
to   (a preposition or the sign of the infinitive; do not confuse with *too,* an adverb meaning "also" or expressing an unacceptable degree, or with *two,* a numeral pronoun or pronominal adjective)
tragedy
transferred
truly

undoubtedly   (note pronunciation)
unnecessary

vacuum
vengeance
view
villain   (note pronunciation)

weather   (a noun referring to atmospheric conditions; do not confuse with *whether,* a subordinating conjunction expressing indeterminacy, or *wether,* an emasculated male sheep)
weird
woman   (cf. the plural *women;* note differences of pronunciation)
writing

MECHANICS

Avoid these common spelling-related errors in mechanics. For additional help, consult the relevant entries of a full-sized desk dictionary.

Capitals

 Capitals mark beginnings and distinguish proper nouns from common nouns.

Capitalize the first words of sentences and of introduced quotations   1
that form sentences.

> His letter said that he would not run for office in the near future.

> His letter said, "I will not get into the race any time soon."

> His letter said that he would not run for office "any time soon."

Capitalization of quoted material may be adjusted to fit the sur-   2
rounding sentence.

> "Any time soon" does, of course, imply that he intends to run.

Capitalize the first and last words of titles and subtitles. Capitalize   3
all other words except articles, short conjunctions and prepositions
(of five or fewer letters), and the sign of the infinitive.

> He belongs to the Book of the Month Club.

> William Stafford's poem "Traveling Through the Dark" has symbolic implications.

> The acronym WAVES refers to Women Accepted for Volunteer Emergency Service.

> William Blake wrote a poem entitled "Three Things to Remember."

Capitalize proper nouns and adjectives: that is, names of specific   4
persons, places, or things, and their derivatives. Do not capitalize
common nouns unless they are used as substitutes for proper nouns.

The sentences below exemplify correct handling of frequent
problem areas.

> To reach the Deep South, one must travel farther south than the Mason-Dixon Line.

> Mount Washington is the highest mountain of the White Mountains in northern New Hampshire.

An Alaskan spring can appear as late as the month of June.

We have learned a great deal of chemistry in Chemistry 101.

It is a fact that Senator Strom Thurmond has served in the Senate longer than any other senator in history.

Tyler's mother told Father about her Aunt Laura.

At the ministerial luncheon Pastor read from the Bible and led the other pastors in prayer.

Hyphens

Word division

Hyphens divide words at the ends of lines. Words should be divided between syllables. Consult a dictionary if syllabification is in doubt. Be sure that syllables of at least three letters' length appear on both sides of the line break. 1

No: The citizens protested having a toll road as the only thoroug-hfare connecting the cities.

No: The citizens of the area protested having a toll road as the on-ly thoroughfare connecting the cities.

Yes: The citizens protested having a toll road as the only thorough-fare connecting the cities.

Compounds

Hyphens form permanent compounds. Consult a dictionary to verify the hyphenation of doubtful instances. 2

great-grandfather, son-in-law, self-evident, ninety-nine, first-rate, up-to-date, fly-by-night, round-the-clock, re-creation (as distinguished from *recreation*)

Hyphens also form temporary compounds. One kind of temporary compound is created by the addition of a standard prefix.

post-World War II, quasi-independent, pro-military

Another kind of temporary compound is a phrasal adjective linked by hyphens into a modifying unit. 3

on-the-job training, hands-on learning, job-related injury, once-in-a-lifetime opportunity, end-of-century issue, foot-long hot dog, late-night bowling, modern-day miracle, last-minute decision, ankle-length dress, five-course meal, full-length portrait, early-blooming rose, well-managed company

Hyphenation is unnecessary when the phrasal adjective follows the noun it modifies (a well-done steak, a steak well done). Hyphenation is also unnecessary when the phrasal adjective is capitalized, is a compound possessive, is a foreign expression, or is otherwise easily recognizable as a unit.

> Roman Catholic doctrine, dining room's size, pro bono work, high school curriculum

When hyphenating phrasal adjectives, do not place a hyphen after an adverb ending in *-ly* or in *-er, -est,* or *-st.*

> badly burned steak, better planned campaign, least damaged fruit

Place a suspensory hyphen after a detached prefix when two or more prefixes share the same base in a compound expression.   4

> pro- and anti-union

Do not mix hyphenated and spelled-out expressions.   5

> No: The drop-in will last from eight-nine o'clock.
>
> Yes: The drop-in will last from eight to nine o'clock.

Abbreviations and Numbers

 Write out most abbreviations, symbols, and numbers.

Some abbreviations that are appropriate within parentheses or   1
within notes to the text are inappropriate in the text itself.

> No: Psalms, Proverbs, Ecclesiastes, etc., should be read as poetry rather than prose.
>
> Yes: Psalms, Proverbs, Ecclesiastes, and the other poetic books should be read as poetry rather than prose.
>
> Yes: The poetic books (Psalms, Proverbs, Ecclesiastes, etc.) should be read as poetry rather than prose.
>
> No: The Pillars of Hercules, viz. the Strait of Gibraltar, stood at the western edge of the classical world.
>
> Yes: The Pillars of Hercules, namely the Strait of Gibraltar, stood at the western edge of the classical world.
>
> Yes: The Pillars of Hercules (viz. the Strait of Gibraltar) stood at the western edge of the classical world.
>
> No: She said she was "flustrated"; i.e., she was both flustered and frustrated.

> She said she was "flustrated"; that is, she was both flustered and frustrated.

Yes: She said she was "flustrated" (i.e., she was both flustered and frustrated).

When an organization has become known primarily by its initials, its name need not be spelled out: FBI, CIA, UNESCO, IBM.   2

Use *U.S.* only as an adjective.   3

No: We returned to the U.S. after ten months abroad.

Yes: We returned to the United States after ten months abroad.

Yes: They insisted on payment in U.S. currency.

Yes: They insisted on payment in United States currency.

Use *A.M.* and *P.M.* only with numerals.   4

No: We leave in the A.M. before dawn.

Yes: We leave in the morning before dawn.

Yes: We leave before dawn at 5:00 A.M.

The abbreviations *B.C.* (before Christ) and *A.D.* (*Anno Domini,* in the year of the Lord) may be used with years expressed in words as well as in numerals. Be aware, however, that *A.D.* precedes the year, whereas *B.C.* follows.   5

No: The First Council of Nicaea convened in 325 A.D.

Yes: The First Council of Nicaea convened in A.D. 325.

No: The Septuagint was translated about B.C. 250.

Yes: The Septuagint was translated about 250 B.C.

wr 2d Do not use numerals with *o'clock.*   1

No: We leave in the morning at 5 o'clock.

Yes: We leave in the morning at five o'clock.

Yes: We leave in the morning at 5:00.

Spell out numbers expressible in one or two words unless they appear in the vicinity of numbers that require numerals.   2

No: Unfortunately 2/3 of the 200 crates of lettuce had spoiled.

Yes: Unfortunately two-thirds of the two hundred crates of lettuce had spoiled.

Yes: Unfortunately more than 130 of the 200 crates of lettuce had spoiled.

Do not begin a sentence with a numeral.   3

> No: 100,000 protesters gathered at the palace.
>
> Yes: One hundred thousand protesters gathered at the palace.

Do not spell out numbers of chapters or other parts of books or   4
works of literature.

> No: It is not until Chapter Three that the action really gets under-
>   way.
>
> Yes: It is not until Chapter 3 that the action really gets underway.

Wr 2e Write out symbols in ordinary writing, including those that
are common in scientific and business writing.

> No: The house was sold at 125% of its appraised value.
>
> Yes: The house was sold at 125 percent of its appraised value.
>
> No: Kerosene and heating oil are selling at sixty-five & seventy cents
>   per gallon.
>
> Yes: Kerosene and heating oil are selling at sixty-five and seventy
>   cents per gallon.
>
> No: Air contamination is usually attributed to exhaust emission from
>   motor vehicles and/or industry.
>
> Yes: Air contamination is usually attributed to exhaust emission from
>   motor vehicles or industry or both.
>
> Yes: Air contamination is usually attributed to exhaust emission from
>   motor vehicles or industry.

Apostrophes

Apostrophes are part of the correct spelling of contractions, certain
plurals, and most possessives.

Contractions

apos 3a The apostrophe indicates omitted elements in contractions.   1
Place the apostrophe precisely at the point of the omission.

> No: His salary doesnt cover his expenses.
>
> No: His salary does'nt cover his expenses.
>
> Yes: His salary doesn't cover his expenses.

Avoid the use of contractions, however, in academic writing.   2

Plurals

An apostrophe followed by *-s* forms plurals of letters, numbers, words referred to as words, and abbreviations followed by periods.

1

The French and the Spanish trill their *r*'s differently.

There are eighteen *whereas*'s in the formal resolution.

Two B.A.'s do not equal an M.A.

Spell out &'s except when they appear in a company's name.

An apostrophe is unnecessary, however, with the plural of years.

2

Any job seemed a good job during the Great Depression of the 1930s.

Possessives

The apostrophe, usually followed by *-s,* indicates possession. Use an apostrophe with *-s* to show possession with nouns and indefinite pronouns that end without *-s.*

1

Austin's opinion is that Brandon is the team's best player.

We got more than our money's worth from the tour.

The parsonage is a stone's throw from the church.

No one's questions were left unanswered.

Do not omit the *-s* that follows the apostrophe in the possessive of singular nouns ending in *-s*. Though some writers drop the *-s* when the resulting pronunciation sounds awkward, academic practice favors keeping the *-s.*

2

One of his jobs is to correct the boss's spelling.

William Butler Yeats's poems are more widely read than his plays.

Randall Jones's hobby is bird watching.

Use an apostrophe without *-s* to show possession with plural nouns that end in *-s* or *-es.*

3

The recent victories raised the soldiers' morale.

In three hours' time the battle was over.

The Joneses' family portrait hangs in the living room.

Use an apostrophe and *-s* to show possession with plural nouns that do not end in *-s* or *-es.*

4

Children's clothes sell quickly at yard sales.

The sheep's names are Fred and Molly.

In summary, use an apostrophe and -*s* to show possession with indefinite pronouns and all nouns other than plural nouns ending in -*s* or -*es*. Plural nouns ending in -*s* or -*es* take only the apostrophe.

In multiple possession use an apostrophe after only the last posses-   5
sor to show joint or group possession. Use an apostrophe after each
possessor to show individual possession.

> Ryan's and Megan's Bibles were found in their aunt and uncle's car.

Avoid the misuse of apostrophes with nonpossessive plurals or with   6
the possessive forms of personal pronouns.

No:	Hundred's of boxes arrived in the afternoon mail.
Yes:	Hundreds of boxes arrived in the afternoon mail.
No:	It's features include an automatic winding mechanism who's action is regulated by quartz.
Yes:	Its features include an automatic winding mechanism whose action is regulated by quartz.

Avoid the misuse of apostrophes with present-tense verb forms.   7

| No: | The pitcher bat's last in the next inning. |
| Yes: | The pitcher bats last in the next inning. |

Avoid misplacement of the apostrophe within the base of a posses-   8
sive noun ending in -*s* or -*es*. Mentally box the nonpossessive base
form of the word and add the apostrophe and -*s* (if needed) to it.

> the ⬚children⬚'s parents   both ⬚boys⬚' parents

No:	John Keat's "On First Looking into Chapman's Homer" contains a factual error.
Yes:	John Keats's "On First Looking into Chapman's Homer" contains a factual error.
No:	The Jones'es flowering apple tree blooms early in the spring.
Yes:	The Joneses' flowering apple tree blooms early in the spring.

PUNCTUATION

End Punctuation

End marks indicate the close of freestanding thought units that can be followed in speech by an extendable silence. For this reason they are called full stops. Formal usage requires that end punctuation be preceded by grammatically complete sentences. Errors in end punctuation are especially noticeable and distracting.

Period

 A period ends a statement, a wish, a mild command, a weak exclamation, a polite request, or an indirect question. (An indirect question is actually a statement; it reports a question rather than forms a question itself.)

The rain has stopped.

I wish the weather were fair.

Leave the room quietly.

How soon the summer passes.

Will everyone please stand.

He asked why he had not been notified.

Periods are used to end most abbreviations (see an up-to-date dictionary).

 Periods also form **ellipses.** An ellipsis consists of three periods, each preceded and followed by a single space. It indicates the omission of a word or words *within* quoted material. It is ordinarily unnecessary at the beginning or end of a quotation.   1

"Charity . . . is kind."

Attach to the three spaced periods of an ellipsis whatever mark from the original is needed for grammatical order and continuity. If the omitted part of the quoted passage ends or begins at a break *between* sentences, the ellipsis adds the end punctuation of the shortened sentence it terminates or of the preceding sentence from which it begins.   2

"Love not the world, neither the things that are in the world. . . . The world passeth away, and the lust thereof: but he that doeth the will of God abideth forever" (I John 2:15–17).

"Who shall lay any thing to the charge of God's elect? . . . It is Christ that died, yea rather, that is risen again, who is even at the right hand of God, who also maketh intercession for us" (Romans 8:33–34).

If the omission ends or begins at a punctuated break *within* a sentence, the ellipsis adds the punctuation that marks the break.

3

"I have, myself, full confidence that if all do their duty, if nothing is neglected, and if the best arrangements are made . . . , we shall prove ourselves once again able to defend our Island home."

"Miss Bates stood in the very worst predicament in the world for having much of the public favour; . . . and yet she was a happy woman, and a woman whom no one named without good will."

An extended ellipsis line indicates the omission of one or more lines of block-indented poetry.

4

But at the coming of the King of Heaven
All's set at six and seven;

. . . .

We entertain him always like a stranger,
And, as at first, still lodge him in the manger.

Question mark

 A question mark ends a direct question.

Have you not heard about the improved health benefits?

When a direct question is only part of a sentence, the question mark appears immediately after the question segment. It is not delayed.

1

You have heard—have you not?—about the improved health benefits.

You have heard about the improved health benefits, have you not?

A question mark ends each part of a series of questions within a sentence.

2

Have the improved health benefits been explained to the company supervisors? to the workers? to their families?

Exclamation point

 An exclamation point ends an emphatic or exclamatory sentence or part of a sentence.

Leave immediately!

What a beautiful view of the mountains!

Now really!

She won—yes!—her race in record time.

Exclamation points belong more to informal emotive expression than to academic and professional writing. Use them only sparingly.

Quotation marks

 Double quotation marks enclose direct quotations, speech   1
in dialogue, titles of short works, and words used in special ways. Single quotation marks set off quotations within quotations or titles within titles. (See Internal Punctuation.)

Place terminal quotation marks correctly in relation to other end   2
punctuation. Periods and commas always precede a closing quotation mark, regardless of the length of the quoted material.

My father enjoyed reciting Kipling's poem "If."

When Kipling wrote "If," he was thinking of his own son.

Semicolons and colons always follow a closing quotation mark.   3

Blake's Clod of Clay declares, "Love seeketh not itself to please"; Blake's Pebble of the Brook replies, "Love seeketh only self to please."

"Readiness is all": these words give Hamlet's final view of death.

Question marks or exclamation points precede closing quotation   4
marks if they apply to the quoted material only. They follow the quotation mark if they apply to more than the quoted material. They precede the quotation mark if they apply to both the quoted material and the entire sentence.

"Did he who made the lamb make thee?"

Should I be pleased that he called my writing "tenebrous"?

Did the groom say "I do" or "I will"?

Did the soloist sing "Were You There?"

"Uncle Sam needs you!"

The sentry cried, "Halt!"

Stop saying everything is "awesome"!

Get moving when he says "Go!"

Dashes appear within closing quotation marks if the break in 5
thought they indicate occurs within the quoted words; they appear
after the quotation mark if the break occurs afterward. In this distinction they follow the rule of question marks and exclamation points.

> "I would have come, but—" was as far as she got with her story.
>
> "I would have come, but visitors showed up unexpectedly"—a likely
> story.

Commas and periods normally necessary are dropped when ques- 6
tion marks, exclamation points, or dashes appear within quotation
marks to end a sentence or part of a sentence. Do not double the
punctuation.

> One of the most beautiful songs in the hymnbook is entitled "Why?"
>
> "Who can estimate the power of a woman's love?" said the speaker.
>
> "Give me liberty, or give me death!" cried Patrick Henry.
>
> "I would have come, but—"

When a source is cited parenthetically, the parenthesis immedi- 7
ately follows the closing quotation mark. The period or other end
mark follows the parenthesis.

> An expression in the King James Version that is a holdover from Old
> English is "all to brake" (Judges 9:53).

Internal Punctuation

Punctuation within a sentence clarifies sentence structure and content. It should be used purposefully, not haphazardly.

Comma

Commas clarify sentence structure either by separating sentence elements or by enclosing them. Single commas separate; pairs of commas enclose.

Commas to separate

 A comma separates two independent clauses joined by 1
a coordinating conjunction.

> The old bridge has been closed, and traffic has been routed to the
> north.

If the independent clauses are fairly short and are preceded by a   2
yoking idea, the comma is commonly dropped.

> Because of the dangerous flooding, the old bridge has been closed and
> traffic has been routed to the north.

A comma separates three or more coordinate elements in a series.   3
Do not omit the comma before the coordinating conjunction.

> She collected nickels, dimes, quarters, and half-dollars.

> A triathlon consists of cross-country running, long-distance swimming,
> and long-distance bicycling.

> We stopped for gas, bought sandwiches, and filled the Thermos jug.

> The police were puzzled to discover that no one was harmed, that
> nothing was missing, and that the house showed no signs of forced
> entry.

Commas separate two or more coordinate adjectives in a series.   4
Coordinate adjectives modify a noun independently rather than
cumulatively. They can be separated by *and* or their order
rearranged with no change of meaning.

> They set sail on a cold, clear morning.

Noncoordinate adjectives in a series modify cumulatively. They have
a fixed order and should not be separated by commas.

> They set sail on a cold October morning.

Commas follow certain introductory elements. These include adverb   5
clauses, participial phrases, gerund-containing phrases, infinitive
phrases, absolute phrases, and long prepositional phrases (of five
or more words). These also include lesser introductory elements:
interjections, conjunctive adverbs (*therefore, however, nevertheless,*
etc.), and transitional phrases (*for example, in addition,* etc.).

> After he had run for three miles, he was too tired to continue.

> Having run for three miles, he was too tired to continue.

> After having run for three miles, he was too tired to continue.

> To prepare for the marathon, he did three-mile practice runs.

> The day of the race being unusually warm, he soon tired.

> For a while after the race, he was antisocial.

> Oh, he moped for about a week.

> However, he eventually returned to normal living.

> For example, he no longer refused to come to meals.

Commas set off introductory adjective phrases and appositives that   6
precede the nouns they normally follow.

> Happy with his present score, Zachary withdrew from further com-
> petition.
>
> The giant of the stringed instruments, the bass viol is also known as the
> double bass.

Commas set off attributive expressions from direct quotations. If the   7
attributive is a statement, a colon is needed. Notice the punctuation
and capitalization of the following.

> The director said, "The end is in sight."
>
> "The end is in sight," said the director.
>
> The director said that the end is in sight.
>
> The director said what we hoped to hear: "The end is in sight."

Commas to enclose

Comma punctuation of introductory elements falls partly
under a more general principle that would require setting
off most of the introductory elements in the examples above
wherever they might appear in the sentence.

> He was too tired to continue, having run for three miles.
>
> He was too tired, having run for three miles, to continue.
>
> He eventually returned to normal living, however.
>
> He eventually returned, however, to normal living.

The general principle is this. Commas mark certain sentence elements as nonessential, as supplying extra information. These commas represent pauses in speech indicating interruptive or loosely
associated ideas. When such an element appears at the beginning or
end of a sentence, it is separated from the rest of the sentence by a
single comma. When it appears in the interior of the sentence, breaking into normal word order, it is set off by commas *on both sides.*

Commas, then, *enclose* nonessential sentence elements to indicate
their parenthetical quality—on one side when these elements appear
at the beginning or end of the sentence, on both sides when they
appear within the sentence.

Pairs of commas enclose nonessential adjective clauses and phrases.   1
These are often referred to as nonrestrictive to distinguish them
from restrictive clauses and phrases. A restrictive clause or phrase
has an essential specifying function. It limits the force of a statement

to one or more individuals among many. It reduces the scope
of a generalization to a subset. It is therefore not set off by commas.

Compare the following sentences.

> Everyone who raised a thousand dollars will receive two free tickets.
>
> Nicole, who raised a thousand dollars, will receive two free tickets.

The adjective clause in the first sentence has an essential restricting
function. The same clause in the second sentence does not; it provides useful, relevant information but is not logically required since
the subject idea is already sufficiently specified. It is nonrestrictive
and therefore nonessential. It must be set off by commas.

Notice how this distinction between essential (restrictive) and
nonessential (nonrestrictive) adjective elements affects comma
punctuation in the following pairs of sentences.

> Concerts that feature light-classical and popular works are the best
> attended.
>
> Outdoor concerts, which feature light-classical and popular works, are
> the best attended.
>
> The teachers retiring in June were honored at a luncheon.
>
> Amanda Wilson, retiring in June, was honored at a luncheon.
>
> The yachts moored in the lagoon survived the hurricane.
>
> The *Sea Sprite,* moored in the lagoon, survived the hurricane.
>
> The guests at the far end of the table were served first.
>
> The honored guest, at the far end of the table, was served first.

The punctuation of adverb clauses also follows this principle,
though less strictly. Adverb clauses loosely related to the main
sentence idea are usually enclosed in commas. Adverb clauses
closely related to the main sentence idea are not, unless they are
introductory.

2

> The fund drive succeeded, though some felt it might have started
> earlier.
>
> The fund drive succeeded even though it might have started earlier.
>
> Everyone enjoyed the outdoor drama, because the weather was fair
> and mild and the actors had learned their parts well.
>
> Colin enjoyed the outdoor drama because his children were in it.
>
> The city will get a new sports stadium, unless the news report was
> mistaken.
>
> The city will get a new sports stadium unless the voters disapprove.

Commas enclose nonessential (nonrestrictive) appositives. 3

> He confused two poets, Keats and Yeats, in his exam essay.
>
> He confused the poets Keats and Yeats in his exam essay.
>
> Dickens's last novel, *The Mystery of Edwin Drood,* was unfinished at his death.
>
> Dickens's novel *The Mystery of Edwin Drood* was unfinished at his death.
>
> A distressing fact, that an ancestor had been hanged for horse thievery, was offered as an explanation for his life of crime.
>
> The fact that an ancestor had been hanged for horse thievery was offered as an explanation for his life of crime.

Commas enclose absolute phrases. 4

> The trial run was, all things considered, a real success.
>
> Meanwhile, the rain holding off, play continued.

Commas enclose other parenthetical expressions, such as interjections and conjunctive adverbs, when they break the flow of the sentence. 5

> He was gone, oh, perhaps five minutes.
>
> The match, however, was played as scheduled.
>
> The benefits include, for example, a lifetime pass to the city zoo.

Commas enclose abruptly contrasting elements. 6

> You were to place the flower, not the flour, in the vase.

Commas enclose names spoken in direct address and speaker tags in dialogue. 7

> This is the way, Jared, to tie a line to a fishhook.
>
> "The world," said Wordsworth, "is too much with us."

Commas enclose units in dates and addresses. Do not omit the comma that follows the final unit. 8

> Talladega Motor Speedway near Anniston, Alabama, has higher, more steeply banked turns than any other speedway on the NASCAR circuit.
>
> The date of April 23, 1564, is traditional for Shakespeare's birthday.

Remember to include both commas where a pair is needed. 9

> No: The League of Nations, the predecessor of the United Nations was founded in 1919 at the Paris Peace Conference.
>
> Yes: The League of Nations, the predecessor of the United Nations, was founded in 1919 at the Paris Peace Conference.

Misuse of commas

 A comma improperly inserted can disrupt meaning as seriously as a comma improperly omitted.

Do not use a comma to separate a pair of words, phrases, or clauses (other than independent clauses) joined by a coordinating conjunction.   1

> No: The House of Representatives, and the Senate were in session.
>
> Yes: The House of Representatives and the Senate were in session.
>
> No: The evidence that the fire had not been started accidentally, and the rumor that the Ku Klux Klan had been involved brought the FBI into the case.
>
> Yes: The evidence that the fire had not been started accidentally and the rumor that the Ku Klux Klan had been involved brought the FBI into the case.
>
> No: He felt comfortable about his performance on the test, but did not display his confidence to his friends.
>
> Yes: He felt comfortable about his performance on the test but did not display his confidence to his friends.
>
> No: He did not want to charge his neighbors with negligence for the broken fence and the cows in his yard, or to accept the entire blame himself.
>
> Yes: He did not want to charge his neighbors with negligence for the broken fence and the cows in his yard or to accept the entire blame himself.

Do not use a comma to separate grammatical unities such as a subject and its verb, a verb and its complement or adverbial modifier, an adjective and its adjacent noun, or adjectives in noncoordinate sequence. The only commas appearing in these positions should be enclosing pairs.   2

> No: The evidence that the fire had not been started accidentally and the rumor that the Ku Klux Klan had been involved, brought the FBI into the case.
>
> Yes: The evidence that the fire had not been started accidentally and the rumor that the Ku Klux Klan had been involved brought the FBI into the case.
>
> No: We found in the cellar behind the potato rack, a stack of valuable old magazines.
>
> Yes: We found in the cellar behind the potato rack a stack of valuable old magazines.
>
> Yes: We found in the cellar, behind the potato rack, a stack of valuable old magazines.

No: Both Thomas Babington Macaulay and Thomas Carlyle became
        in their later years, pessimistic and despondent.

Yes: Both Thomas Babington Macaulay and Thomas Carlyle became
        in their later years pessimistic and despondent.

Yes: Both Thomas Babington Macaulay and Thomas Carlyle became,
        in their later years, pessimistic and despondent.

No: Mark Antony, in pretense, came to the Forum, "to bury Caesar,
        not to praise him."

Yes: Mark Antony, in pretense, came to the Forum "to bury Caesar,
        not to praise him."

Yes: Mark Antony came to the Forum, he said, "to bury Caesar, not
        to praise him."

No: The huge, indescribably beautiful, sky canopied the Western
        plains.

Yes: The huge, indescribably beautiful sky canopied the Western
        plains.

Yes: The huge sky, indescribably beautiful, canopied the Western
        plains.

No: He pondered the difficult, algebraic problem.

Yes: He pondered the difficult algebraic problem.

Do not use a comma to separate conjunctions and prepositions   3
from what follows them.

No: Sir Arthur Conan Doyle did not want to resurrect Sherlock
        Holmes; but, the public demand was overwhelming.

No: Sir Arthur Conan Doyle did not want to resurrect Sherlock
        Holmes but, the public demand was overwhelming.

Yes: Sir Arthur Conan Doyle did not want to resurrect Sherlock
        Holmes, but the public demand was overwhelming.

No: Sergei Prokofiev's early work was too avant-garde for Soviet
        authorities, though, they referred to it as decadent.

Yes: Sergei Prokofiev's early work was too avant-garde for Soviet
        authorities, though they referred to it as decadent.

Yes: Sergei Prokofiev's early work was too avant-garde for Soviet
        authorities; they referred to it, though, as decadent.

No: She faced a difficult choice between, enjoyable eating and
        enjoyable health.

Yes: She faced a difficult choice between enjoyable eating and
        enjoyable health.

Yes: She faced a difficult choice between, on the one hand, enjoy-
        able eating and, on the other, enjoyable health.

Do not use a pair of commas to enclose essential (restrictive) elements. 4

No:	Robert Frost's poem, "Birches," expresses the boundless aspirations of youth.
Yes:	Robert Frost's poem "Birches" expresses the boundless aspirations of youth.
No:	Fish fillets, lightly basted and broiled on a grill, taste better and are more healthful than fish baked in sauce.
Yes:	Fish fillets lightly basted and broiled on a grill taste better and are more healthful than fish baked in sauce.
No:	The Queen Elizabeth, who ruled four centuries ago, gave her name to the period of her reign.
Yes:	The Queen Elizabeth who ruled four centuries ago gave her name to the period of her reign.
Yes:	Queen Elizabeth I, who ruled four centuries ago, gave her name to the period of her reign.

Semicolon

 Semicolons separate coordinate elements where grammar or clarity requires more than a comma.

Semicolons separate elements in a series that contains commas. 1

Philip has lived in Bangor, Maine; Newark, New Jersey; and Asheville, North Carolina.

Semicolons separate independent clauses joined by coordinate conjunctions when a comma would be inadequate to clarify the dividing point because of other commas in the sentence. 2

Classical ethics based the moral life on prudence, justice, temperance, and fortitude; but medieval ethics added faith, hope, and charity.

Semicolons separate independent clauses that are not joined by a coordinating conjunction. The use of a comma instead of a semicolon for this purpose is a serious grammatical error known as a *comma splice*. (See p. 99.)

No:	Classical ethics based the moral life on the four cardinal virtues, medieval ethics added the three virtues of I Corinthians 13:13.
Yes:	Classical ethics based the moral life on the four cardinal virtues; medieval ethics added the three virtues of I Corinthians 13:13.
Yes:	Classical ethics based the moral life on the four cardinal virtues; however, medieval ethics added the three virtues of I Corinthians 13:13.

Do not use semicolons to separate unequal elements. 3

No: Classical ethics based the moral life on the four cardinal virtues; whereas medieval ethics added the three virtues of I Corinthians 13:13.

Yes: Classical ethics based the moral life on the four cardinal virtues, whereas medieval ethics added the three virtues of I Corinthians 13:13.

No: Whereas classical ethics based the moral life on the four cardinal virtues; medieval ethics added the three virtues of I Corinthians 13:13.

Yes: Whereas classical ethics based the moral life on the four cardinal virtues, medieval ethics added the three virtues of I Corinthians 13:13.

Accordingly, do not use a semicolon in place of a colon. 4

No: Classical ethics based the moral life on the four cardinal virtues; prudence, justice, temperance, and fortitude.

Yes: Classical ethics based the moral life on the four cardinal virtues: prudence, justice, temperance, and fortitude.

Colon

 A colon shows a resultant relationship between what precedes it and what follows it in the sentence. What precedes it must be a complete statement. 1

No: The purposes of marriage in the Anglican *Book of Common Prayer* are: to produce offspring, to provide comfort, and to preserve moral purity.

Yes: The purposes of marriage in the Anglican *Book of Common Prayer* are three: to produce offspring, to provide comfort, and to preserve moral purity.

Yes: The purposes of marriage in the Anglican *Book of Common Prayer* are to produce offspring, to provide comfort, and to preserve moral purity.

A colon is a more precise mark than a semicolon when the second of two statements in a sentence stems logically from the first. 2

No: The prosecution case had a major setback; its key witness refused to testify.

Yes: The prosecution case had a major setback: its key witness refused to testify.

Colons separate titles from subtitles.   3

> No: The class was assigned to read Richard Rodriguez's essay "Aria, A Memoir of a Bilingual Childhood."
>
> No: The class was assigned to read Richard Rodriguez's essay "Aria; A Memoir of a Bilingual Childhood."
>
> Yes: The class was assigned to read Richard Rodriguez's essay "Aria: A Memoir of a Bilingual Childhood."

Dash

 Dashes set off interruptive sentence expansions and extensions.

A typewritten dash consists of two hyphens without spacing on either side. It prints as a long hyphen.   1

> No: Peaches and lemons - cars, that is - can look exactly alike.
>
> Yes: Peaches and lemons--cars, that is--can look exactly alike.
>
> Yes: Peaches and lemons—cars, that is—can look exactly alike.

Dashes enclose appositives that contain commas.   2

> In classical ethics the four cardinal virtues—prudence, justice, temperance, and fortitude—form the foundation of the moral life.

Dashes set off afterthoughts and other breaks in thought.   3

> If you respect the land you farm, it will repay you—or so we were taught.
>
> Donald Duck's three nephews—are they Huey, Dewey, and Louie?—seem as egotistical as their uncle.
>
> Cable television, VCRs, digital sound equipment, computers—all have become necessities of modern life.

Do not use the dash as an informal colon in academic writing.   4

> No: Only one job remained to be done—mowing the grass.
>
> Yes: Only one job remained to be done: mowing the grass.

Parentheses

 Parentheses enclose supplementary, ignorable items (explanations, examples, directions, asides).   1

> The Authorized (King James) Version was never officially authorized by James I (1603-25).
>
> Angola in Southwest Africa should not be confused with the tiny country of Andorra (pop. 32,700) in the Eastern Pyrenees between France and Spain (see map).

Parentheses enclose numbers or letters marking a series within a sentence. 2

> The purposes of marriage in the Anglican *Book of Common Prayer* are (1) to produce offspring, (2) to provide comfort, and (3) to preserve moral purity.

Parentheses at the end of a sentence go before, not after, the closing punctuation. 3

Brackets

 Brackets enclose parenthetical elements within parentheses. 1

> The California coastal trail laid by Spanish missionaries (known as El Camino Real [The Royal Road]) was divided into day's-length journeys by missions.

> Lewis Carroll (Charles Lutwidge Dodgson [1832-98]) was an Oxford professor of mathematics with an affection for children (especially for a daughter of friends [Alice Liddell]).

Brackets enclose parenthetical material inserted into quotations. 2

> He wrote, "There is little that is angelic about the City of the Angels [Los Angeles]."

> He wrote, "There is little that is angelic about the City of the Angles [*sic*]."

Discretionary punctuation

 In some sentence situations punctuation is variable or even optional. How or whether a writer sets off an element of uncertain importance indicates how much he wishes it to be noticed by the reader and to affect the thought.

In the set of examples below, the enclosed phrase is less and less closely tied to the rest of the sentence and its idea made less essential.

> We finally found Father, writing poetry, in the tool shed.

> We finally found Father—writing poetry—in the tool shed.

> We finally found Father (writing poetry) in the tool shed.

In the next series of examples, the enclosed phrase is more and more boldly emphasized as a unit in itself and its idea made to stand out more strikingly.

> We finally found Father (writing poetry) in the tool shed.
>
> We finally found Father, writing poetry, in the tool shed.
>
> We finally found Father—writing poetry—in the tool shed.

Quotation marks

 Quotation marks enclose direct quotations and dialogue.   1

> Was Thomas Paine speaking of family vacations when he wrote, "These are the times that try men's souls"?
>
> In *Emma* Jane Austen introduces George Knightley as "a sensible man."
>
> "Dinner is served," he said, "between 5:30 and 9:00. No reservations are necessary."
>
> "Thank you," replied the caller.

Quotation marks enclose lines of poetry (three or fewer) that are   2
run into a paragraph. Notice the use of the slash mark to show line division and the retained capitalization of the words that begin successive lines.

> Alexander Pope wisely urged, "Trust not thyself; but, thy defects to know, / Make use of every friend, and every foe."

Quotation marks and italics

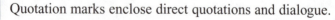 Place in quotation marks titles of short or unpublished works   1
(such as short poems and speeches), parts of published works, published essays and articles, translations of terms, and words used in special senses or for special purposes.

Italicize titles of books, magazines, newspapers, plays, operas and   2
other long musical works (though not when the title consists only of the class of work, number, and key), long poems, paintings and other works of visual art, films, and recordings.

Italicize names of specific trains, ships, aircraft, spacecraft, and   3
satellites.

Italicize foreign words and phrases. (Check an up-to-date diction-   4
ary to determine whether an expression is considered foreign or has become naturalized.)

Italicize words, letters, and numbers that are referred to as them- 5
selves and characters used as symbols in special disciplines such as
mathematics.

Do not set off in quotation marks or italics generic titles of poems 6
(e.g., Sonnet 6) or titles of sacred works and public documents.

> Compare the uses of quotation marks and italics in the following
> examples. Notice also the titles for which neither is necessary.
>
> "Tactics," Chapter 17 in *Companion to College English,* contains an
> excerpt from "Lifeboat Ethics: The Case Against Helping the
> Poor," an article in *Psychology Today,* September, 1974.
>
> In *Alice in Wonderland* the Mock Turtle parodies the Victorian par-
> lor song "Beautiful Star."
>
> The Broadway musical *My Fair Lady* is an adaptation of George
> Bernard Shaw's play *Pygmalion.*
>
> The *New York Times* reviewer praised last night's performance of
> Bizet's opera *Carmen.*
>
> Milton's Sonnet 19, "On His Blindness," looks forward to his epic
> poem *Paradise Lost.*
>
> Hawthorne's short story "The Maypole of Merrymount" can serve
> as a guide to the interpretation of his novel *The Scarlet Letter.*
>
> Because of the steep grade and its tall "drivers," the Union Pacific
> *Daylight* was "doubleheaded" for its climb over the Santa
> Margarita pass.
>
> The fallacy of *post hoc ergo propter hoc,* "after this, therefore
> because of this," is common in statistical arguments.
>
> Some scholars question whether the moral concepts of the Bible
> supplied the groundwork for the Declaration of Independence.

Single quotation marks set off quotations within quotations or titles 7
within titles.

> "One of my students," he groaned, "wrote that O. Henry's stories have
> 'surprised endings.' "
>
> His essay was titled "Irony in Hawthorne's 'Rappacini's Daughter.' "

For italicized titles within italicized titles, return to roman letters 8
for the enclosed title.

> His book was titled *The Muse's Method: An Introduction to* Paradise Lost.

Do not use quotation marks to "apologize" for expressions of 9
doubtful appropriateness such as slang and clichés.

No: The elderly aunt "parked" herself in the nearest chair.

Yes: The elderly aunt settled into the nearest chair.

Do not use quotation marks or italics to set off the title of your   10
own paper on the title page or above the text of page one.

No: "The Dangers of Sleep Deprivation"

No: *The Dangers of Sleep Deprivation*

Yes: The Dangers of Sleep Deprivation

Do not use quotation marks or italics (or capital letters) to empha-   11
size important words or ideas. Use syntax instead.

No: The government needs new "principles," not new policies.

No: The government needs new *principles,* not new policies.

No: The government needs new PRINCIPLES, not new policies.

Yes: What the government needs is not new policies but new prin-
        ciples.

No: In 1973 the Supreme Court "legalized murder."

No: In 1973 the Supreme Court *legalized murder.*

No: In 1973 the Supreme Court LEGALIZED MURDER.

Yes: It was in 1973 that the Supreme Court announced a decision
        that legalized murder.

No: The "chief of police" is mainly responsible for the drop in crime.

No: The *chief of police* is mainly responsible for the drop in crime.

No: The CHIEF OF POLICE is mainly responsible for the drop in
        crime.

Yes: The drop in crime is due mainly to the work of one man: the
        chief of police.

Do not add quotation marks to block-indented quotations. The   12
indentation serves the purpose of quotation marks.

Punctuation of Compound Sentences

Punctuation is based on sentence structure. The most important punctuation is end punctuation, whether closing a sentence or closing an independent clause within a sentence. Improper closing of an independent clause within a sentence causes serious punctuation errors.

Two independent clauses forming a compound sentence must be joined with a comma and a coordinating conjunction or with a semicolon. Or they may be written as two sentences.

> The banks close Monday, but they will be open Tuesday.
>
> The banks close Monday; they will be open Tuesday.
>
> The banks close Monday. They will be open Tuesday.

To use only a comma is to create a *comma splice*.   1

> No: The banks close Monday, they will be open Tuesday.

To use no punctuation is to create a *fused sentence*.   2

> No: The banks close Monday they will be open Tuesday.

Notice that inserting an adverb at the joining point does not solve   3
the problem.

> No: The banks close Monday, however they will open Tuesday.
>
> No: The banks close Monday, then they will open Tuesday.

Readers need a clear signal that they have finished a self-contained unit of thought. The absence of such a signal hinders reading and shows either ignorance of sentence structure or extreme carelessness.

Keep in mind, however, the difference between a compound sen-   4
tence that joins two independent clauses and a complex sentence that joins an independent clause with an adverbial clause. An introductory adverbial clause, preceding an independent clause, is followed with a comma. A trailing adverbial clause, following an independent clause, is also set off with a comma when it gives loosely related information.

To use a semicolon rather than a comma to join an independent and a dependent clause is to misrepresent a complex sentence as compound and cause the reader momentarily to stumble. A semicolon between clauses signals a division between complete statements.

When one of the clauses is not a full statement, the semicolon is a false marker.

No:　　Whereas the banks close Monday; they will open Tuesday.

Yes:　Whereas the banks close Monday, they will open Tuesday.

No:　　The banks close Monday; whereas they will open Tuesday.

Yes:　The banks close Monday, whereas they will open Tuesday.

It is almost as serious to overpunctuate a complex sentence with a semicolon as it is to underpunctuate a compound sentence with a comma or with no punctuation when it needs a semicolon.

Sentence Fragments

A sentence fragment is a pseudosentence punctuated as if it were an actual sentence. Usually it is a phrase or clause left over from a preceding sentence.

The first year of law school is similar in purpose to a cadet's first year at a military academy. A period of controlled pressure designed to weed out those who lack the necessary aptitude and will.

But a sentence fragment can also be a phrase or clause dismembered from a following sentence.

Because he had been blinded to the cruelty of the Soviet dictatorship by his advisors' belief that both Russia and the United States were developing into modern social democracies. Franklin D. Roosevelt made disastrous concessions to Stalin at Yalta.

To correct a sentence fragment, you can attach it to the sentence to which it belongs.　　　　1

The first year of law school is similar in purpose to a cadet's first year at a military academy: a period of controlled pressure designed to weed out those who lack the necessary aptitude and will.

Because he had been blinded to the cruelty of the Soviet dictatorship by his advisors' belief that both Russia and the United States were developing into modern social democracies, Franklin D. Roosevelt made disastrous concessions to Stalin at Yalta.

You can also correct a fragment by forming it into a new sentence.　　　2

The first year of law school is similar in purpose to a cadet's first year at a military academy. It is a period of controlled pressure designed to weed out those who lack the necessary aptitude and will.

Franklin D. Roosevelt had been blinded to the cruelty of the Soviet dictatorship by his advisors' belief that both Russia and the United States were developing into modern social democracies. As a result, Roosevelt made disastrous concessions to Stalin at Yalta.

Writers sometimes use sentence fragments intentionally for informality of tone or special effect. 3

So much for that. Now on to the next business.

Indeed! A pet inheriting a million dollars!

He walked off without saying a word. Which is to say, he refused the offer.

Unintentional fragments are prime indicators of carelessness or incompetence in writing. Avoid sentence fragments, both unintentional and intentional, in academic writing.

COORDINATION
AND SUBORDINATION

A sentence can expand in two ways. Its parts can spread equally like the tines of a pitchfork. Or they can branch progressively like an antler, with primary elements supporting lesser elements, these lesser supporting still lesser, and so forth. The first method is known as coordination; the second, as subordination.

Coordination

 Coordination requires, first, that the ideas of a coordinate structure form a logical set. That is, they must be similar in nature and importance and must not overlap.

It is an error to coordinate dissimilar ideas.   1

> No: Maude Tilly was from Landrum and died Thursday. She was a truck driver and a Baptist.

> Yes: Maude Tilly from Landrum died Thursday. Though her truck driving often kept her away on weekends, she was a faithful member of her Baptist church.

> No: *God and General Longstreet* explores printed material about the historical Lost Cause and was written by Thomas Connelly and Barbara Bellows.

> Yes: *God and General Longstreet,* written by Thomas Connelly and Barbara Bellows, explores printed material about the historical Lost Cause.

It is also an error to coordinate overlapping ideas.   2

> No: The victim denounced the courts and railed at the criminal justice system.

> Yes: The victim denounced the courts, indeed railed at the entire criminal justice system.

These errors are known as errors in logical parallelism.

Coordination requires, second, that the parts of a coordi-   1
nate structure be grammatically similar and complete.

No: Dvořák's piano quintet requires two violins, a viola, a cello, and piano.

Yes: Dvořák's piano quintet requires two violins, a viola, a cello, and a piano.

No: An orchestra and choir seem unnecessary for a wedding.

Yes: An orchestra and a choir seem unnecessary for a wedding.

No: He liked surfing of all kinds: boardsurfing, bodysurfing, windsurfing, shore-break surfing, and even to channel surf when the waves were down.

Yes: He liked surfing of all kinds: boardsurfing, bodysurfing, windsurfing, shore-break surfing, and even channel surfing when the waves were down.

No: He is an actor, a poet, and plays the violin.

No: He is an actor, a poet, and he plays the violin.

Yes: He is an actor, a poet, and a violinist.

Yes: He is an actor and a poet, and he plays the violin.

Yes: He acts, composes poetry, and plays the violin.

No: She was dedicated to her profession and a good mother.

Yes: She was a dedicated professional and a good mother.

Yes: She was dedicated to her profession and devoted to her children.

No: The governor came to the flood-stricken town to show support for the homeless victims and also because he saw a good photo opportunity.

Yes: The governor came to the flood-stricken town to show support for the homeless victims and also to take advantage of a good photo opportunity.

No: The sign at the ferryboat landing stated the amount of the fare, the departure schedule, the distance and duration of the trip, and how many vehicles were allowed at one time.

Yes: The sign at the ferryboat landing stated the amount of the fare, the departure schedule, the distance and duration of the trip, and the number of vehicles allowed at one time.

No: His three responsibilities were to mow the grass, to water the houseplants, and walking the dog twice daily.

No: His three responsibilities were to mow the grass, to water the houseplants, and walk the dog twice daily.

Yes: His three responsibilities were to mow the grass, to water the houseplants, and to walk the dog twice daily.

Yes: His three responsibilities were to mow the grass, water the houseplants, and walk the dog twice daily.

Yes: His three responsibilities were mowing the grass, watering the houseplants, and walking the dog twice daily.

No: Saving extra money for a special need may be easier than to earn it.

No: To save extra money for a special need may be easier than earning it.

Yes: Saving extra money for a special need may be easier than earning it.

Yes: To save extra money for a special need may be easier than to earn it.

A special problem area in coordination is the managing of correlative conjunctions so that they join identical grammatical constructions.

2

No: He neither carried his checkbook nor his credit card.

Yes: He carried neither his checkbook nor his credit card.

No: Garaging a car will not only save the external paint but also the interior.

No: Garaging a car not only will save the external paint but also save the interior.

Yes: Garaging a car will not only save the external paint but also save the interior.

Yes: Garaging a car will save not only the external paint but also the interior.

No: His responses both irritated the prosecuting attorney and the judge.

Yes: His responses irritated both the prosecuting attorney and the judge.

Yes: His responses both irritated the prosecuting attorney and annoyed the judge.

No: We have won more games than ever before, both because we have played unselfishly and we have followed the coach's instructions.

Yes: We have won more games than ever before, both because we have played unselfishly and because we have followed the coach's instructions.

Another special problem in coordination occurs when one element   3 in a pair of coordinated verbs is missing. Each verb of the pair must be fully formed and connectable with what follows.

No: Nova Scotia always has and always will be my favorite place to visit.

Yes: Nova Scotia always has been and always will be my favorite place to visit.

Subordination

Subordination requires that unequal elements be joined in such a way as to indicate their inequality and also their logical relationship.

 Errors in subordination occur when ideas logically inequivalent are joined equivalently in a coordinate structure (see Coordination above) or when the lesser of two ideas is emphasized over the more important. Express the foreground idea in the main clause and the background idea in the subordinate clause or phrase.

No: One of the finest hymn writers of the eighteenth century was Philip Doddridge, and his poems generally end strongly.

No: One of the finest hymn writers of the eighteenth century was Philip Doddridge, whose poems generally end strongly.

Yes: The poems of Philip Doddridge, one of the finest hymn writers of the eighteenth century, generally end strongly.

No: The home of the British prime minister is at 10 Downing Street, and it is a brick townhouse.

No: The home of the British prime minister, which is a brick townhouse, is at 10 Downing Street.

Yes: The home of the British prime minister, at 10 Downing Street, is a brick townhouse.

No: The branches are waving violently, and the wind is strong.

No: Because the branches are waving violently, the wind is strong.

Yes: Because the wind is strong, the branches are waving violently.

The second sentence in the last set of examples illustrates another error in subordination. This error occurs when a lesser idea is subordinated to a more important idea but in an inexact way. Choose a subordinating conjunction that shows the precise logical connection between the clauses it joins.

No: Because the nights are shortening, the days are lengthening.

Yes: When the nights are shortening, the days are lengthening.

No: Even if his sister preferred her steak broiled medium well, he liked his medium rare.

No: Though his sister preferred her steak broiled medium well, he liked his medium rare.

Yes: Whereas his sister preferred her steak broiled medium well, he liked his medium rare.

No: Softbound books seem a bargain unless their covers get worn.

Yes: Softbound books seem a bargain until their covers get worn.

No: Think twice when you speak.

Yes: Think twice before you speak.

Correcting improper subordination may require supplying an important idea left unstated.

Yes: Because the branches are waving violently, one can be sure that the wind is strong.

Yes: Because it is true that the nights are shortening, it is also true that the days are lengthening.

Yes: Though his sister preferred her steak broiled medium well and though he followed her judgment in most things, he liked his steak medium rare.

Yes: Softbound books seem a bargain, and indeed they are unless their covers are so poorly made as to be soon worn.

AGREEMENT

Since the rules concerning the agreement of subject and verb and the agreement of pronoun and antecedent overlap, violations of these rules are largely parallel errors. Therefore, the two problem areas are treated here together.

Agreement of Subject and Verb

 The verb of a clause must agree with (match in form) its subject in number and person. Disagreement in person is a problem only with the verb *be,* which is unique among English verbs in having a separate first-person-singular form in the present tense. Since few are likely to err with "I" and "am," we can concentrate on problems of agreement in number.

These problems arise from the fact that third-person-singular present-tense verb forms end in *-s* or *-es,* whereas third-person-plural forms do not, adhering to the general pattern. Though the percentage of sentence situations that cause agreement problems is small for a native speaker of English, these situations need to be mastered; for errors in agreement are considered serious flaws.

The ability to recognize a verb's true subject is necessary to accurate agreement. Mistakes resulting from misidentification of the subject most often occur in the following situations.

Linking verbs

When two noun elements differing in number are joined by a linking verb, consider the one preceding the verb to be the verb's subject and make the verb agree with it.

No:	The healthiest kind are traditional roses.
Yes:	The healthiest kind is traditional roses.
No:	Traditional roses is the healthiest kind.
Yes:	Traditional roses are the healthiest kind.

Intervening modifiers

Phrases that come between a verb and its subject are common sources of disagreement. Errors of this sort are most frequent when the intervening phrase is long.

One kind of confusing intervening phrase is the prepositional phrase 2
whose object is closely related to the subject of the verb and yet differs from the subject in number.

No:	The healthiest kind of roses are the traditional varieties.
Yes:	The healthiest kind of roses is the traditional varieties.
No:	A combination of factors are responsible for the delay.
Yes:	A combination of factors is responsible for the delay.

Another kind of intervening prepositional phrase that can cause an 3
error in agreement is one that creates with the subject a plural idea.
Logical plurality, however, is not the same as grammatical plurality.
Treat such constructions as pseudoplurals.

No:	Lady Macbeth as well as her husband are guilty of Duncan's death.
Yes:	Lady Macbeth as well as her husband is guilty of Duncan's death.
No:	The old locomotive along with its tender, caboose, and freight cars were sold for scrap.
Yes:	The old locomotive along with its tender, caboose, and freight cars was sold for scrap.
No:	A Confederate Army buckle in addition to some shell casings and scraps of gray cloth were found on the battlefield.
Yes:	A Confederate Army buckle in addition to some shell casings and scraps of gray cloth was found on the battlefield.

Remember that an object of a preposition can never be the subject of
a verb or be any other skeletal element of a sentence.

Inverted order

Do not assume that subjects always precede verbs or, when the order
is reversed, that the first noun following the verb is the full subject.

Errors from inverted order usually happen when the subject is plural. 4

No:	Chosen from among the audience was a man and his wife.
Yes:	Chosen from among the audience were a man and his wife.
No:	In the middle of the stack of papers was the bill and the receipt.
Yes:	In the middle of the stack of papers were the bill and the receipt.

Errors from inverted order often occur in questions.   5

No: Where is the hammer and screwdriver?

Yes: Where are the hammer and screwdriver?

No: Has Jacob and Kevin left yet?

Yes: Have Jacob and Kevin left yet?

Errors from inverted order are common in expletive constructions.   6

No: There is a suitcase and a golf bag yet to be loaded.

Yes: There are a suitcase and a golf bag yet to be loaded.

Singular compound subjects

Mistakes in subject-verb agreement occur not only from misidentifying the subject but also from misconstruing the subject's number. Subjects can look plural and be singular. They can also look singular and be plural. Still others are singular or plural according to logical context.

Compound subjects are singular if they refer to the same person or   7
thing or to a unit.

No: Her pride and joy were her garden.

Yes: Her pride and joy was her garden.

No: His colleague, mentor, and friend are writing his biography.

Yes: His colleague, mentor, and friend is writing his biography.

No: Sauerkraut and wieners are a family favorite.

Yes: Sauerkraut and wieners is a family favorite.

Compound subjects joined by *or* or *nor* or by the correlative con-   8
junctions *either . . . or, neither . . . nor,* or *not only . . . but also* are
singular if both parts are singular, plural if both parts are plural. If
one part is singular and the other is plural, the verb agrees with the
nearer part.

No: Neither Robert nor Nicholas were available.

Yes: Neither Robert nor Nicholas was available.

No: Either Mariah or her parents is home by now.

Yes: Either Mariah or her parents are home by now.

Yes: Either Mariah's parents or Mariah is home by now.

No: Not only pollen but also dust affect my sinuses.

Yes: Not only pollen but also dust affects my sinuses.

When *each* or *every* precedes a compound subject, the subject is   9
singular.

> No: Each boy and girl were given a front-row seat.
>
> Yes: Each boy and girl was given a front-row seat.

Singular subjects ending in -*s*

Some subjects formed of words ending in -*s* are considered singular 10
in idea and take a singular verb.

Subjects specifying amounts are singular.

> No: Two months are too little time to finish this project.
>
> Yes: Two months is too little time to finish this project.
>
> No: Five dollars were added to the coffee fund.
>
> Yes: Five dollars was added to the coffee fund.

Titles and other phrases designating a unit that end in -*s* are singular. 11

> No: The Five Pillars are basic Muslim doctrine.
>
> Yes: The Five Pillars is basic Muslim doctrine.
>
> No: The United States have the highest living standard in the world.
>
> Yes: The United States has the highest living standard in the world.

Certain words ending in -*s* always take a singular verb *(news,*   12
measles, molasses).

> No: Measles are a potentially serious disease.
>
> Yes: Measles is a potentially serious disease.

Words ending in -*ics* take a singular verb when they refer to a body 13
of knowledge, an academic discipline or course of instruction, or a
profession but can take a plural verb when they refer to separate
instances, activities, or characteristics *(ethics, athletics, aesthetics,*
acoustics, politics, physics, mathematics, statistics).

> No: Mathematics are daunting to some who have not been taught
>   well.
>
> Yes: Mathematics is daunting to some who have not been taught
>   well.
>
> Yes: Acoustics is an important study for industrial architects.
>
> Yes: The acoustics of this auditorium have never been right.

Some nouns ending in -*s* that refer to objects thought of as pairs take a plural verb (*pants, slacks, jeans, eyeglasses, scissors, clippers,* etc.). If *pair of* is used with such words, *pair* becomes the subject and the verb is singular.

14

> Yes: The new hedge clippers cut better than the old.
>
> Yes: The new pair of hedge clippers cuts better than the old.

The words *series, species,* and *means* have the same form for both singular and plural. Their number must therefore be indicated by that of the verb.

15

> Yes: Last year's concert series was better than the previous year's.
>
> Yes: The concert series of the past two years were exceptional.

Collective nouns

When the subject of a verb is a collective noun such as *team, committee, jury, crowd,* or *couple,* regard it as singular and give it a singular verb unless the context requires otherwise.

16

> Yes: The committee holds public hearings next week.
>
> Yes: The committee are bickering about whether to have public hearings.

People and *police* are always plural, as are adjectival nouns referring to groups.

> Yes: In the outcome of the referendum, the people have spoken.
>
> Yes: The poor are always with us.

Collective nouns with Latin endings such as *media, criteria, phenomena,* and *curricula* take plural verbs. Distinguish these plural forms from the singular *medium, criterion, phenomenon,* and *curriculum.*

17

> No: The public media is protected by the First Amendment.
>
> Yes: The public media are protected by the First Amendment.
>
> Yes: The print medium is protected by the First Amendment.

Indefinite pronouns

Mistakes in agreement can result from failure to realize that the following indefinite pronouns are always singular: *anyone, everyone, someone, anybody, everybody, somebody, either, neither, each, one,*

18

and *no one*. Even when expressing a plural idea, they refer to individuals and take a singular verb.

No: Each of the students were individually praised.

Yes: Each of the students was individually praised.

No: Everyone on the picket lines are irritable.

Yes: Everyone on the picket lines is irritable.

No: Neither of the campsites are occupied.

Yes: Neither of the campsites is occupied.

The pronouns *some, all, more, most, any, part,* and *none* are singular 19
or plural according to context.

Some of the pie was eaten.

Some of the pies were eaten.

The pronouns *few, many, both,* and *several* are always plural.

Relative pronouns

The relative pronouns *who, which,* and *that* take singular or plural   20
verbs according to whether their antecedents are singular or plural.

She served the pie that was made yesterday.

She served the pies that were made yesterday.

We wrote the senator who favors the legislation.

We wrote the senators who favor the legislation.

Agreement of Pronoun and Antecedent

Pronouns and pronominal adjectives agree with their antecedents in person, gender, and number. Since few mistakes in person or gender are likely to be made by a native speaker of English, we can concentrate on number. The areas of difficulty parallel those of subject-verb agreement. For more detail, see the corresponding sections above.

The following rules concerning pronouns (*it, they,* etc.) also apply to pronominal adjectives (*its, their, her, our,* etc.).

Compound antecedents

Ordinarily a compound antecedent is plural and requires a plural   1
pronoun.

The car and the truck were recovered soon after they were stolen.

Compound antecedents that refer to one person or thing or to a unit   2
are singular and require singular pronouns.

> My friend and coworker found himself in a predicament Thursday.
>
> That man reveres the Stars and Stripes who has defended it with his life.
>
> We order corned beef and cabbage whenever we see it on the menu.
>
> Five dollars and seven cents in pennies will not buy much, but it will take a while to count.

Compound antecedents with singular parts joined by *or, nor,*   3
either . . . or, neither . . . nor, or *not only . . . but also* are singular
and require singular pronouns.

> Almost every week we hear of a stolen car or truck left unlocked by its owner.

Compound antecedents preceded by *each* or *every* are singular and
require singular pronouns.

> Every car and truck in the parking lot had an advertising flyer on its windshield.

Collective nouns

Collective nouns as antecedents are singular and require singular   4
pronouns unless the context requires otherwise.

> The scout troop found itself in a natural amphitheater.
>
> The scout troop seated themselves on the stumps and boulders.

Indefinite pronouns

The following indefinite pronouns are always singular: *anyone,*   5
everyone, someone, anybody, everybody, somebody, either, neither,
each, one, and *no one.* Even when expressing a plural idea, they
refer to individuals and are referred to by singular pronouns.

> No: Everyone enjoyed themselves at the county fair.
>
> Yes: Everyone enjoyed himself at the county fair.
>
> Yes: All enjoyed themselves at the county fair.

Do not mistake as the antecedent the object of a modifying prepositional phrase.

> No: Neither of the boys hurt themselves badly.
>
> Yes: Neither of the boys hurt himself badly.

Indefinite nouns

Nouns such as *person* and *individual* are singular and are referred   6
to by singular pronouns.

No: Even when a customer is unreasonable, they must be treated
        politely.

Yes: Even when a customer is unreasonable, he must be treated
        politely.

Yes: Even when customers are unreasonable, they must be treated
        politely.

Agreement of Noun and Adjective

agr
10c   Do not use the plural demonstrative adjective *these* to modify
        singular nouns such as *kind* or *type*.

No: These kind of apples grow better in cold climates.

Yes: These kinds of apples grow better in cold climates.

Yes: This kind of apples grows better in cold climates.

Yes: This kind of apple grows better in cold climates.

PRONOUN REFERENCE

The relationship between a pronoun or pronominal adjective and its antecedent must be certain and clear.

Ambiguous Reference

 Pronoun reference is faulty when a pronoun can refer to more than one antecedent.

No: Sarah told Emily that she needed to replace her pencil.

Yes: Sarah told Emily, "I need to replace your pencil."

Yes: Sarah told Emily, "You need to replace my pencil."

Yes: Sarah told Emily, "I need to replace my pencil."

Yes: Sarah told Emily, "You need to replace your pencil."

Remote Reference

 Pronoun reference is faulty when pronouns follow their antecedents at too great a distance to be easily associated.

No: Franklin Delano Roosevelt once joked, "The secret of eternal youth is arrested development." If so, most of the spectators at yesterday's game will live forever. They behaved like inmates of an institution. The behavior he described was laughable; yesterday's was disgusting.

Yes: Franklin Delano Roosevelt once joked, "The secret of eternal youth is arrested development." If so, most of the spectators at yesterday's game will live forever. They behaved like inmates of an institution. The behavior Roosevelt described was laughable; yesterday's was disgusting.

Do not separate a pronoun from its antecedent by a paragraph break.   1

No: They behaved like inmates of an institution. The behavior Roosevelt described was laughable; yesterday's was disgusting.

      Eventually they became so unruly that the umpire awarded a forfeit to the visiting team. . . .

Yes: They behaved like inmates of an institution. The behavior Roosevelt described was laughable; yesterday's was disgusting.

      Eventually the spectators became so unruly that the umpire awarded a forfeit to the visiting team. . . .

In the first sentence of your paper, do not use a pronoun whose antecedent is in the title. The paper's text should be independent of its title.

Irony in "The Unknown Citizen"

No: This poem uses irony for social satire.

Yes: W. H. Auden's "The Unknown Citizen" uses irony for social satire.

Weak Reference

Pronoun reference is faulty when the antecedent is only implied.   1

No: Jeremy took violin lessons for five years but never mastered it.

Yes: Jeremy took violin lessons for five years but never mastered the instrument.

Pronoun reference is faulty when the antecedent is a possessive noun or pronoun. A possessive may, however, serve as the antecedent for another possessive. Also a possessive may precede its antecedent at a short distance.   2

No: The company's charitable contributions helped it regain public esteem.

Yes: The charitable contributions of the company helped it regain public esteem.

Yes: The company's charitable contributions helped restore its public esteem.

Yes: Its charitable contributions helped the company regain public esteem.

Broad Reference

Pronoun reference is faulty when a demonstrative or relative pronoun has no expressed antecedent but refers only vaguely to an idea.

No: The dormitory student spends most of his time on campus; this provides him many opportunities to make friends.

No: The dormitory student spends most of his time on campus, which provides him many opportunities to make friends.

Yes: The dormitory student spends most of his time on campus; this circumstance provides him many opportunities to make friends.

The dormitory student spends most of his time on campus, a circumstance that provides him many opportunities to make friends.

Yes: Because the dormitory student spends most of his time on campus, he has many opportunities to make friends.

No: The post-and-beam building withstood the earthquake. This shows that some older methods of construction are not inferior to new.

No: The post-and-beam building withstood the earthquake, which shows that some older methods of construction are not inferior to new.

Yes: The fact that the post-and-beam building withstood the earthquake shows that some older methods of construction are not inferior to new.

Yes: The post-and-beam building withstood the earthquake. Evidently some older methods of construction are not inferior to new.

Yes: The post-and-beam building withstood the earthquake—an evidence that some older methods of construction are not inferior to new.

Indefinite Reference

ref
11e Pronoun reference is faulty when the pronouns *you, they,* and *it* have only a general reference.   1

No: You do not have to be especially mathematical to learn computer programming.

Yes: A person does not have to be especially mathematical to learn computer programming.

Yes: One does not have to be especially mathematical to learn computer programming.

Yes: Computer programming does not require unusual ability in mathematics.

No: To avoid injury to your hands, you need proper piano technique.

Yes: To avoid injury to his hands, a pianist needs proper technique.

No: In the military they insist on proper respect.

Yes: In the military, superiors insist on proper respect.

Yes: The military insists on proper respect.

No: They say that girls develop mathematical ability later than boys.

Yes: Studies have indicated that girls develop mathematical ability later than boys.

No: In Numbers 32:23 it says, "Be sure your sin will find you out."

Yes: Numbers 32:23 says, "Be sure your sin will find you out."

Yes: The Bible says, "Be sure your sin will find you out" (Num. 32:23).

No: It said on the morning news that the escapees had been caught.

Yes: The morning news reported that the escapees had been caught.

Yes: According to the morning news, the escapees have been caught.

It without an antecedent may be used correctly as an expletive, a word filling the place of a delayed subject.   2

Yes: It is impossible to meet the deadline.

Yes: To meet the deadline is impossible.

Yes: It is now clear who the winner will be.

Yes: Who the winner will be is now clear.

It also may be used correctly without an antecedent in reference to time, distance, or weather.   3

Yes: It was eight o'clock when he left the office.

Yes: It was dark by the time he got home.

Yes: It is two blocks from the courthouse to the town square.

Yes: It rained steadily on the day of the wedding.

MISPLACED AND DANGLING MODIFIERS

Misplaced Modifiers

 Place modifying words, phrases, and clauses in a sentence so that the meaning is not uncertain or awkwardly suspended.

Only and similar words

Place limiting adverbs such as *almost, especially, even, hardly, just, merely, nearly, only,* and *simply* immediately before the word they modify rather than (as is common in spoken English) before the verb.

1

No:	She only hesitated one minute before entering the room.
Yes:	She hesitated only one minute before entering the room.
No:	He almost lost a year's salary in fines and court fees.
Yes:	He lost almost a year's salary in fines and court fees.
No:	He had hardly slept a wink all night.
Yes:	He had slept hardly a wink all night.

Squinting modifiers

Do not position a modifier so that it can modify the words both before and after it.

2

No:	The driver approaching the judge's bench fervently began to speak.
Yes:	The driver fervently approaching the judge's bench began to speak.
Yes:	The driver approaching the judge's bench began to speak fervently.
Yes:	Fervently the driver approaching the judge's bench began to speak.
No:	The agitator who was carrying a sign to gain attention cleared his throat loudly and began to speak.
Yes:	The agitator who to gain attention was carrying a sign cleared his throat loudly and began to speak.

Yes: The agitator who was carrying a sign cleared his throat loudly to gain attention and began to speak.

Yes: To gain attention, the agitator who was carrying a sign cleared his throat loudly; then he began to speak.

Other confusing misplacements

Avoid illogical misplacement of modifying words, phrases, or clauses. 3

No: All teenagers are not ready to drive at the age of fifteen.

Yes: Not all teenagers are ready to drive at the age of fifteen.

No: The former ambassador predicted that a free market will bring democracy to China at the end of his lecture.

Yes: The former ambassador predicted at the end of his lecture that a free market will bring democracy to China.

Yes: At the end of his lecture, the former ambassador predicted that a free market will bring democracy to China.

No: Rusty from years of disuse and exposure to the weather, the new owner looked dismally at the farm equipment.

Yes: The new owner looked dismally at the farm equipment, rusty from years of disuse and exposure to the weather.

No: The package was delivered by the mail carrier that was sent from overseas.

Yes: The package that was sent from overseas was delivered by the mail carrier.

Split infinitives

Avoid inserting words between the sign of the infinitive *(to)* and the verb base. If, however, an infinitive is less awkward split than unsplit, leave it split; or, better, revise the sentence so as to eliminate the infinitive construction. Infinitives incorporating verb phrases are less awkward when split than are simple infinitives. 4

No: He intended to as soon as possible complete the plans for the renovation.

Yes: He intended to complete the plans for the renovation as soon as possible.

No: If you want to really do well in this course, you must do your reading as it is assigned.

Yes: If you want to do really well in this course, you must do your reading as it is assigned.

Awkward splitting of other grammatical unities

Avoid awkward separation of basic sentence elements.

Do not awkwardly separate the subject from the verb. 5

No: The rookie outfielder, though he had led his league in batting through the earlier half of the season, was not chosen for the all-star team.

Yes: The rookie outfielder was not chosen for the all-star team, though he had led his league in batting through the earlier half of the season.

Yes: Though he had led his league in batting through the earlier half of the season, the rookie outfielder was not chosen for the all-star team.

Do not awkwardly separate a verb or verbal from its complement. 6

No: Her report uses as much as possible original source material.

Yes: Her report uses original source material as much as possible.

No: He enjoyed refereeing despite all of its hazards international soccer.

Yes: He enjoyed refereeing international soccer despite all of its hazards.

Do not awkwardly separate the parts of a verb phrase. 7

No: He had until the day before yesterday read only one chapter.

Yes: He had read only one chapter until the day before yesterday.

Yes: Until the day before yesterday, he had read only one chapter.

Dangling Modifiers

 Unlike misplaced modifiers, dangling modifiers cannot be corrected by repositioning. They are structurally and logically disjoined from the rest of the sentence. To correct them requires a rewriting of the sentence.

Introductory dangling elements

An introductory verbal phrase or elliptical clause dangles when 1 its implied subject is not identical with the expressed subject of the independent clause that follows. To correct the sentence,

expand the dangling element into a fully formed dependent clause
or change the subject of the independent clause so that it agrees with
the implied subject of the dangling element.

No: Having entered the room, our attention was drawn immediately to a stuffed owl on a bookcase.

No: On entering the room, our attention was drawn immediately to a stuffed owl on a bookcase.

No: When entering the room, our attention was drawn immediately to a stuffed owl on a bookcase.

Yes: When we entered the room, our attention was drawn immediately to a stuffed owl on a bookcase.

Yes: Having entered the room, we immediately noticed a stuffed owl on a bookcase.

Yes: On having entered the room, we immediately noticed a stuffed owl on a bookcase.

No: To reach the upper shelf, a small ladder was brought from the kitchen.

No: To reach the upper shelf, it was necessary to bring a small ladder from the kitchen.

Yes: Because the upper shelf was high, a small ladder was brought from the kitchen.

Yes: Because the upper shelf was high, it was necessary to bring a small ladder from the kitchen.

Yes: To reach the upper shelf, we brought a small ladder from the kitchen.

A dangling phrase can sometimes be corrected by expansion into an 2
absolute phrase.

Yes: The upper shelf being high, a small ladder was brought from the kitchen.

Yes: The upper shelf being high, it was necessary to bring a small ladder from the kitchen.

A dangling gerund-containing phrase can often be corrected by 3
giving the gerund a possessive subject.

No: On entering the room, our attention was drawn immediately to a stuffed owl on a bookcase.

Yes: On our entering the room, our attention was drawn immediately to a stuffed owl on the bookcase.

Trailing dangling elements

An introductory verbal phrase or elliptical clause that dangles   4
does not cease to dangle when it is shifted to the end of the sentence. The original problem remains. Its implied subject still must
be identical with the expressed subject of the independent clause
it formerly preceded and now follows.

No: It was necessary to bring a small ladder from the kitchen to reach the upper shelf.

Yes: We had to bring a small ladder from the kitchen to reach the upper shelf.

No: The fire could have been stopped by simply shutting off the gas supply.

Yes: We could have stopped the fire by simply shutting off the gas supply.

Yes: The fire could have been stopped by our simply shutting off the gas supply.

Trailing dangling elements are especially common where an inexpe-   5
rienced writer has moved from an example to a generalization or
from a generalization to an example.

No: The major advertiser dropped its support of the television show, proving that the threat of a boycott can be effective.

Yes: The fact that the major advertiser dropped its support of the television show proves that the threat of a boycott can be effective.

Yes: The major advertiser dropped its support of the television show. Clearly, the threat of a boycott can be effective.

No: The threat of a boycott can be effective, as seen when the major advertiser dropped its support of the television show.

Yes: That the threat of a boycott can be effective was apparent when the major advertiser dropped its support of the television show.

Yes: Clearly the threat of a boycott can be effective: the major advertiser dropped its support of the television show.

Acceptable dangling elements

Phrases such as *as expected, to be exact, to summarize,* and *to make*   6
matters worse are considered general modifiers that stand in absolute
relation to the rest of the sentence. They do not require revision.

Yes: He could not remember where we had parked the car. To make matters worse, he could not remember what it looked like.

SENTENCE LOGIC

Some grammatical errors belong to the borderlands of sentence structure and logic.

Illogical Predication

 The core elements of a clause, when lifted out, should make basic sense. If the subject, verb, and complement do not logically connect, the clause is fundamentally flawed and must be reconstructed. Notice especially the following problems.

Logical inequivalence

Be sure that the subject of a linking verb equates logically with the predicate noun.

No:	The farmer's best-paying crop is raising turnips.
Yes:	The farmer's best-paying crop is turnips.
No:	The vocation for which she prepared was a schoolteacher.
Yes:	The vocation for which she prepared was school teaching.

1

Grammatical inequivalence

Be sure that the subject of a linking verb equates grammatically with the predicate noun. Only noun elements can be subjects or predicate nouns. Do not use an adverbial element for the subject or predicate noun of a linking verb.

No:	In the midafternoon is when I feel the drowsiest.
Yes:	The midafternoon is the time I feel the drowsiest.
Yes:	In the midafternoon I feel the drowsiest.
No:	By reading the want ads is how I found my job.
Yes:	Reading the want ads is how I found my job.
Yes:	By reading the want ads, I found my job.
No:	The only basis on which I will come is if my family is invited also.
Yes:	The only basis on which I will come is that my family be invited also.
Yes:	I will come only if my family is invited also.

2

When defining something, state what, not where or when, it is.   3

No: A double fault in tennis is when the player serving fails to place his first and second serves within the proper area on his opponent's side of the net.

Yes: A double fault in tennis is the failure of the player serving to place his first and second serves within the proper area on his opponent's side of the net.

No: The post hoc fallacy is where one assumes that because one thing happened before another it caused the other.

Yes: The post hoc fallacy is the assumption that because one thing happened before another it caused the other.

Do not use a *because* phrase or clause as the subject or predicate   4
noun of a sentence expressing causation.

No: Because of his desire to be a writer is why Isaac Singer came to America.

Yes: Because of his desire to be a writer, Isaac Singer came to America.

No: Because he wanted to be a writer is why Isaac Singer came to America.

Yes: Because he wanted to be a writer, Isaac Singer came to America.

No: The reason Isaac Singer came to America is because he wanted to be a writer.

Yes: The reason Isaac Singer came to America is that he wanted to be a writer.

Yes: Isaac Singer came to America because he wanted to be a writer.

No: Because the strength to resist is gone does not mean the will has gone also.

Yes: The fact that the strength to resist is gone does not mean the will has gone also.

Yes: Because the strength to resist is gone, the will is not necessarily gone also.

Yes: Though the strength to resist be gone, the will need not be gone also.

Do not use a prepositional phrase as the subject or predicate   5
noun of a sentence expressing purpose.

No: The purpose of a liberal arts education is for improving the person.

Yes: The purpose of a liberal arts education is the improvement of the person.

Other illogical predication

A weak sense of the sentence core can result in a variety of mixed   6
constructions.

No: The fact that the axis of the earth is tilted in relation to the sun
        is responsible for the seasons.

Yes: The tilt of the earth's axis in relation to the sun is responsible for
        the seasons.

No: The conclusion of the study shows that most toxic substances
        are eventually broken down by soil bacteria.

Yes: The conclusion of the study is that most toxic substances are
        eventually broken down by soil bacteria.

Yes: The study concludes that most toxic substances are eventually
        broken down by soil bacteria.

No: From the shore they watched the changing reflection of the
        autumn moon rise slowly in the sky.

Yes: From the shore they watched the changing reflection of the
        autumn moon rising slowly in the sky.

Incomplete Predication

  Supply all words necessary to complete the sense and syntax of
the predicate.

Incomplete causation

Do not omit the consequence in a statement using *so* or *such*.   1

No: The birthday party was such a pleasant surprise.

Yes: The birthday party was such a pleasant surprise that he wrote
        thank-you notes to all who came.

Yes: The birthday party was a most pleasant surprise.

No: This sonata is so hard to learn.

Yes: This sonata is so hard to learn that teachers rarely assign it.

Yes: This sonata is exceptionally hard to learn.

Discontinued comparison

Do not omit the second part of a comparison.   2

No: Mabel's Tables serves better fried chicken.

Yes: Mabel's Tables serves better fried chicken than any other restau-
        rant in town.

No: Andrew's taste in clothes is surely different.

Yes: Andrew's taste in clothes is surely different from yours and
        mine.

Elliptical comparison

Do not omit necessary words in a comparison containing a paral-   3.
lel construction. Ellipsis is possible only at the end of the sentence.

No: On certain days artificial lures work as well if not better than live
bait.

Yes: On certain days artificial lures work as well as if not better than
live bait.

Yes: On certain days artificial lures work as well as live bait, if not
better.

No: Thickety Cove is one of the best, if not the best, place on the
lake to catch bass.

No: Thickety Cove is one of the best, if not the best, places on the
lake to catch bass.

No: Thickety Cove is one of the best places on the lake, if not the
best, to catch bass.

Yes: Thickety Cove is one of the best places on the lake, if not the
best place, to catch bass.

Yes: Thickety Cove is one of the best places on the lake to catch
bass, if not the best.

Illogical comparison

Do not compare items that are of different sorts or are interinvolved.   4

Avoid illogical comparisons that omit a required possessive.

No: Hailey's knowledge of cooking is as great as her mother.

Yes: Hailey's knowledge of cooking is as great as her mother's.

Avoid illogical comparisons that omit a required *other.* A thing
cannot reasonably be compared to itself or a person to himself.

No: Pennsylvania is as beautiful as any state in the Union.

Yes: Pennsylvania is as beautiful as any other state in the Union.

No: Langley practices harder than any player on his team.

Yes: Langley practices harder than any other player on his team.

Awkward Shifts

Maintain consistency within and among sentences in person, number, subject, voice, tense, and mood.

Shifts in person

 Do not shift arbitrarily to the second person in first- or third-person discourse.

No: I prefer aggressive stock trading, even though you never know when the market will drop.

Yes: I prefer aggressive stock trading, even though I never know when the market will drop.

No: Summer visitors to England will find the weather pleasant, but you still need to take warm coats.

Yes: Summer visitors to England will find the weather pleasant, but they still need to take warm coats.

Shifts in number

 Do not shift unnecessarily between singular and plural.

Do not shift haphazardly between singular and plural nouns referring   1 to the same person or thing. Though a lesser error than disagreement of pronoun and antecedent, it also disrupts continuity.

No: Visitors to the National Gallery of Art wander with delight through a maze of treasure-filled rooms. In so engaging a setting, the wanderer cares little about getting lost.

Yes: Visitors to the National Gallery of Art wander with delight through a maze of treasure-filled rooms. In so engaging a setting, the wanderers care little about getting lost.

Another awkward shift in number occurs when a plural possessive   2 is joined to a generic singular. Stay with the plural.

No: After the concluding fireworks display, all the families picked up their ice chest and blanket and headed for their car.

Yes: After the concluding fireworks display, all the families picked up their ice chests and blankets and headed for their cars.

Shifts in subject

 Do not shift unnecessarily between sentence subjects.

No: In the Apache museum the women studied the hunting weapons, whereas the cooking implements interested the men!

Yes: In the Apache museum the women studied the hunting weapons, whereas the men examined the cooking implements!

Shifts in voice

 Do not shift unnecessarily between the active and the passive voice.

No: Chess draws heavily upon left-brain computational skills, but right-brain creativities are also engaged by it.

Yes: Chess draws heavily upon left-brain computational skills, but it also engages right-brain creativities.

Shifts in tense

 Do not shift haphazardly between tenses. Establish a govern- 1 ing tense and hold to it.

No: Clara first emptied her purse and then begins checking all the pockets of her clothes.

Yes: Clara first emptied her purse and then began checking all the pockets of her clothes.

In writing about a historical event or a fictional incident, you may 2 decide to adopt the present tense (the historical or literary present). In writing about another writer's work, you may choose to treat that work as if it were being written or spoken in the present (the editorial present). Whatever your decision, be consistent.

No: When Peter saw the waves and became fearful, he begins to sink.

No: When Peter sees the waves and becomes fearful, he began to sink.

Yes: When Peter saw the waves and became fearful, he began to sink.

Yes: When Peter sees the waves and becomes fearful, he begins to sink.

No: First, Paul re-established his spiritual authority. Then he addresses specific problems in the Corinthian church.

Yes: First, Paul re-established his spiritual authority. Then he addressed specific problems in the Corinthian church.

Yes: First, Paul re-establishes his spiritual authority. Then he addresses specific problems in the Corinthian church.

An idea expressed as a general fact or universal truth must, however, 3
be stated in the present tense. Whether the idea is true or false is not
a factor.

No: It was believed at one time that primitive forms of life, under
favorable conditions, could generate spontaneously.

Yes: It was believed at one time that primitive forms of life, under
favorable conditions, can generate spontaneously.

Shifts between direct and indirect discourse

 Do not shift arbitrarily from indirect to direct discourse.

No: He did not understand why his invitation was rejected, and how
could she have been so cruel?

Yes: He did not understand why his invitation was rejected and how
she could have been so cruel.

Yes: He did not understand. Why was his invitation rejected, and
how could she have been so cruel?

No: She asked did we enjoy our meal?

Yes: She asked whether we enjoyed our meal.

Yes: She asked, "Did you enjoy your meal?"

Shifts in mood

shft
14g
Do not shift arbitrarily between moods. The indicative mood
comprises statements and questions; the imperative, commands and requests; the subjunctive, expressions of uncertainty or unreality.

Do not shift arbitrarily between the imperative and indicative moods. 1

No: First make a deep cut in the side facing the direction in which
you want the tree to fall, and then you meet it with a lesser cut
from the opposite side.

Yes: First make a deep cut in the side facing the direction in which
you want the tree to fall, and then meet it with a lesser cut
from the opposite side.

Yes: First you make a deep cut in the side facing the direction in
which you want the tree to fall, and then you meet it with a
lesser cut from the opposite side.

Do not shift arbitrarily between the subjunctive and indicative 2
moods. The subjunctive mood is a survival from a subjunctive tense
in an earlier stage of our language. It consists of several departures

from ordinary verb usage when the idea expressed is of uncertain fulfillment or is contrary to fact.

In a noun clause following a command or a strong request, formal   3
English uses *be* or an *s*-less third-person form of the verb for all
persons. Notice that the forms of the subjunctive mood are identical
with those of the imperative in an imperative context.

> I insist that he be present for the vote.

> The court required that he pay double damages.

For *if* clauses expressing a condition contrary to fact, formal English   4
uses *were* for all persons.

> If I were you, I would take your father's advice.

For *if* clauses expressing uncertainty, formal English uses *were* for   5
all persons or *should* in an indefinite, futuristic sense.

> If a guest were to come early, we would not be prepared.

> If a guest should come early, we would not be prepared.

Avoid these awkward shifts to or from the subjunctive.   6

> No: We will not be prepared if a guest should come early.

> Yes: We will not be prepared if a guest comes early.

> Yes: We would not be prepared if a guest should come early.

> No: Economists warn that if the U.S. economy were to lose its for-
>   eign investors to Japan it will sink rapidly.

> Yes: Economists warn that if the U.S. economy were to lose its for-
>   eign investors to Japan it would sink rapidly.

> Yes: Economists warn that if the U.S. economy loses its foreign
>   investors to Japan it will sink rapidly.

> No: The rules require that campers be out of bed by seven o'clock
>   and that they will be present for the raising of the flag at seven-
>   thirty.

> Yes: The rules require that campers be out of bed by seven o'clock
>   and that they be present for the raising of the flag at seven-
>   thirty.

Redundant Syntax

 Avoid careless repetition of a preposition or conjunction.

No: Monday was not the kind of day about which most campers
       would feel they had to write home about.

Yes: Monday was not the kind of day most campers would feel they
       had to write home about.

Yes: Monday was not the kind of day about which most campers
       would feel they had to write home.

No: He decided that if he received no response after another month
       that he would withdraw his request.

Yes: He decided that if he received no response after another month
       he would withdraw his request.

Other Awkward Syntax

 Avoid dangling adjective phrases.   1

No: As moral conservatives, our beliefs are challenged almost daily
       in the national media.

Yes: As moral conservatives, we find our beliefs being challenged
       almost daily in the national media.

Yes: Our beliefs, morally conservative, are challenged almost daily in
       the national media.

Avoid momentarily ambiguous omissions.   2

No: After forcing the door, the police detectives found the escapee
       with the stolen money and firearms had fled.

Yes: After forcing the door, the police detectives found that the
       escapee with the stolen money and firearms had fled.

Avoid awkward separation. Two phrases or clauses modifying the   3
same element should be kept together rather than positioned before
and after the element.

No: After lunch take a short nap before the next appointment.

Yes: After lunch and before the next appointment, take a short nap.

No: If we have our typical winter, we will have a good peach crop, if
       we do not have a late freeze.

Yes: If we have our typical winter and if we do not have a late
       freeze, we will have a good peach crop.

Yes: If we have our typical winter and do not have a late freeze, we
       will have a good peach crop.

PRONOUN USE

This section treats questions of pronoun use not covered above under pronoun agreement and reference, including the very important area of pronoun case. Review as necessary the explanation of sentence parts in Appendix A, Basic Sentence Analysis.

Pronoun Case

 Grammatical variations in word forms are greatly diminished in English from the time, a millennium ago, when Old English had cases (differences in form according to function) for nouns, pronouns, and adjectives similar to those of modern German. Modern English has only one case ending for nouns, the possessive, which appears in written language as an -*s* preceded by an apostrophe. The -*s* is dropped if the word has a plural -*s* or -*es* ending already. (See Mechanics.)

Case survives mainly in pronouns. It affects choices in personal pronouns and, to a lesser extent, in relative and interrogative pronouns. For these pronouns modern English has three cases: the subjective, the objective, and the possessive. Since almost all errors in case result from the confusion of the subjective and objective forms, we will begin with them and reserve the possessive case with its one problem area for the end of the discussion.

A full explanation of pronoun case can make the subject seem more difficult than it need be. Native speakers of English use the forms of pronoun case accurately without thought. They do so consistently except in certain problem areas, in which formal educated usage retains traditional distinctions that popular usage ignores. To understand what is correct in these areas, we need the whole scheme of pronoun case before us. Notice the variations between the subjective and objective case forms in the chart below.

Personal Pronouns	Subjective Case	Objective Case
Singular		
first	I	me
second	you	you
third	he	him
	she	her
	it	it
Plural		
first	we	us
second	you	you
third	they	them

Relative and Interrogative Pronouns		
	who	whom
	whoever	whomever

When we drop from the list the pronouns that have the same subjective and objective forms, we simplify the picture.

Subjective Case	Objective Case
I	me
he	him
she	her
we	us
they	them
who	whom
whoever	whomever

The governing rule of pronoun case is simple. The forms of the subjective case in the left column are used for subjects of verbs and their equivalents; those of the objective case in the right column are used for objects and their equivalents. That is, the subjective case is used for subjects of verbs, predicate nouns, and their appositives, whereas the objective case is used for direct and indirect objects, objects of prepositions, objects of verbals, objective complements, and their appositives.

We may now turn to the specific areas in which mistakes in pronoun case most often occur.

Linking verbs

Pronouns acting as predicate nouns are in the subjective case.　　1

No:	Surprisingly the winner was him.
Yes:	Surprisingly the winner was he.
No:	The only ones questioned were them.
Yes:	The only ones questioned were they.
No:	Yes, this is her.
Yes:	Yes, this is she.
No:	Whom is this?
Yes:	Who is this?

Reversing the construction makes the proper case more evident.

No:	Him was the winner.
Yes:	He was the winner.
No:	Them were the only ones questioned.
Yes:	They were the only ones questioned.
No:	This is whom?
Yes:	This is who?

Compound elements

The case of pronouns in compound constructions is unaffected by　　2
the compounding. Pronouns that are part of a compound subject are
in the subjective case; those that are part of a compound object are
in the objective case.

No:	Brian, Trent, and him led the team to victory.
Yes:	Brian, Trent, and he led the team to victory.
No:	The team honored Brian, Trent, and he.
Yes:	The team honored Brian, Trent, and him.
No:	Neither her nor me received a second chance.
Yes:	Neither she nor I received a second chance.
No:	The rules allowed neither she nor I a second chance.
Yes:	The rules allowed neither her nor me a second chance.
No:	The agreement between he and Mr. Abernathy was only oral.
Yes:	The agreement between him and Mr. Abernathy was only oral.
No:	Give the certificate to Jill or I.
Yes:	Give the certificate to Jill or me.

No: Just between you and I, the family business is doing well.

Yes: Just between you and me, the family business is doing well.

No: The money was divided equally among Tyler, Sarah, and I.

Yes: The money was divided equally among Tyler, Sarah, and me.

The inclination to use *I* in compounds may be the result of overcorrection. As children we were corrected for using the following nonstandard construction, which we were told was impolite.

No: Me and Eric won the rowing contest.

Yes: Eric and I won the rowing contest.

Polite use requires putting self-references at the end of a compound. It does not authorize using *I* for *me* in the object position.

No: The rowing contest was won by Eric and I.

Yes: The rowing contest was won by Eric and me.

A simple test will clarify the case of the pronoun in most compound constructions. Mentally drop all of the construction except the pronoun and notice what is left. Notice how *I* would sound jarring after the preposition as would *me* before the verb.

No: Just between [you and] I the family business is doing well.

No: Me [and Eric] won the rowing contest.

No: The rowing contest was won by [Eric and] I.

Appositives

The case of a pronoun used as an appositive is determined by the use   3
of the noun or pronoun with which it is in apposition. Pronouns that
are appositives of subjects and predicate nouns are in the subjective
case. Pronouns that are appositives of objects are in the objective
case. Be especially careful when the appositive is a compound construction.

No: The winning doubles team, Deanna and her, accepted the applause modestly.

Yes: The winning doubles team, Deanna and she, accepted the applause modestly.

No: The article featured the winning doubles team, Deanna and she.

Yes: The article featured the winning doubles team, Deanna and her.

No: Let's you and I be the first to volunteer.

Yes: Let's you and me be the first to volunteer.

Again, mentally drop the noun or pronoun to which the appositive refers along with the remainder of the compound construction. The proper case should then be evident.

> No: [The winning doubles team, Deanna and] her[,] accepted the applause modestly.

> No: The article featured [the winning doubles team, Deanna and] she.

> No: Let['s you and] I be the first to volunteer.

A similar test will indicate the proper case of the first-person-plural 4
pronoun *we* or *us* when it is followed by an appositive. Mentally drop the appositive.

> No: Us [boys] will repair the roof.

> Yes: We boys will repair the roof.

> No: The highest grades were made by we [girls].

> Yes: The highest grades were made by us girls.

Elliptical comparisons

In an elliptical comparison, part of the comparison is unstated. 5
When such a comparison contains a pronoun whose case depends upon what is unstated, mentally supply the missing part.

> No: Her friend tries harder than her.

> Yes: Her friend tries harder than she [tries].

> No: His sister is as fine a pianist as him.

> Yes: His sister is as fine a pianist as he [is].

> No: The coach chose Chad rather than he.

> Yes: The coach chose Chad rather than [choosing] him.

In constructions in which alternatives are possible, the case deter- 6
mines the meaning.

> Yes: He likes Jessica more than I [like Jessica].

> Yes: He likes Jessica more than [he likes] me.

You can eliminate uncertainty by filling in part or all of such comparisons.

> Yes: He likes Jessica more than I do.

> Yes: He likes Jessica more than he likes me.

Relative clauses

The relative pronouns *who* (subjective) and *whom* (objective) introduce clauses known as relative clauses. They join these clauses to
an antecedent in a preceding clause. They have a possessive form,
whose, which causes no problem for us and will not enter this
discussion.

The case of relative pronouns is determined by their function within   7
the relative clause they introduce, not by what precedes or surrounds
the relative clause. For this reason, bracket mentally the relative
clause and analyze its internal structure until the function of the
who or *whom* becomes clear (whether it serves within its clause as
subject, direct object, predicate noun, object of preposition, etc.).
Who is correct wherever subjective pronouns such as *I* or *he* are
appropriate; *whom,* wherever objective pronouns such as *me* or
him are proper.

> [Who will be the first to scale the walls] has not been determined.
>
> [Whom she prefers] will be revealed in due time.
>
> The candidate [who spends the most money] will probably win.
>
> The candidate [whom the party chooses] must unite the party.

It may be helpful to substitute mentally *he* for *who* and *him* for *whom.*

> He will be the first to scale the walls.
>
> She prefers him.
>
> He spends the most money.
>
> The party chooses him.

When relative pronouns introduce a clause acting as an object in the   8
main sentence, do not assume that the pronoun heading the clause is
the object and therefore belongs in the objective case and fail to see
that the entire clause itself is the object.

> No: We were not told [whom would go].
>
> Yes: We were not told [who would go].
>
> No: We were uninformed about [whom would go].
>
> Yes: We were uninformed about [who would go].

Unless a relative pronoun is the object of a preposition that appears
with it, its case will be unaffected by anything ahead of it in the sentence.

> Only Mother knew [who was to receive the gift].
>
> Only Mother knew [for whom the gift was intended].

The *-ever* forms of *who* and *whom* introduce noun clauses and fol- 9
low the same rule concerning case.

> [Whomever I assign to the phone] should get [whoever calls]
> [whomever he asks for].

Questions

When *who* and *whom* introduce questions, they are called inter- 10
rogative pronouns. As with the relative pronouns *who* and *whom,*
their case is determined by their use within the clause in which
they appear. However, an interrogative clause, unlike the clauses
introduced by relative pronouns, is the main clause of the sentence.

> Who received a bonus this month?
>
> Whom did the company reward this month?
>
> Of whom were you speaking?
>
> Whom were you referring to?

The use of *whom* to begin a clause has faded in both speech and
informal writing. However, formal writing still requires *whom*
whenever the objective case is needed.

Verbal phrases

Pronoun case with verbal phrases departs from the general rule that
connects subjective case with subject function and objective case
with object function. Place the phrases in mental parentheses to see
better how they relate to the sentence.

Subjects as well as complements of infinitives are in the objective 11
case.

> The spectators wanted (her to defeat him in tennis).
>
> The new guide mistakenly thought (us to be them).

A single exception is the complement of *to be* when *to be* has no
subject. In this construction the infinitive complement takes on the
quality and role of a predicate noun renaming the subject of the sentence. For this reason, the complement is in the subjective case.

> The caller had to be he.

Subjects of gerunds are adjectival and are therefore in the possessive 12
case.

> No: We have no record of (him leaving work early).
>
> Yes: We have no record of (his leaving work early).

Do not confuse this construction with that of a noun or pronoun in the objective case modified by a participial phrase.

> **Yes:**   We watched him (leaving work early).

Reflexive and Intensive Pronouns

 Reserve the *-self* pronouns for their specialized uses.   1

Reflexive pronouns are pronouns used as objects that refer to the subject of their clause. They require the objective case.

> Daniel hurt himself.
>
> Daniel built the fence by himself.
>
> Daniel gave himself a scolding.

Intensive pronouns emphasize the noun or pronoun they follow. They are grammatically nonessential in the sentence.

> Daniel himself built the fence.
>
> Daniel built the fence himself.

Do not use *-self* pronouns except in these two functions. They must rename a noun or another pronoun occurring earlier in the sentence.

> **No:**   You can leave the gift with my wife or myself.
>
> **Yes:**   You can leave the gift with my wife or me.
>
> **No:**   As for my wife and myself, we will eat at home.
>
> **Yes:**   As for my wife and me, we will eat at home.

Do not use the possessive case to form third-person reflexive and   2
intensive pronouns.

> **No:**   Daniel hurt hisself.
>
> **No:**   They built the fence by theirselves.

ADJECTIVES AND ADVERBS

Confusion of Adjectives and Adverbs

Most errors with adjectives and adverbs result from confusing their grammatical functions. If necessary, review the parts of speech.

Misuse of adjectives for adverbs

 Use adverbs, not adjectives, to modify verbs, adjectives, and other adverbs.

No:	The car ran good during the first fifty laps.
Yes:	The car ran well during the first fifty laps.
No:	They sure took a long time to service the car.
Yes:	They surely took a long time to service the car.
No:	She feels some better after three days in bed.
Yes:	She feels somewhat better after three days in bed.
No:	He tried real hard to make the team.
Yes:	He tried really hard to make the team.
No:	We are reasonable sure of good weather.
Yes:	We are reasonably sure of good weather.

Misuse of adverbs for adjectives

 Do not use adverbs for predicate adjectives. Errors are common with linking verbs of sense.

No:	The company feels badly about the error in billing.
Yes:	The company feels bad about the error in billing.
No:	He looks well in a double-breasted suit.
Yes:	He looks good in a double-breasted suit.
No:	The deer meat on the stove smells awfully.
Yes:	The deer meat on the stove smells awful.
No:	Home-baked bread tastes especially well fresh out of the oven.
Yes:	Home-baked bread tastes especially good fresh out of the oven.

Misuse of Comparative Forms

Most adjectives and adverbs have, in addition to their basic form (the positive), two forms of comparison expressing degrees of intensity. The *comparative* form uses the ending *-er* or the adverbs *more* or *less*. The *superlative* form uses the ending *-est* or the adverbs *most* or *least*.

Use the comparative form in a comparison of two persons or things. 1

No: Of the two Olympics, the Winter has the most exciting events.

Yes: Of the two Olympics, the Winter has the more exciting events.

Use the superlative form in a comparison of three or more persons or things or in a comparison of an undetermined number.

No: The better athlete of the three is Jared.

Yes: The best athlete of the three is Jared.

Use the endings *-er* and *-est* to form comparisons with one- and 2
two-syllable adjectives and one-syllable adverbs. Use the adverbs *more* and *most* or *less* and *least* to form comparisons with adjectives of three or more syllables and adverbs of two or more syllables. Use *more* and *most* or *less* and *least* also with adjectives ending in *-ful* and adverbs ending in *-ly*. These are general guidelines.

No: The yellow pencil is more sharp than the brown one.

Yes: The yellow pencil is sharper than the brown one.

No: Children become gratefuller as they get older.

Yes: Children become more grateful as they get older.

No: The current moved swiftlier than before.

Yes: The current moved more swiftly than before.

Insert an *-ly* adverb between *more, most, less, least,* or *very* and 3
a past-participle modifier.

No: He was more injured in the crash than his copilot.

Yes: He was more severely injured in the crash than his copilot.

Avoid double comparatives. Errors are most frequent with 4
adjectives that already contain the idea of comparative or superlative degree.

No: The atmosphere is more denser at sea level than at high elevations.

Yes: The atmosphere is denser at sea level than at high elevations.

No: Traveling by air is more preferable than traveling by car.

Yes: Traveling by air is preferable to traveling by car.

Yes: Traveling by air is more desirable than traveling by car.

No: Vanilla is my most preferred flavor.

Yes: Vanilla is my preferred flavor.

Distinguish between *less,* referring to amount, and *fewer,* referring   5
to number.

No: We picked less peaches today than yesterday.

Yes: We picked fewer peaches today than yesterday.

No: For its size, Alaska has fewer population than any other state.

Yes: For its size, Alaska has less population than any other state.

Avoid degrees of comparison with absolute modifiers.   6

No: The most ideal place to live is a small town a half-hour's drive from a large city.

Yes: The ideal place to live is a small town a half-hour's drive from a large city.

No: He skated the most perfect figure eight in the skating technicals.

Yes: He skated the most nearly perfect figure eight in the skating technicals.

No: As homes of strange animal species, Australia and New Zealand are the most unique land areas on earth.

Yes: As homes of strange animal species, Australia and New Zealand are unique among the land areas on earth.

Yes: As homes of strange animal species, Australia and New Zealand are the most extraordinary land areas on earth.

Avoid illogical comparisons that mix the superlative and comparative constructions.   7

No: Derrick has the most excuses for tardiness of any student in the class.

Yes: Derrick has more excuses for tardiness than any other student in the class.

Yes: Derrick has the most excuses for tardiness of all the students in his class.

VERB USE

Correcting errors in verb forms requires some knowledge of the general grammatical scheme of verbs. Refer as necessary to the discussion of verbs under Parts of Speech. The following are some areas of confusion.

Principal Parts

The principal parts of verbs are those forms of the verb base that combine with auxiliary verbs to form the tenses, voices, and moods of the verb. The first principal part is the present form. The second is the past form. The third is the past-participle form.

With regard to the formation of principal parts, grammarians distinguish between regular and irregular verbs. Regular verbs have identical second and third principal parts, which they form by adding -*d* or -*ed* to the first principal part. Irregular verbs form their second and third principal parts without the help of these suffixes.

Regular verbs

Be sure to include the -*d* or -*ed* ending when the second or third principal part of a regular verb is required.   1

No:	He use to walk with a cane.
Yes:	He used to walk with a cane.
No:	They were suppose to be here by five o'clock.
Yes:	They were supposed to be here by five o'clock.
No:	She had ask Danielle to call her.
Yes:	She had asked Danielle to call her.

Be aware that a few regular verbs substitute -*t* for -*d* or -*ed*.

No:	The large fish bended the hook almost straight.
Yes:	The large fish bent the hook almost straight.
No:	She builded her house by herself.
Yes:	She built her house by herself.

Irregular verbs

Choose the second principal part for the past tense. Choose the third principal part for the perfect tenses and the passive voice. (The perfect tenses use *have, has,* etc., as auxiliaries. The passive voice uses *is, are, was, were, been,* etc.) The chart below lists the principal parts of some irregular verbs that cause problems. Consult a college dictionary for the principal parts of verbs not listed.

First Principal Part	Second Principal Part	Third Principal Part
beat	beat	beaten
begin	began	begun
blow	blew	blown
break	broke	broken
bring	brought	brought
burst	burst	burst
catch	caught	caught
choose	chose	chosen
come	came	come
cost	cost	cost
dig	dug	dug
dive	dived, dove	dived
drive	drove	driven
do	did	done
draw	drew	drawn
drink	drank	drunk
eat	ate	eaten
fly	flew	flown
forgive	forgave	forgiven
freeze	froze	frozen
give	gave	given
go	went	gone
grow	grew	grown
hang	hung	hung
hang (execute by hanging)	hanged	hanged
hold	held	held
hurt	hurt	hurt
know	knew	known
lead	led	led
lie	lay	lain

First Principal Part	Second Principal Part	Third Principal Part
quit	quit	quit
ride	rode	ridden
rise	rose	risen
run	ran	run
see	saw	seen
shake	shook	shaken
shrink	shrank	shrunk
sing	sang	sung
sink	sank	sunk
sit	sat	sat
slay	slew	slain
sling	slung	slung
speak	spoke	spoken
steal	stole	stolen
swim	swam	swum
swing	swung	swung
teach	taught	taught
tear	tore	torn
throw	threw	thrown
wear	wore	worn
write	wrote	written

No: The thirsty patient drunk the offered juice.

Yes: The thirsty patient drank the offered juice.

No: The pond had froze overnight.

Yes: The pond had frozen overnight.

No: The egg whites were beat until they were fluffy.

Yes: The egg whites were beaten until they were fluffy.

Troublesome Pairs

Three pairs of verbs *(lie, lay; sit, set; rise, raise)* are a common source of errors in grammatical usage. These errors resist correction for two reasons. First, the errors are widely prevalent and deeply ingrained in spoken English—so much so that avoiding them requires erasing long-standing habits. The wrong forms may sound more natural than the correct ones. Second, correcting the errors requires some technical grammatical knowledge. One must understand the difference between transitive and intransitive verbs.

One verb of each pair is transitive and the other is intransitive. That is, one verb takes a direct object and the other does not. Compare the principal parts and progressive *(-ing)* forms of these verbs in the two columns. (The adverbs *up* and *down* are included only for context and do not affect the choice of verb forms.)

Principal Parts and Progressive

	Intransitive	Transitive
Now they	*lie* down	*lay* the book down
Yesterday they	*lay* down	*laid* the book down
By now they	have *lain* down	have *laid* the book down
Now they	are *lying* down	are *laying* the book down
Now they	*sit* down	*set* the book down
Yesterday they	*sat* down	*set* the book down
By now they	have *sat* down	have *set* the book down
Now they	are *sitting* down	are *setting* the book down
Now they	*rise* up	*raise* the book up
Yesterday they	*rose* up	*raised* the book up
By now they	have *risen* up	have *raised* the book up
Now they	are *rising* up	are *raising* the book up

Transitive verbs also have passive voice forms, which use the third principal part. In the passive voice the subject rather than the object of the verb receives the verb's action.

The book	is/was/has been *laid* down
The book	is/was/has been *set* down
The book	is/was/has been *raised* up

It should be clear that the governing distinction is grammatical rather than logical. The correct choice has nothing to do with physical nature or posture. It is irrelevant whether the subject of the verb is human or animal, animate or inanimate.

No:	I usually lay down after lunch.
Yes:	I usually lie down after lunch.
No:	The cat is laying on the new sofa.
Yes:	The cat is lying on the new sofa.
No:	The paper has laid in the driveway since this morning.
Yes:	The paper has lain in the driveway since this morning.

No:	The flowerpot sets on the windowsill.
Yes:	The flowerpot sits on the windowsill.
No:	He raised up suddenly from his chair.
Yes:	He rose up suddenly from his chair.
No:	A thousand hands raised at once.
Yes:	A thousand hands rose at once.

Notice from these examples that it is the transitive form that tends to invade the territory of the intransitive form rather than the reverse. Errors almost always consist of choosing a transitive form where the corresponding intransitive form is required.

An exception to the above is the verb *set,* which normally is transitive but is intransitive when it refers to the sun or to material that is hardening.

| Yes: | The sun sets quickly over the ocean. |
| Yes: | A gelatin salad sets only when it is refrigerated. |

Sequence of Tenses

We have seen that the forms of a verb vary to show the person and number of the subject. They also vary to show the time and manner of the action or condition the verb expresses. Changes of form to show time are called tenses. Most native speakers of English use the tenses accurately without forethought. They know that the simple present, past, and future tenses indicate action in the present, past, and future. They know that the present-, past-, and future-perfect tenses (those using *have*) indicate action completed by a specific time in the present, past, and future. They know that the progressive forms of the simple and the perfect tenses express continuing action in the times indicated by those tenses.

However, certain areas require special attention for even competent native speakers of English. Under Sentence Logic we noted the importance of consistency in tenses in narration or in commentary. We also noted the requirement of the present tense for stating a general fact or a universal truth.

Another area needing explanation is tense sequence within sentences. The tenses of dependent clauses and verbal phrases must accurately relate to the time established by the governing verb of the sentence. A full account of tense sequence would be cumbersome and is unnecessary. The following are situations in which errors often occur.

Past-perfect tense

Use the past-perfect tense to express action preceding other past   1
action.

> No: We realized that our guests came and left.
>
> Yes: We realized that our guests had come and left.

Present infinitives and participles

Use the present infinitive and present participle to express action   2
at the same time as that of the governing verb.

> No: I wanted to have seen him.
>
> Yes: I wanted to see him.
>
> No: I enjoyed having seen him.
>
> Yes: I enjoyed seeing him.
>
> No: I would like to have seen him.
>
> Yes: I would have liked to see him.

Present-perfect infinitives and participles

Use the present-perfect infinitive and participle to express action   3
before that of the governing verb.

> No: He was satisfied to finish the race among the leaders.
>
> Yes: He was satisfied to have finished the race among the leaders.
>
> No: She was an old woman now, being born before the First World War.
>
> Yes: She was an old woman now, having been born before the First World War.
>
> No: Banking most of his earnings for fifty years, he was wealthier than anyone realized.
>
> Yes: Having banked most of his earnings for fifty years, he was wealthier than anyone realized.

Subjunctive Mood

The subjunctive mood consists of several departures in verb form from the normal indicative mood used for statements and questions. These are survivals from an earlier stage of English, when the language contained a subjunctive tense. Formal English uses subjunctive forms when the action of the sentence is of uncertain fulfillment or is contrary to fact. See Sentence Logic for an explanation of the indicative, imperative, and subjunctive moods.

No:	I advise that he is corrected in private.
Yes:	I advise that he be corrected in private.
No:	The consultant recommends that the company hires only experienced workers.
Yes:	The consultant recommends that the company hire only experienced workers.
No:	She lived every day as if it was her last.
Yes:	She lived every day as if it were her last.
No:	If the test was today, I would not pass it.
Yes:	If the test were today, I would not pass it.
Yes:	If the test had been today, I would not have passed it.
Yes:	Had the test been today, I would not have passed it.
No:	If Aaron was to quit, the company would fold.
Yes:	If Aaron were to quit, the company would fold.
Yes:	If Aaron should quit, the company would fold.

Modal Auxiliaries

 Modal auxiliaries are helping verbs that affect the action of the verb in much the same way as the imperative and subjunctive mood—thus the term *modal*.

They indicate condition, possibility, necessity, and intent. They do not stand alone as main verbs except in shortened expressions. They have two tenses, present and past, but otherwise do not change their forms to show person, time, and so forth, as do other verbs. They are as follows:

Present	Past
can	could
may	might
must	must
shall	should
will	would

(The present forms *shall* and *will* are modals when they express determination.)

May and *can*

Distinguish *may,* which expresses permission or possibility, from *can,* which expresses ability.

1

No:	You can leave your seat when the bell rings.
Yes:	You may leave your seat when the bell rings.
No:	Can we use pencils to write the essay?
Yes:	May we use pencils to write the essay?

Would

Do not use *would* as a timid declarative.

2

No:	It would be true that Shakespeare put something of himself into all of his plays.
Yes:	It is true that Shakespeare put something of himself into all of his plays.
Yes:	Shakespeare put something of himself into all of his plays.
No:	The Norsemen would be the first Europeans to set foot in the New World.
No:	The Norsemen would have been the first Europeans to set foot in the New World.
Yes:	The Norsemen were the first Europeans to set foot in the New World.
Yes:	The Norsemen were likely the first Europeans to set foot in the New World.

Personal Pronouns and Verb Tense in Scholarly Writing

Scholarly writing in some fields still prohibits the use of the first-person pronoun. Statements about what the author thinks or has done must refer to "the writer" or be put in the passive voice. If describing the process of his research, they must be expressed in the past tense.

These restrictions have been largely abandoned in the humanities but continue in the sciences, most notably in the social sciences. Thus the researcher must not write, "I conclude that the data do not support the original hypothesis." He must write, "It was concluded that the data did not support the original hypothesis." He did not "discover" a result, but the result "was discovered."

The required past tense in the description of research has a meaningful rationale behind it, since the process being described is in the past. The case is less compelling for the avoiding of the first person.

Apart from the general awkwardness and affectation it produces, the prohibiting of the first-person pronoun almost forces the writer into **dangling modifiers** at transition points in his text. Notice in the first of the examples below that the participial phrase "Having established the role of Factor A" points toward a first-person pronoun for the grammatical subject of the main statement. When the subject is instead impersonal, the phrase grammatically dangles and the sentence is forced into the **passive voice.** The next example corrects the problem by replacing the expletive *it* with *we.*

No: Having established the role of Factor A, it can now be understood how Factors B and C interact with A to form the desired environment.

Yes: Having established the role of Factor A, we can now understand how Factors B and C interact with A to form the desired environment.

When the personal pronoun is permitted and not overused, scholarly writing is the better for it. Disallowing its use is responsible for some of the most laborious, pretentious prose ever written. Nevertheless, follow your instructor's directions in this as in other matters.

Be aware that the dilemma of the dangling phrase can often be avoided by predicating what you are saying on your factual subject rather than on yourself.

Yes: Factor A then is necessary but insufficient in itself to form the desired environment. It must interact with Factors A and B.

The problem of the dangling phrase and awkward passive is largely due to your adopting a personal tone during explanation without your being allowed the personal pronouns necessary to that tone. You want to engage your reader while conducting him down your thought path all the while maintaining a scholarly, impersonal stance. You can usually avoid the problem by simply stating facts.

Standard Form

This chapter acquaints you with general standards in the form and style of written documents submitted for credit in college classrooms. Details of format and layout will vary from instructor to instructor. Documentation styles differ somewhat among disciplines. But the general scheme presented here is typical of what is insisted upon in college written work, especially in courses whose instructors feel a commitment to teach the apparatus of scholarly discussion.

After describing standard format and layout, chapter 9 gives detailed coverage of the forms of citation specified by the Modern Language Association (MLA), the documentation style in widest use in the humanities. It then gives lesser comparative coverage of three other common styles: that of the American Psychological Association (APA), dominant in the social sciences, education, and business; the *Chicago Manual of Style* (CMS), prevalent in history, philosophy, religion, and the fine arts; and the Council of Biology Editors (CBE), established in the life sciences. Finally, it offers guidelines for documenting material from online and electronic sources.

For clarity's sake the documentation forms appear in the uniform spacing of typewriter font (pica, ten spaces per inch), rather than in the variable spacing used almost universally in printed text and provided by your word processor. Use tabs if necessary to duplicate the indentation indicated for bibliography entries and notes. Book and periodical titles are underlined here rather than presented in italic type, the equivalent of underlining, in keeping with the typewriter mode and for greater visibility of distinctions. You may either underline or use italics wherever underlining appears in the examples.

Details such as these warrant close attention. There is no other area in the preparation of papers in which scrupulous care has a more direct payoff than in the particulars of this chapter. Your instructor, by training and habit, cares about small things. So does the God he serves. Concerning the Hebrew Scriptures Jesus said that all must be fulfilled, down to the merest pen strokes—each jot and tittle—of the law.

FORMAT AND LAYOUT

Manuscript correctness and neatness indicate respect for your reader as well as for academic standards. Type or print on 8½" × 11" regular bond paper, using only one side of the sheet. Maintain margins of an inch and a half at the left of all pages and above page titles, and an inch elsewhere. Vertically space any footnotes so that the one-inch bottom margin is preserved.

Page numbers begin with page 2 of the body and continue throughout the pages that list references and sources. Preliminary pages are numbered with lowercase roman numerals, with the title page counting as page i but left unnumbered. Place page numbers in the upper-right corner and double space beneath them to continue the text.

Triple space between titles and text. Double space all other content, including blocked quotations, notes, and reference lists.

If printing, set tabs for a half-inch indentation for paragraph beginnings and an inch indentation for blocked quotations (of five or more lines). (If typing, indent for these purposes five and ten spaces respectively.) Indent the first lines of paragraphs beginning within blocked quotations an additional half inch. (Remember not to add quotation marks to blocked quotations.)

Use a standard readable font (not script) and type size (10–12 pt.). Do not italicize, underline, or place in quotation marks your own title. Leave the right margin ragged, not justified.

Standard format and layout are illustrated in the sample paper on pages 47–62.

VERSE QUOTATIONS

Verse quotation of four or more lines should be block indented an inch from the left margin, after which the indentation conforms to the typographical display of the passage in the source. Fewer than four lines should be set off in quotation marks within the paragraph, with the line breaks indicated by slash marks.

The indication "lines" is helpful with the first citation, after which only the line numbers need be given. (Quotations below are from George Herbert's "Love III.")

At the door, the guest "drew back, / Guilty of dust and sin" (lines 1-2). The host quickly responded, engaging the guest in comforting conversation.

> But quick-ey'd Love, observing me grow slack
>> From my first entrance in,
> Drew nearer to me, sweetly questioning,
>> If I lack'd any thing. (3-6)

MLA DOCUMENTATION

In the MLA style, sources are identified briefly in the text by author and page number within parentheses and fully in a reference list, usually titled Works Cited, following the text. An additional reference list titled Works Consulted may complement the Works Cited page. Or all works, those cited and those only consulted, may be combined in a single list titled Bibliography. If you use the bibliography format, avoid padding your list with unexamined sources or with examined sources that have provided no help.

The MLA style reserves footnotes and endnotes for subordinated information or explanation: content that has genuine purpose but that, if incorporated into the text, would break the pace and burden the line of thought. Notes can have real importance. One kind that is quite necessary is a note giving full information for a frequently cited source that will be referred to subsequently only by pages or, if a poem or play, only by lines or sections and lines. An essay discussing a work of literature should provide with the first reference to the work a footnote identifying the edition to which that and every subsequent citation of location will refer and the mode (by page numbers, lines, etc.) of citation. If notes are collected as endnotes, list them in the order of citation on a page titled Notes preceding the Works Cited or Bibliography page.

FREQUENT REFERENCES TO A SOURCE

Be aware of ways to economize frequent references to a source. The following patch of text shows how to cite a work that will be referred to repeatedly. The footnote number should be placed at the point of the first reference to the source.

> Jane Austen's *Emma* shows the maturing of the main character, Emma Woodhouse, from a selfish, intolerant girl to a kind, sincere woman with a genuine appreciation for others. Emma's encounters with Jane Fairfax, Miss Bates's beautiful and accomplished niece, show Emma's growth.
>
> Emma's first two encounters with Jane demonstrate most of Emma's faults and few of her virtues. On her welcoming visit to Jane, Emma feels dislike for her, perhaps out of jealousy, but has enough fairness to admit that Jane is beautiful and to determine that

she "will dislike her no longer" (112),[1] although the resolution seems almost against Emma's will. Emma leaves with "softened, charitable feelings" (112); these feelings are based on Emma's overactive imaginings about what Jane is suffering and why.

[1] All references to *Emma* are from Jane Austen, *Emma*, ed. Stephen M. Parrish (New York: Norton, 1972).

Works with long titles can be abbreviated after first mention as follows.

Among the documentary styles to be compared, that of the *Chicago Manual of Style* (CMS) is most widely used by academic publishers, that of *Words into Type* (WT) among trade publishers. CMS provides style guidelines in extraordinary detail and thoroughness, suited to the special needs of academic publication. WT is . . .

Notice the differences in content and form of the reference list entries (B), parenthetical citations (P), and endnotes and footnotes (N) for each kind of source illustrated below. Give close attention to what is and is not included, to the order and spacing of items, and to capitalization and punctuation.

Standard book entry

B   Keller, Karl. The Example of Edward Taylor.

   Amherst: U of Massachusetts P, 1975.

P   (Keller 51)

N   [1] Karl Keller, The Example of Edward

   Taylor (Amherst: U of Massachusetts P, 1975)

   51.

Book with subtitle

B   Axtell, James. <u>Natives and Newcomers: The</u>
        <u>Cultural Origins of North America</u>. New
        York: Oxford, 2001.

P   (Axtell 15)

N   [1] James Axtell, <u>Natives and Newcomers: The</u>
    <u>Cultural Origins of North America</u> (New York:
    Oxford, 2001) 15.

Book with a title of a published work within its own title

B   Lewis, C. S. <u>A Preface to</u> Paradise Lost.
        London: Oxford UP, 1942.

P   (Lewis 43)

N   [1] C. S. Lewis, <u>A Preface to</u> Paradise Lost
    (London: Oxford UP, 1942) 43.

Pamphlet or book with missing publication information (place, publisher, date of publication)

B   Haycock, Ruth C. <u>God's Truth in School</u>
        <u>Subjects</u>. N.p.: n.p., 1978.

P   (Haycock 18)

N   [1] Ruth C. Haycock, <u>God's Truth in School</u>
    <u>Subjects</u> (n.p.: n.p., 1978) 18.

B Dow Jones Newspaper Fund, Inc. <u>Newspapers,</u>
<u>Diversity, and You: 1995-1997</u>. N.p.: n.p.,
n.d.

P (Dow Jones 21-23)

N [1] Dow Jones Newspaper Fund, Inc.,
<u>Newspapers, Diversity, and You: 1995-1997</u>
(n.p.: n.p., n.d.) 21-23.

Book published by a branch, or under an imprint, of a large company

B Jennings, Edward M. <u>Science and Literature: New</u>
<u>Lenses for Criticism</u>. Garden City, NY:
Anchor-Doubleday, 1970.

P (Jennings ix)

N [1] Edward M. Jennings, <u>Science and</u>
<u>Literature: New Lenses for Criticism</u> (Garden
City, NY: Anchor-Doubleday, 1970), ix.

Book republished in paperback under a publisher's imprint

B Bowra, C. M. <u>The Romantic Imagination</u>. 1949.
New York: Galaxy-Oxford UP, 1961.

P (Bowra 181)

N [1] C. M. Bowra, <u>The Romantic Imagination</u>
(1949; New York: Galaxy-Oxford UP, 1961) 181.

Book in subsequent edition

B   Horton, Ronald A. <u>Companion to College English</u>.

      2nd ed. Greenville, SC: Bob Jones UP,

      2000.

P   (Horton 268)

N   [1] Ronald A. Horton, <u>Companion to College</u>

    <u>English</u>, 2nd ed. (Greenville, SC: Bob Jones UP,

    2000) 268.

Book with two, three, or more than three authors

B   Marshall, Madeleine Forell, and Janet Todd.

      <u>English Congregational Hymns in the</u>

      <u>Eighteenth Century</u>. Lexington: UP of

      Kentucky, 1982.

P   (Marshall and Todd 26)

N   [1] Madeleine Forell Marshall and Janet

    Todd, <u>English Congregational Hymns in the</u>

    <u>Eighteenth Century</u> (Lexington: UP of Kentucky,

    1982) 26.

B   Anson, Chris M., Robert A. Schwegler, and

      Marcia F. Muth. <u>The Longman Writer's</u>

      <u>Companion</u>. New York: Longman, 2000.

P   (Anson, Schwegler, and Muth 34)

N   [1] Chris M. Anson, Robert A. Schwegler, and Marcia F. Muth, <u>The Longman Writer's Companion</u> (New York: Longman, 2000) 34.

B   Chodorow, Stanley, MacGregor Knox, Conrad Schirokauer, Joseph R. Strayer, and Hans W. Gatzke. <u>The Mainstream of Civilization</u>. 6th ed. Fort Worth: Harcourt, 1994.

or

Chodorow, Stanley, et al. <u>The Mainstream of Civilization</u>. 6th ed. Fort Worth: Harcourt, 1994.

P   (Chodorow et al. 73)

N   [1] Stanley Chodorow, MacGregor Knox, Conrad Schirokauer, Joseph R. Strayer, and Hans W. Gatzke, <u>The Mainstream of Civilization</u>, 6th ed. (Fort Worth: Harcourt, 1994) 73.

or

     [1] Stanley Chodorow, et al., <u>The Mainstream of Civilization</u>, 6th ed. (Fort Worth: Harcourt, 1994) 73.

Book with no named author

B   <u>Readings for College English</u>. Greenville, SC: Bob Jones UP, 1990.

P   (Readings 248-49)

N   [1] Readings for College English
(Greenville, SC: Bob Jones UP, 1990) 248-49.

Book with no named author and with name supplied

B   [Horton, Ronald A.]. Objectionable Elements:
          The Biblical Approach. Greenville, SC: Bob
          Jones UP, 1990.

P   ([Horton] 6)

N   [1] [Ronald A. Horton], Objectionable
Elements: The Biblical Approach (Greenville,
SC: Bob Jones UP, 1990) 6.

Book with pseudonymous author and with name supplied

B   Twain, Mark [Samuel Clemens]. The Mysterious
          Stranger. Ed. William M. Gibson. Berkeley:
          U of California P, 1969.

P   ([Clemens] 310)

N   [1] Mark Twain [Samuel Clemens], The
Mysterious Stranger, ed. William M. Gibson
(Berkeley: U of California P, 1969) 310.

Two or more works by the same author

B   Stumpf, Samuel Enoch. Philosophy: History and
          Problems. 5th ed. New York: McGraw-Hill,
          1994.

     ---. <u>Socrates to Sartre: A History of Philosophy</u>.
        6th ed. New York: McGraw-Hill, 1999.

     ---, ed. <u>Philosophical Problems: Selected</u>
        <u>Readings</u>. 4th ed. New York: McGraw-Hill,
        1994.

     ---, and Donald C. Abel. <u>Elements of</u>
        <u>Philosophy: An Introduction</u>. 4th ed.
        Boston: McGraw-Hill, 2002.

P   (Stumpf, <u>Socrates</u> 356)

    (Stumpf, <u>Philosophy</u> 43)

    (Stumpf, <u>Philosophical</u> 149)

    (Stumpf and Abel, <u>Elements</u> 232)

N   [1] Samuel Enoch Stumpf, <u>Philosophy: History</u>
<u>and Problems</u>, 5th ed. (New York: McGraw-Hill,
1994) 43.

    [1] Samuel Enoch Stumpf, <u>Socrates to Sartre:</u>
<u>A History of Philosophy</u>, 6th ed. (New York:
McGraw-Hill, 1999) 356.

    [1] Samuel Enoch Stumpf, ed. <u>Philosophical</u>
<u>Problems: Selected Readings</u>, 4th ed. (New York:
McGraw-Hill, 1994) 149.

    [1] Samuel Enoch Stumpf and Donald C. Abel,
<u>Elements of Philosophy: An Introduction</u>, 4th
ed. (Boston: McGraw-Hill, 2002) 232.

Two or more authors with the same last name

B   Lewis, C. S. <u>The Allegory of Love: A Study of Medieval Tradition</u>. London: Oxford UP, 1936.

Lewis, Wyndham. <u>Men Without Art</u>. New York: Russell, 1964.

P   (Lewis, <u>Allegory</u> 36)

(Lewis, <u>Men</u> 128)

N   [1] C. S. Lewis, <u>The Allegory of Love: A Study of Medieval Tradition</u> (London: Oxford UP, 1936) 36.

[1] Wyndham Lewis, <u>Men Without Art</u> (New York: Russell, 1964) 128.

Book with organization as author

B   The American Society of Journalists and Authors. <u>Tools of the Writer's Trade</u>. Ed. Dodi Schultz. New York: HarperCollins, 1990.

P   (American 108)

N   [1] The American Society of Journalists and Authors, <u>Tools of the Writer's Trade</u>, ed. Dodi Schultz (New York: HarperCollins, 1990) 108.

Edited book (emphasis on editor)

B   Rivers, Elias L., ed. <u>Renaissance and Baroque</u>
       <u>Poetry of Spain</u>. Prospect Heights, IL:
       Waveland, 1966.

P   (Rivers 13)

N   [1] Elias L. Rivers, ed. <u>Renaissance and</u>
     <u>Baroque Poetry of Spain</u> (Prospect Heights, IL:
     Waveland, 1966) 13.

Edited book (emphasis on title)

B   <u>Renaissance and Baroque Poetry of Spain</u>. Ed.
       Elias L. Rivers. Prospect Heights, IL:
       Waveland, 1966.

P   (<u>Renaissance</u> 13)

N   [1] <u>Renaissance and Baroque Poetry of Spain</u>,
     ed. Elias L. Rivers (Prospect Heights, IL:
     Waveland, 1966) 13.

Book with editor and author (emphasis on editor)

B   Parrish, Stephen, ed. <u>Emma</u>. By Jane Austen. New
       York: Norton, 1972.

P   (Parrish 93-94)

N   [1] Stephen Parrish, ed., <u>Emma</u>, by Jane
     Austen (New York: Norton, 1972) 93-94.

Book with editor and author (emphasis on author)

B   Austen, Jane. <u>Emma</u>. Ed. Stephen Parrish. New

        York: Norton, 1972.

P   (Austen 93-94)

N   [1] Jane Austen, <u>Emma</u>, ed. Stephen Parrish

    (New York: Norton, 1972) 93-94.

Book with multiple editors

B   Bartlett, Kenneth R., Konrad Eisenbichler, and

        Janice Liedl, eds. <u>Love and Death in the</u>

        <u>Renaissance</u>. Ottawa: Dovehouse, 1991.

P   (Bartlett ix)

N   [1] Kenneth R. Bartlett, Konrad

    Eisenbichler, and Janice Liedl, eds., <u>Love and</u>

    <u>Death in the Renaissance</u> (Ottawa: Dovehouse,

    1991) ix.

B   Spiller, Robert E., Willard Thorp, Thomas H.

        Johnson, Henry Seidel Canby, and Richard

        M. Ludwig, eds. <u>Literary History of the</u>

        <u>United States</u>. 3rd ed. New York:

        Macmillan, 1963.

    or

    Spiller, Robert E., et al., eds. <u>Literary</u>

        <u>History of the United States</u>. New York:

        Macmillan, 1963.

P   (Spiller 65)

N   [1] Robert E. Spiller, Willard Thorp, Thomas
      H. Johnson, Henry Seidel Canby, and Richard M.
      Ludwig, eds., <u>Literary History of the United
      States</u>, 3rd ed. (New York: Macmillan, 1963) 65.
      or
         [1] Robert E. Spiller, et al., eds.,
      <u>Literary History of the United States</u>, 3rd ed.
      (New York: Macmillan, 1963) 65.

Book with editor and translator

B   Aristotle. <u>Aristotle's Poetics: A Translation
         and Commentary for Students of Literature</u>.
         Trans. Leon Golden. Ed. O. B. Hardison,
         Jr. Englewood Cliffs, NJ: Prentice-Hall,
         1968.

P   (Aristotle 282)

N   [1] Aristotle, <u>Aristotle's Poetics: A
      Translation and Commentary for Students of
      Literature</u>, trans. Leon Golden, ed. O. B.
      Hardison, Jr. (Englewood Cliffs, NJ: Prentice-
      Hall, 1968) 282.

Book with named author of preface, introduction, foreword, or afterword

B   Barth, John. Afterword. <u>Roderick Random</u>. By

       Tobias Smollett. New York: Signet-New

       American Library, 1964. 469-79.

P   (Barth 473)

N   [1] John Barth, Afterword, <u>Roderick Random</u>,

by Tobias Smollett (New York: Signet-New

American Library, 1964) 473.

B   Hughes, Hugh Price. Introduction. <u>The Journal</u>

       <u>of John Wesley</u>. By John Wesley. Ed. Percy

       Livingstone Parker. Chicago: Moody,

       [1951]. 11-13.

P   (Hughes 12)

N   [1] Hugh Price Hughes, Introduction, <u>The</u>

<u>Journal of John Wesley</u>, by John Wesley, ed.

Percy Livingstone Parker (Chicago: Moody,

[1951]) 12.

B   Brooks, Cleanth. "A Retrospective

       Introduction." <u>Modern Poetry and the</u>

       <u>Tradition</u>. 1939. New York: Galaxy-Oxford

       UP, 1965. vii-xxvii.

P   (Brooks xii)

N   [1] Cleanth Brooks, "A Retrospective Introduction," <u>Modern Poetry and the Tradition</u>, 1939 (New York: Galaxy-Oxford UP, 1965) xii.

Book in a series

B   Lewis, C. S. <u>English Literature in the Sixteenth Century Excluding Drama</u>. Oxford Hist. of Eng. Lit. 3. Oxford: Clarendon, 1954.

P   (Lewis 173)

N   [1] C. S. Lewis, <u>English Literature in the Sixteenth Century Excluding Drama</u>, Oxford Hist. of Eng. Lit. 3 (Oxford: Clarendon, 1954) 173.

Translated book

B   de Lorris, Guillaume, and Jean de Meun. <u>The Romance of the Rose</u>. Trans. Charles Dahlberg. Princeton: Princeton UP, 1971.

P   (de Lorris 61)

or

(<u>Romance</u> 61)

N   [1] Guillaume de Lorris and Jean de Meun, <u>The Romance of the Rose</u>, trans. Charles Dahlberg (Princeton: Princeton UP, 1971) 61.

B Curtius, Ernst Robert. <u>European Literature and</u>
       <u>the Latin Middle Ages</u>. Trans. Willard R.
       Trask. Bollingen Ser. 36. 1953. Princeton:
       Princeton UP, 1973.

P (Curtius 273)

N   [1] Ernst Robert Curtius, <u>European</u>
<u>Literature and the Latin Middle Ages</u>, trans.
Willard R. Trask, Bollingen Ser. 36 (1953;
Princeton: Princeton UP, 1973) 273.

Multivolume book

B Abrams, M. H., et al., eds. <u>The Norton</u>
       <u>Anthology of English Literature</u>. 7th ed. 2
       vols. New York: Norton, 2000.

P (Abrams et al. 2: 221)

N   [1] M. H. Abrams et al., eds., <u>The Norton</u>
<u>Anthology of English Literature</u>, 7th ed. (New
York: Norton, 2000) 2: 221.

B Jones, W. T. <u>A History of Western Philosophy</u>.
       2nd ed. 5 vols. New York: Harcourt, 1975.

P (Jones 3: 159)

N   [1] W. T. Jones, <u>A History of Western</u>
<u>Philosophy</u>, 2nd ed. (New York: Harcourt, 1975)
3: 159.

One volume in a multivolume book

B M. H. Abrams et al., eds. <u>The Norton Anthology of English Literature</u>. Vol. 2. New York: Norton, 2000. 2 vols.

P (Abrams et al. 221)

N   [1] M. H. Abrams et al., eds., <u>The Norton Anthology of English Literature</u>, vol. 2 (New York: Norton, 2000) 221.

B Jones, W. T. <u>Hobbes to Hume</u>. 2nd ed. New York: Harcourt, 1969. Vol. 3 of <u>A History of Western Philosophy</u>. 2nd ed. 5 vols. 1969-75.

P (Jones 159)

N   [1] W. T. Jones, <u>Hobbes to Hume</u>, 2nd ed. (New York: Harcourt, 1969), vol. 3 of <u>A History of Western Philosophy</u>, 2nd ed. 5 vols. (New York: Harcourt, 1969-75) 159.

Article in a reference book
General
Signed

B Sankovitch, Tilde. "Montaigne." <u>The New Encyclopaedia Britannica: Macropaedia</u>. 15th ed. 1994.

P (Sankovitch 345)

N   ¹ Tilde Sankovitch, "Montaigne," <u>The New</u>
<u>Encyclopaedia Britannica: Macropaedia</u>, 15th
ed., 1997, 24: 345.

B   Holman, C. Hugh. "Figures of Speech."
      <u>Encyclopedia Americana</u>. 1998 ed.

P   (Holman 197)

N   ¹ C. Hugh Holman, "Figures of Speech,"
<u>Encyclopedia Americana</u>, 1998 ed., 11: 197.

Unsigned
B   "Alliteration." <u>Encyclopedia Americana</u>.
      1998 ed.

P   ("Alliteration")

N   ¹ "Alliteration," <u>Encyclopedia Americana</u>,
1998 ed.

Topical
B   Popkin, Richard. "Blaise Pascal." <u>Encyclopedia</u>
      <u>of Philosophy</u>. Ed. Paul Edwards. 8 vols.
      New York: Macmillan, 1967.

P   (Popkin 52)

N   ¹ Richard Popkin, "Blaise Pascal,"
<u>Encyclopedia of Philosophy</u>, ed. Paul Edwards,
8 vols. (New York: Macmillan, 1967) 6: 52.

Article in a collection

B Austern, Linda Phyllis. "Love, Death, and Ideas
      of Music in the English Renaissance." <u>Love
      and Death in the Renaissance</u>. Ed. Kenneth
      R. Bartlett, Konrad Eisenbichler, and Jan-
      ice Liedl. Ottawa: Dovehouse, 1991. 17-36.

P (Austern 20)

N   [1] Linda Phyllis Austern, "Love, Death, and
   Ideas of Music in the English Renaissance,"
   <u>Love and Death in the Renaissance</u>, ed. Kenneth
   R. Bartlett, Konrad Eisenbichler, and Janice
   Liedl (Ottawa: Dovehouse, 1991) 20.

Selection(s) in an anthology

B Melville, Herman. "Bartleby the Scrivener." <u>The
      American Tradition in Literature</u>. Shorter
      ed. Ed. George Perkins and Barbara Per-
      kins. Boston: McGraw-Hill, 1999. 672-94.

P (Melville 674)

N   [1] Herman Melville, "Bartleby the
   Scrivener," <u>The American Tradition in Liter-
   ature</u>, shorter ed., ed. George Perkins and
   Barbara Perkins (Boston: McGraw-Hill, 1999)
   674. All citations of "Bartleby" will refer by
   page number to this edition.

Government publication

B Hunter, Laura Grace. <u>The Language of Audit</u>
       <u>Reports</u>. US Gen. Acct. Off. Washington:
       GPO, 1957.

P (Hunter 28)

N   [1] Laura Grace Hunter, <u>The Language of</u>
<u>Audit Reports</u>, US Gen. Acct. Off. (Washington:
GPO, 1957) 28.

B United States. Cong. Senate. <u>National</u>
       <u>Environmental Education Amendments Act of</u>
       <u>1996</u>. 104th Cong., 2nd sess. Washington:
       GPO, 1996.

P (United States 2-3)

N   [1] United States, Cong., Senate, <u>National</u>
<u>Environmental Education Amendments Act of 1996</u>,
104th Cong., 2nd sess. (Washington: GPO, 1996)
2-3.

Dissertation

B Blitch, Alice. "Etymon and Image in <u>The Faerie</u>
       <u>Queene</u>." Diss. Michigan State U, 1965.

P (Blitch 197)

N   [1] Alice Blitch, "Etymon and Image in <u>The Faerie Queene</u>," diss., Michigan State U, 1965, 197.

Unpublished manuscript

B   Miller, Russell E., Jr. "The Authority of
            Biblical Translations: A Layman's Guide to
            the KJV Controversy." Unpublished manu-
            script.

P   (Miller 23)

N   [1] Russell E. Miller, Jr., "The Authority
of Biblical Translations: A Layman's Guide to
the KJV Controversy," unpublished manuscript,
23.

Article in a monthly or bimonthly periodical

B   Walruff, Barbara. "What Global Language?"
            <u>Atlantic Monthly</u> Nov. 2000: 52-66.

P   (Walruff 55)

N   [1] Barbara Walruff, "What Global Language?"
<u>Atlantic Monthly</u> Nov. 2000: 55.

B   Cummins, David L. "Roots of the First
            Amendment." <u>Frontline</u> May-June 2001: 22.

P   (Cummins)

N   [1] David L. Cummins, "Roots of the First Amendment," <u>Frontline</u> May-June 2001: 22.

Article in a weekly or biweekly periodical

B   Olasky, Marvin. "Off with His Head." <u>World</u> 16 June 2001: 30-36.

P   (Olasky 36)

N   [1] Marvin Olasky, "Off with His Head," <u>World</u> 16 June 2001: 36.

B   MacFarquhar, Roderick. "India: The Imprint of Empire." <u>New York Review of Books</u> 23 Oct. 1997: 26-32.

P   (MacFarquhar 32)

N   [1] Roderick MacFarquhar, "India: The Imprint of Empire," <u>New York Review of Books</u> 23 Oct. 1997: 32.

Newspaper article

B   Hoover, Dan. "Hunley Guards Secrets It's Kept Since 1864." <u>Greenville News</u> 8 July 2001: A1+.

P   (Hoover A12)

N   [1] Dan Hoover, "Hunley Guards Secrets It's Kept Since 1864," <u>Greenville News</u> 8 July 2001: A12.

B   Howlett, Debbie. "Legendary News Bureau to Close." <u>USA Today</u> 26 Feb. 1999: 4A.

P   (Howlett)

N   [1] Debbie Howlett, "Legendary News Bureau to Close," <u>USA Today</u> 26 Feb. 1999: 4A.

B   "Public Values Internet for Being a Library, Not a Shopping Mall." <u>Wall Street Journal</u> 10 July 2001: A8.

P   ("Public")

N   [1] "Public Values Internet for Being a Library, Not a Shopping Mall," <u>Wall Street Journal</u> 10 July 2001: A8.

Editorial

B   "The Earth Rebalanced." Editorial. <u>Wall Street Journal</u> 10 July 2001: A18.

P   ("Earth")

N   [1] "The Earth Rebalanced," editorial, <u>Wall Street Journal</u> 10 July 2001: A18.

B   Hendrix, Marcia. "The Sixth of June."

Editorial. <u>The State</u> 6 June 2001. A11.

P   (Hendrix)

N   [1] Marcia Hendrix, "The Sixth of June,"
editorial, <u>The State</u> 6 June 2001: A11.

Syndicated column

B   Greene, Bob. "Some Things Don't Show Up in
Surveys." <u>Gaffney Ledger</u> 24 Apr. 1998: 4A.

P   (Greene)

N   [1] Bob Greene, "Some Things Don't Show Up
in Surveys," <u>Gaffney Ledger</u> 24 Apr. 1998: 4A.

Letter to an editor

B   Horton, Ron. Letter. <u>USA Today</u> 26-28 Feb. 1999:
13A.

P   (Horton)

N   [1] Ron Horton, letter, <u>USA Today</u> 26-28 Feb.
1999: 13A.

Article in a journal paginated by issue

B   Mills, Jerry Leath. "Recent Studies in
Herbert." <u>English Literary Renaissance</u> 6.1
(1976): 105-18.

P   (Mills 106-07)

N   [1] Jerry Leath Mills, "Recent Studies in Herbert," <u>English Literary Renaissance</u> 6.1 (1976): 106-07.

Article in a journal paginated by volume   CQ Researcher.

B Newman, Lance. "Wordsworth in America and the Nature of Democracy." <u>New England Quarterly</u> 72 (1999): 517-38.

P (Newman 533)

N   [1] Lance Newman, "Wordsworth in America and the Nature of Democracy," <u>New England Quarterly</u> 72 (1999): 533.

Article in a journal with more than one series

B Price, Diana. "Reconsidering Shakespeare's Monument." <u>Review of English Studies</u> ns 48.190 (1997): 168-82.

P (Price 171)

N   [1] Diana Price, "Reconsidering Shakespeare's Monument," <u>Review of English Studies</u> ns 48.190 (1997): 171.

Review

B   Kermode, Frank. "Art Among the Ruins." Rev. of
<u>Practicing New Historicism</u>, by Catherine
Gallagher and Stephen Greenblatt, and
<u>Shakespeare After Theory</u>, by David Scott
Kastan. <u>New York Review of Books</u> 5 July
2001: 59-63.

P   (Kermode 62)

N   [1] Frank Kermode, "Art Among the Ruins,"
rev. of <u>Practicing New Historicism</u>, by
Catherine Gallagher and Stephen Greenblatt, and
<u>Shakespeare After Theory</u>, by David Scott
Kastan, <u>New York Review of Books</u> 5 July 2001:
62.

B   Waterman, Sue. Rev. of <u>A History of Reading in
the West</u>. Ed. Guglierma Cavallo and Roger
Chartier. Trans. Lydia Cochrane. <u>Modern
Language Notes</u> 116 (2001): 596-601.

P   (Waterman 599)

N   [1] Sue Waterman, rev. of <u>A History of
Reading in the West</u>, ed. Guglierma Cavallo and
Roger Chartier, trans. Lydia Cochrane, <u>Modern
Language Notes</u> 116 (2001): 599.

Published letter

B   Paulding, James Kirke. "To James Fenimore
           Cooper." 20 May 1839. Letter 190 in The
           Letters of James Kirke Paulding. Ed. Ralph
           M. Aderman. Madison: U of Wisconsin P,
           1962. 256-57.

P   (Paulding 257)

N   [1] James Kirke Paulding, "To James Fenimore
     Cooper," 20 May 1839, letter 190 in The Letters
     of James Kirke Paulding, ed. Ralph M. Aderman
     (Madison: U of Wisconsin P, 1962) 257.

Unpublished letter

B   Hardison, O. B., Jr. Letter to Ronald Horton.
           14 May 1990.

    or

    Hardison, O. B., Jr. Letter to the author. 14
           May 1990.

P   (Hardison)

    or

    (Hardison, letter)

N   [1] O. B. Hardison, Jr., letter to Ronald
     Horton, 14 May 1990.

    or

           [1] O. B. Hardison, Jr., letter to the
     author, 14 May 1990.

Personal interview

B   Custer, Stewart. Personal Interview. 8 February

1999.

P   (Custer)

N   [1] Stewart Custer, personal interview, 8

February 1999.

Published or broadcast interview

B   Bennett, William J. "The Virtue of the

Marketplace." Interview with Eric S.

Cohen. <u>Campus</u> 9.2 (1998): 12-13.

P   (Bennett 13)

N   [1] William J. Bennett, "The Virtue of the

Marketplace," interview with Eric S. Cohen,

<u>Campus</u> 9.2 (1998): 13.

B   Gould, Glenn. Interview with CBC producer

Vincent Tovell. Project 20: At Home with

Glenn Gould. 4 Dec. 1959.

P   (Gould)

N   [1] Glenn Gould, interview with CBC producer

Vincent Tovell, Project 20: At Home with Glenn

Gould, 4 Dec. 1959.

Unpublished lecture, public address, or other speech

B   Salter, Guenter. "The Christian Philosophy of
        Education." Bob Jones University faculty
        session. Stratton Hall, Bob Jones
        University, Greenville, SC. 16 Aug. 2001.

P   (Salter)

N   1 Guenter Salter, "The Christian
     Philosophy of Education," Bob Jones University
     faculty session, Stratton Hall, Bob Jones
     University, Greenville, SC, 16 Aug. 2001.

Map or chart

B   <u>Africa</u>. Map. Chicago: Denoyer-Geppert, 1966.

P   (<u>Africa</u>)

N   1 <u>Africa</u>, map, (Chicago: Denoyer-Geppert),
     1966.

Film, videocassette, or digital versatile disc

B   <u>Our Mutual Friend</u>. By Charles Dickens. Adapt.
        Sandy Welch. Dir. Julian Farino. Prod.
        Catherine Wearing. Perf. Paul McGann,
        Keeley Hawes, Anna Friel, Stephen
        Mackintosh, Peter Vaughan, Pam Ferris, and
        David Morrissey. Videocassette. BBC, 1998.

P   (<u>Our Mutual Friend</u>)

N   [1] <u>Our Mutual Friend</u>, by Charles Dickens, adapt. Sandy Welch, dir. Julian Farino, prod. Catherine Wearing, perf. Paul McGann, Keeley Hawes, Anna Friel, Stephen Mackintosh, Peter Vaughan, Pam Ferris, and David Morrissey, videocassette, BBC, 1998.

B <u>Chariots of Fire</u>. Screenplay by Colin Welland. Dir. Hugh Hudson. Prod. David Puttnam. Perf. Ben Cross, Ian Charleson, Nigel Havers, Ian Holm, Sir John Gielgud, Lindsay Anderson, David Yelland, Nicholas Farrell. DVD. 1981.

P (<u>Chariots of Fire</u>)

N   [1] <u>Chariots of Fire</u>, screenplay by Colin Welland, dir. Hugh Hudson, prod. David Puttnam, perf. Ben Cross, Ian Charleson, Nigel Havers, Ian Holm, Sir John Gielgud, Lindsay Anderson, David Yelland, Nicholas Farrell, DVD, 1981.

Audio recording

B Tchaikovsky, Pyotr Ilyitch. Symphony no. 4 in F minor, op. 36. Cond. Georg Solti. Chicago Symph. Orch. 1984. Decca-London, 1985.

P (Tchaikovsky)

N   [1] Pyotr Ilyitch Tchaikovsky, Symphony no.
4 in F minor, op. 36, cond. Georg Solti,
Chicago Symph. Orch., 1984, Decca-London, 1985.

B   Estes, Simon. Spirituals. Howard Roberts
         Chorale. Philips, 1984.

P   (Estes)

N   [1] Simon Estes, Spirituals, Howard Roberts
Chorale, Philips, 1984.

B   Gould, Glenn. Goldberg Variations. By Johann
         Sebastian Bach. Rec. June 1955. Prod.
         Howard Scott. LP. Angel, 1956.

P   (Gould)

N   [1] Glenn Gould, Goldberg Variations, by
Johann Sebastian Bach, rec. June 1955, prod.
Howard Scott, LP, Angel, 1956.

Television or radio broadcast

B   The Law and the Prophets. Project 20. NBC.
         WYFF, Greenville, SC. 23 April 1972.

P   (Law and Prophets)

N   1 The Law and the Prophets, Project 20,
NBC, WYFF, Greenville, SC, 23 April 1972.

Performance

B   Gould, Glenn, pianist. <u>Pavane</u>. By Orlando
       Gibbons. Five Sinfonias and Partita no. 5.
       By Johann Sebastian Bach. <u>Variations for
       Piano</u>, op. 27. By Anton Webern. Sonata
       no. 30 in E Major, op. 109. By Ludwig van
       Beethoven. Sonata. By Alban Berg. Concert.
       Town Hall, New York. 11 Jan. 1955.

P   (Gould)

N   [1] Glenn Gould, pianist, <u>Pavane</u>, by Orlando
   Gibbons, five Sinfonias and Partita no. 5, by
   Johann Sebastian Bach, <u>Variations for Piano</u>,
   op. 27, by Anton Webern, Sonata no. 30 in E
   Major, op. 109, by Ludwig van Beethoven,
   Sonata, by Alban Berg, concert, Town Hall, New
   York, 11 Jan. 1955.

Work of art or photograph

B   Vignon, Claude. <u>St. Jerome</u>. Bob Jones
       University Museum and Gallery, Inc.,
       Greenville, SC.

P   (Vignon)

N   [1] Claude Vignon, <u>St. Jerome</u>, Bob Jones
   University Museum and Gallery, Inc.,
   Greenville, SC.

Musical composition

B   Chopin, Frederick. Piano Sonata no. 3 in B
        minor, op. 58.

P   (Chopin)

N   [1] Frederick Chopin, Piano Sonata no. 3
in B minor, op. 58.

B   Hansen, Howard. <u>Three Miniatures</u>. New York:
        Fischer, 1964.

P   (Hansen)

N   [1] Howard Hansen, <u>Three Miniatures</u> (New
York: Fischer, 1964).

A COMPARISON OF STYLES

The sets of examples below illustrate the differences between the most common documentation styles. The examples include forms for the types of sources cited most frequently. Though the non-MLA styles cannot be as fully represented here as is the MLA style above, the range of examples should be sufficient for the needs of most undergraduate research.

Graduate students will find it convenient to have their own copies of the style manuals used in their disciplines. The manuals on which the styles compared below are based are the following:

Gibaldi, Joseph. *MLA [Modern Language Association] Style Manual and Guide to Scholarly Publishing.* 2nd ed. New York: MLA, 1998.

The Chicago Manual of Style. 14th ed. Chicago: U of Chicago P, 1993.

Publication Manual of the American Psychological Association. 5th ed. Washington: APA, 2001.

Scientific Style and Format: The CBE [Council of Biology Editors] Manual for Authors, Editors, and Publishers. 6th ed. Chicago: Cambridge UP, 1994.

Reference List

The term "Reference List" rather than "Bibliography" heads this section because it includes only works cited and because "Reference List" is more common among the disciplines represented than "Works Cited," preferred by MLA.

Book with one author in a subsequent edition

MLA

```
Fussell, Paul. Poetic Meter and Poetic Form. Rev.
     ed. New York: Random, 1979.
```

CMS

```
Fussell, Paul. Poetic Meter and Poetic Form. Rev.
     ed. New York: Random House, 1979.
```

APA

Fussell, P. (1979). <u>Poetic meter and poetic form</u>.

    (Rev. ed.). New York: Random House.

CBE

Fussell P. Poetic meter and poetic form. Rev. ed.

    New York: Random House; 1979. 188 p.

Book with two or three authors

MLA

Geisler, Norman, and Ronald M. Brooks. <u>When Skep-</u>

    <u>tics Ask: A Handbook of Christian Evidences</u>.

    Grand Rapids: Baker, 1990.

CMS

Geisler, Norman, and Ronald M. Brooks. <u>When</u>

    <u>Skeptics Ask: A Handbook of Christian</u>

    <u>Evidences</u>. Grand Rapids: Baker Book House,

    1990.

APA

Geisler, N., & Brooks, R. M. (1990). <u>When skeptics</u>

    <u>ask: A handbook of Christian evidences</u>. Grand

    Rapids: Baker Book House.

CBE

Geisler N, Brooks RM. When skeptics ask: A hand-

    book of Christian evidences. Grand Rapids:

    Baker; 1990. 348 p.

Book with more than three authors

MLA

Alberts, Bruce, et al. <u>Essential Cell Biology: An Introduction to the Molecular Biology of the Cell</u>. New York: Garland, 1998.

CMS

Alberts, Bruce, et al. <u>Essential Cell Biology: An Introduction to the Molecular Biology of the Cell</u>. New York: Garland Publishing, 1998.

APA

Alberts, B., Bray, D., Lewis, J., Raff, M., Roberts, K., & Walter, P. (1998). <u>Essential cell biology: An introduction to the molecular biology of the cell</u>. New York: Garland Publishing.

CBE

Alberts B, Bray D, Lewis J, Raff M, Roberts K, Walter P. Essential cell biology: An introduction to the molecular biology of the cell. New York: Garland; 1998. 630 p.

More than one work by the same author

MLA

Hamilton, Edith. <u>The Great Age of Greek Literature</u>. New York: Norton, 1942.

---. <u>The Roman Way</u>. New York: Norton, 1932.

CMS

Hamilton, Edith. <u>The Great Age of Greek
Literature</u>. New York: Norton, 1942.

——. <u>The Roman Way</u>. New York: Norton, 1932.

APA

Hamilton, E. (1942) <u>The great age of Greek litera-
ture</u>. New York: Norton.

Hamilton, E. (1932) <u>The Roman way</u>. New York: Norton.

CBE

Hamilton E. The great age of Greek literature.
New York: Norton; 1942. 347 p.

Hamilton E. The Roman way. New York: Norton; 1932.
281 p.

Edited book

MLA

Sanders, Russell Scott, ed. <u>Audubon Reader: The
Best Writings of John James Audubon</u>. Bloomington: U of Indiana P, 1986.

or

Audubon, John James. <u>Audubon Reader: The Best
Writings of John James Audubon</u>. Ed. Russell
Scott Sanders. Bloomington: U of Indiana P,
1986.

CMS

Sanders, Russell Scott, ed. <u>Audubon Reader: The Best Writings of John James Audubon</u>. Bloomington: University of Indiana Press, 1986.

or

Audubon, John James. <u>Audubon Reader: The Best Writings of John James Audubon</u>. Edited by Russell Scott Sanders. Bloomington: University of Indiana Press, 1986.

APA

Sanders, R. S. (Ed.). (1986). <u>Audubon reader: The best writings of John James Audubon</u>. Bloomington: University of Indiana Press.

CBE

Sanders RS, editor. Audubon reader: The best writings of John James Audubon. Bloomington: Univ Indiana Pr; 1986. 245 p.

Book with an organization as author and publisher

MLA

National Association of Science Writers. <u>Communicating Science: A Guide for Scientists, Physicians, and Public Information Officers</u>. Greenlawn, NY: National Association of Science Writers, n.d.

CMS

National Association of Science Writers. <u>Communi-
    cating Science: A Guide for Scientists,
    Physicians, and Public Information Officers</u>.
    Greenlawn, N.Y.: National Association of
    Science Writers, n.d.

APA

National Association of Science Writers. (n.d.).

   <u>Communicating science: A guide for scien-</u>

   <u>tists, physicians, and public information</u>

   <u>officers</u>. Greenlawn, NY: author.

CBE

[NASW] National Association of Science Writers.

   Communicating science: A guide for scien-

   tists, physicians, and public information

   officers. Greenlawn (NY): NASW; n.d. 35 p.

Reprinted book in a series with translator

MLA

Curtius, Ernst Robert. <u>European Literature and the</u>

        <u>Latin Middle Ages</u>. Trans. Willard R.

        Trask. Bollingen Ser. 36. 1953. Princeton,

        NJ: Princeton UP, 1967.

CMS

Curtius, Ernst Robert. <u>European Literature and the
    Latin Middle Ages</u>. Translated by Willard R.
    Trask. Bollingen Series 36. 1953. Reprint,
    Princeton, N.J.: Princeton University Press,
    1967.

APA

Curtius, E. R. (1967). <u>European literature and the Latin Middle Ages</u>. (W. R. Trask, Trans.; Bollingen Series No. 36). Princeton, NJ: Princeton University Press.

CBE

Curtius ER. European literature and the Latin Middle Ages. Trask WR, translator. Princeton: Princeton Univ Pr; 1967. 662 p. Translation of: Europäische literatur und lateinisches Mittelalter.

Article in a multivolume book

MLA

Kinder, Donald R. "Opinion and Action in the Realm of Politics." <u>The Handbook of Social Psychology</u>. Ed. Daniel T. Gilbert, Susan T. Fiske, and Gardner Lindzey. 4th ed. 2 vols. Boston: McGraw-Hill, 1998. 2: 778-867.

CMS

Kinder, Donald R. "Opinion and Action in the Realm of Politics." In <u>The Handbook of Social Psychology</u>, ed. Daniel T. Gilbert, Susan T. Fiske, and Gardner Lindzey, 4th ed., vol. 2, 778-867, Boston: McGraw-Hill, 1998.

APA

Kinder, D. R. (1998). Opinion and action in the realm of politics. In D. T. Gilbert, S. T. Fiske, and G. Lindzey (Eds.), <u>The handbook of social psychology</u> (4th ed., vol. 2, pp. 778-867). Boston: McGraw-Hill.

CBE

Kinder, DR. Opinion and action in the realm of politics. In: Gilbert DT, Fiske ST, Lindzey G, editors. The handbook of social psychology. 4th ed. Volume 2. Boston: McGraw-Hill; 1998. p 778-867.

Encyclopedia article

MLA

Sturgeon, Theodore. "Science Fiction." <u>Encyclopedia Americana</u>. 1998 ed.

CMS

<u>Encyclopedia Americana</u>. 1998 ed. S.v. "science fiction."

APA

Sturgeon, T. (1998). Science fiction. In <u>Encyclopedia Americana</u> (Vol. 24, pp. 391-393). Danbury (CT): Grolier.

CBE

Sturgeon T. Science fiction. In: Encyclopedia

　　　Americana. Danbury (CT): Grolier; 1998.

　　　p 391-393.

Article in a periodical published weekly

MLA

Conlin, Michelle. "Religion in the Workplace."

　　　<u>Business Week</u> 1 Nov. 1999: 151+.

CMS

Conlin, Michelle. "Religion in the Workplace."
　　　<u>Business Week</u>, 1 November 1999, 151-54, 156,
　　　158.

APA

Conlin, M. (1999, November 1). Religion in the

　　　workplace. <u>Business Week</u>, 151-154, 156, 158.

CBE

Conlin M. 1999 Nov 1. Religion in the workplace.

　　　Business Week:151-4, 156, 158.

Newspaper article

MLA

Ross, Emma. "Thinness Loses to Exercise in Study."

　　　<u>Charlotte Observer</u> 18 July 2001: A1+.

CMS

Ross, Emma. "Thinness Loses to Exercise in Study."
　　　<u>Charlotte Observer</u>, 18 July 2001, sec. A,
　　　pp. 1, 9.

APA

Ross, E. (2001, July 18). Thinness loses to exer-
    cise in study. <u>Charlotte Observer</u>, pp. A1,
    A9.

CBE

Ross E. 2001 July 18. Thinness loses to exercise
    in study. Charlotte Observer;Sect A:1,9.

Article in a journal paginated by issue

MLA

Cohen, Paula Marantz. "Helen Keller and the Ameri-
    can Myth." <u>Yale Review</u> 85.1 (1997): 1-20.

CMS

Cohen, Paula Marantz. "Helen Keller and the Ameri-
    can Myth." <u>Yale Review</u> 85, no. 1 (1997): 1-20.

APA

Cohen, P. M. (1997). Helen Keller and the American
    myth. <u>Yale Review, 85</u>(1), 1-20.

CBE

Cohen PM. 1997. Helen Keller and the American
    myth. Yale Rev. 85(1):1-20.

Article in a journal paginated by volume

MLA

Reichle, Joe. "Communication Intervention with
    Persons Who Have Severe Disabilities." <u>Jour-
    nal of Special Education</u> 31 (1997): 110-34.

CMS

Reichle, Joe. "Communication Intervention with
Persons Who Have Severe Disabilities."
Journal of Special Education 31 (1997):
110-34.

APA

Reichle, J. (1997). Communication intervention

with persons who have severe disabilities.

Journal of Special Education, 31, 110-34.

CBE

Reichle J. 1997. Communication intervention with

persons who have severe disabilities. J Spec

Ed 31:110-34.

In-Text Citation

This section shows how passages, drawn from the excerpts below, would be incorporated and cited according to the featured documentation styles. Assume that the text is a middle paragraph of a paper ended by the reference list. Recall that the content within the parentheses varies according to what is supplied in the text. Notice the absence of parenthetical documentation with CMS, which prefers footnotes. Notice also the insertion of *sic* (Latin, *thus*) in the second passage immediately below to attribute an error, here grammatical, to the original source, clearing the present writer of responsibility.

Cited passages

1. Lastly, in a very general sense, the Great Awakening may be said to have promoted democracy in America. Its message that all people (including, according to the Baptists and Whitefield, slaves) had the possibility of winning salvation meant that all people were equal before God. As a result, the ordinary member won a far greater voice in the management of church affairs, even including the selection of the minister. It was not long before these same churchgoers began wondering why so much inequality existed in secular affairs and why the "lesser orders" had so little influence in political matters. The two great mass movements in colonial history were the Great Awakening and the American Revolution: Both challenged "establishments"—either religious or political—and both used similar strategies and tactics. (Reich)

2. During the years since the first publication of the book my various experiences with the functioning of our plutocratic society—in the occupation of Germany, in Washington, and in the control and administration of several different academic institutions—has [*sic*], if anything, strengthened rather than weakened my conviction that the closer we could approach the Puritan ideal of the distribution of power in our society and its government the better off we should be. (Knappen)

3. Christian morality is qualified to survive because its design agrees with the design of human nature, if it be granted that conscience and reason are human faculties which even in their dethronement are never destroyed but remain as deep potentialities which define the direction of human effort. And Christian morality is qualified to survive because love and agreement, which unite men, are stronger than hate and fear, which divide them. (Perry)

MLA

Scholarly support is not lacking for the positive effects of fervent Christianity on American democratic society. A standard account of early America considers the Great Awakening one of "the two great mass movements in colonial history" that encouraged the spread of democracy in America, the Revolution being the other (Reich 222). Another author of an acclaimed study believes that the Puritans had a grasp of political realities much needed today. The quarter century since the appearance of the first edition of his study, writes M. M. Knappen, "has, if anything, strengthened rather than weakened my conviction that the closer we could approach the Puritan ideal of the distribution of power in our society and its government the better off we should be" (vi). Still another noted historian has argued for the staying power of the moral core of Puritanism. "Christian morality is qualified to survive because its design agrees with the design of human nature" and "because love and agreement, which unite men, are stronger than hate and fear, which divide them" (Perry, <u>Puritanism</u> 640). Puritanism, he maintains, was not only a benign political influence; it remains a social necessity.

Andrews, Dee E. <u>The Methodists and Revolutionary America, 1760-1800: The Shaping of an Evangelical Culture</u>. Princeton, NJ: Princeton UP, 2000.

Carden, Allen. <u>Puritan Christianity in America: Religion and Life in Seventeenth-Century Massachusetts</u>. Grand Rapids: Baker, 1990.

Degler, Carl N. <u>Out of Our Past: The Forces That Shaped Modern America</u>. 3rd ed. New York: Harper Perennial-Harper, 1984.

Dickens, A. G. <u>The English Reformation</u>. New York: Schocken, 1964.

Knappen, M. M. <u>Tudor Puritanism: A Chapter in the History of Idealism</u>. 1939. Chicago: Phoenix-U of Chicago P, 1965.

Perry, Ralph Barton. <u>The Citizen Decides: A Guide to Responsible Thinking in Time of Crisis</u>. Bloomington: Indiana UP, 1951.

---. <u>Puritanism and Democracy</u>. 1944. New York: Harper, 1964.

Reich, Jerome R. <u>Colonial America</u>. 5th ed. Upper Saddle River, NJ: Prentice, 2001.

Ziff, Larzer. "The Social Bond of Church Covenant." <u>American Quarterly</u> 10.4 (1958): 454-62.

CMS

Scholarly support is not lacking for the positive effects of fervent Christianity on American democratic society. A standard account of early America considers the Great Awakening one of "the two great mass movements in colonial history" that encouraged the spread of democracy in America, the Revolution being the other.[3] Another author of an acclaimed study believes that the Puritans had a grasp of political realities much needed today. The quarter century since the appearance of the first edition of his study, writes M. M. Knappen, "has, if anything, strengthened rather than weakened my conviction that the closer we could approach the Puritan ideal of the distribution of power in our society and its government the better off we should be."[4] Still another noted historian has argued for the staying power of the moral core of Puritanism. "Christian morality is qualified to survive because its design agrees with the design of human nature" and "because love and agreement, which unite men, are stronger than hate and fear, which divide them."[5] Puritanism, he maintains, was not only a benign political influence; it remains a social necessity.

Notes

    3. Jerome R. Reich, <u>Colonial America</u>, 5th ed. (Upper Saddle River, N.J.: Prentice Hall, 2001), p. 222.

    4. M. M. Knappen, preface to <u>Tudor Puritanism: A Chapter in the History of Idealism</u> (Chicago: University of Chicago Press, 1939; Phoenix Books, 1965), p. vi.

    5. Ralph Barton Perry, <u>Puritanism and Democracy</u> (New York: Vanguard Press, 1944; reprint, New York: Harper & Row, 1964), p. 640 (page citations are to the reprint edition).

Reference List

Andrews, Dee E. <u>The Methodists and Revolutionary America, 1760-1800: The Shaping of an Evangelical Culture</u>. Princeton, N.J.: Princeton University Press, 2000.

Carden, Allen. <u>Puritan Christianity in America: Religion and Life in Seventeenth-Century Massachusetts</u>. Grand Rapids: Baker Book House, 1990.

Degler, Carl N. <u>Out of Our Past: The Forces That Shaped Modern America</u>. 3d ed. New York: Harper & Row, Harper Perennial, 1984.

Dickens, A. G. <u>The English Reformation</u>. New York: Schocken Books, 1964.

Knappen, M. M. Preface to <u>Tudor Puritanism: A Chapter in the History of Idealism</u>. Chicago: University of Chicago Press, 1939; Phoenix Books, 1965.

Perry, Ralph Barton. <u>The Citizen Decides: A Guide to Responsible Thinking in Time of Crisis</u>. Bloomington: Indiana University Press, 1951.

_____. <u>Puritanism and Democracy</u>. New York: Vanguard Press, 1944. Reprint, New York: Harper & Row, 1964.

Reich, Jerome R. <u>Colonial America</u>, 5th ed. Upper Saddle River, NJ: Prentice Hall, 2001.

Ziff, Larzer. "The Social Bond of Church Covenant." <u>American Quarterly</u> 10 (1958): 454-62.

APA

Scholarly support is not lacking for the positive effects of fervent Christianity on American democratic society. A standard account of early America considers the Great Awakening one of "the two great mass movements in colonial history" that encouraged the spread of democracy in America, the Revolution being the other (Reich, 2001, p. 222).

Another author of an acclaimed study believes that the Puritans had a grasp of political realities much needed today. The quarter century since the appearance of the first edition of his study, writes Knappen, "has, if anything, strengthened rather than weakened my conviction that the closer we could approach the Puritan ideal of the distribution of power in our society and its government the better off we should be" (1965, p. vi). Still another noted historian has argued for the staying power of the moral core of Puritanism. "Christian morality is qualified to survive because its design agrees with the design of human nature" and "because love and agreement, which unite men, are stronger than hate and fear, which divide them" (Perry, 1964, p. 640). Puritanism, he maintains, was not only a benign political influence; it remains a social necessity.

Andrews, D.E. (2000). <u>The Methodists and Revolutionary America, 1760-1800: The shaping of an evangelical culture</u>. Princeton, NJ: Princeton University Press.

Carden, A. (1990). <u>Puritan Christianity in Amer-
ica: Religion and life in seventeenth-century
Massachusetts</u>. Grand Rapids, MI: Baker Book
House.

Degler, C. N. (1984). <u>Out of our past: The forces
that shaped modern America</u>. (3rd ed.). New
York: Harper & Row.

Dickens, A. G. (1964). <u>The English Reformation</u>.
New York: Schocken Books.

Knappen, M. M. (1965). <u>Tudor puritanism: A chapter
in the history of idealism</u>. Chicago: University of Chicago Press.

Perry, R. B. (1951). <u>The citizen decides: A guide
to responsible thinking in time of crisis</u>.
Bloomington: Indiana University Press.

Perry, R. B. (1964). <u>Puritanism and democracy</u>. New
York: Harper & Row.

Reich, J. R. (2001). <u>Colonial America</u> (5th ed.).
Upper Saddle River, NJ: Prentice Hall.

Ziff, L. (1958). The social bond of church
covenant. <u>American Quarterly 10,</u> 454-62.

CBE Author-Year

Scholarly support is not lacking for the positive effects of fervent Christianity on American democratic society. A standard account of early America considers the Great Awakening one of "the two great mass movements in colonial history" that encouraged the spread of democracy in America, the Revolution being the other (Reich 2001: 222). Another author of an acclaimed study believes that the Puritans had a grasp of political realities much needed today. The quarter century since the appearance of the first edition of his study "has, if anything, strengthened rather than weakened my conviction that the closer we could approach the Puritan ideal of the distribution of power in our society and its government the better off we should be" (Knappen 1965: vi). Still another noted historian has argued for the staying power of the moral core of Puritanism. "Christian morality is qualified to survive because its design agrees with the design of human nature" and "because love and agreement, which unite men, are stronger than hate and fear, which divide them" (Perry 1964: 640). Puritanism, he maintains, was not only a benign political influence; it remains a social necessity.

Andrews DE. 2000. The Methodists and Revolutionary America, 1760-1800: The shaping of an evangelical culture. Princeton (NJ): Princeton Univ Pr. 367 p.

Carden A. 1990. Puritan Christianity in America: Religion and life in seventeenth-century Massachusetts. Grand Rapids: Baker. 239 p.

Degler CN. 1984. Out of our past: The forces that shaped modern America. 3rd ed. New York: Harper & Row. 648 p.

Dickens AG. 1964. The English Reformation. New York: Schocken. 374 p.

Knappen MM. 1965. Tudor puritanism: A chapter in the history of idealism. Chicago: Univ Chicago Pr. 555 p.

Perry RB. 1951. The citizen decides: A guide to responsible thinking in time of crisis. Bloomington: Indiana Univ Pr. 225 p.

Perry RB. 1964. Puritanism and democracy. New York: Harper & Row. 688 p.

Reich JR. 2001. Colonial America. 5th ed. Upper
     Saddle River (NJ): Prentice Hall. 326 p.

Ziff L. 1958. The social bond of church covenant.
     American Quarterly 10:454-62.

CBE Alphabetical Numbering

Scholarly support is not lacking for the positive
effects of fervent Christianity on American democratic society. A standard account of early America[8] considers the Great Awakening one of "the two
great mass movements in colonial history" that
encouraged the spread of democracy in America, the
Revolution being the other. Another author of an
acclaimed study[5] believes that the Puritans had a
grasp of political realities much needed today.
The quarter century since the appearance of the
first edition of his study "has, if anything,
strengthened rather than weakened my conviction
that the closer we could approach the Puritan
ideal of the distribution of power in our society
and its government the better off we should be."
Still another noted historian[7] has argued for the
staying power of the moral core of Puritanism.

"Christian morality is qualified to survive because its design agrees with the design of human nature" and "because love and agreement, which unite men, are stronger than hate and fear, which divide them." Puritanism, he maintains, was not only a benign political influence; it remains a social necessity.

1. Andrews DE. The Methodists and Revolutionary America, 1760-1800: The shaping of an evangelical culture. Princeton (NJ): Princeton Univ Pr; 2000. 367 p. (p 14)

2. Carden A. Puritan Christianity in America: Religion and life in seventeenth-century Massachusetts. Grand Rapids: Baker; 1990. 239 p. (p 143)

3. Degler CN. Out of our past: The forces that shaped modern America. 3rd ed. New York: Harper & Row; 1984. 648 p. (p 598)

4. Dickens AG. The English Reformation. New York: Schocken; 1964. 374 p. (p 331)

5. Knappen MM. Tudor puritanism: A chapter in the history of idealism. Chicago: Univ Chicago Pr; 1965. 555 p. (p vi)

6. Perry RB. The citizen decides: A guide to responsible thinking in time of crisis. Bloomington: Indiana Univ Pr; 1951. 225 p. (p 130)

7. Perry RB. Puritanism and democracy. New York: Harper & Row; 1964. 688 p. (p 640)

8. Reich JR. Colonial America. 5th ed. Upper Saddle River (NJ): Prentice Hall; 2001. 326 p. (p 222)

9. Ziff L. The social bond of church covenant. American Quarterly 1958; 10:454-62. (p 459)

CBE Consecutive Numbering

Scholarly support is not lacking for the positive effects of fervent Christianity on American democratic society. A standard account of early America[3] considers the Great Awakening one of "the two great mass movements in colonial history" that encouraged the spread of democracy in America, the Revolution being the other. Another author of an acclaimed study[4] believes that the Puritans had a grasp of political realities much needed today. The quarter century since the appearance of the first edition of his study "has, if anything,

strengthened rather than weakened my conviction
that the closer we could approach the Puritan
ideal of the distribution of power in our society
and its government the better off we should be."
Still another noted historian[5] has argued for the
staying power of the moral core of Puritanism.
"Christian morality is qualified to survive
because its design agrees with the design of human
nature" and "because love and agreement, which
unite men, are stronger than hate and fear, which
divide them." Puritanism, he maintains, was not
only a benign political influence; it remains a
social necessity.

1. Perry RB. The citizen decides: A guide to
   responsible thinking in time of crisis. Bloomington: Indiana Univ Pr; 1951. 225 p. (p 130)

2. Degler CN. Out of our past: The forces that
   shaped modern America. 3rd ed. New York: Harper
   & Row; 1984. 648 p. (p 513)

3. Reich JR. Colonial America. 5th ed. Upper
   Saddle River (NJ): Prentice Hall; 2001. 326 p.
   (p 222)

4. Knappen MM. Tudor puritanism: A chapter in the history of idealism. Chicago: Univ Chicago Press; 1964. 555 p. (p vi)

5. Perry RB. Puritanism and democracy. New York: Harper & Row; 1964. 688 p. (p 640)

6. Dickens AG. The English Reformation. New York: Schocken; 1964. 374 p. (p 331)

7. Ziff L. The social bond of church covenant. American Quarterly 1958;10:454-62. (p 459)

8. Carden A. Puritan Christianity in America: Religion and life in seventeenth-century Massachusetts. Grand Rapids: Baker; 1990. 239 p. (p 143)

9. Andrews DE. The Methodists and Revolutionary America, 1760-1800: The shaping of an evangelical culture. Princeton (NJ): Princeton Univ Pr; 2000. 367 p. (p 14)

Footnotes and Endnotes

Only one of the notation styles covered in this section (CMS) favors traditional footnotes or endnotes for citing sources. However, notes are widely used for other purposes: for example, cross-referencing the text and providing information valuable to the specialist but ignorable to the general reader. These are known as content notes, distinct from notes identifying source and location.

The first notation method illustrated below, using numbers, is standard for most styles of documentation. The second, using letters, is common in the sciences.

MLA, CMS, APA, and CBE Author-Year

Let us consider Shakespeare's scope of life in relation to that of his plays. First, it is interesting that his dates span an exact, or nearly exact, fifty-two years.[1] This figure, rendered as weeks, reminds us of Shakespeare's interest in all the seasons of earthly life—its generation, flourishing, and decline.[2] More important is the fact that Shakespeare by middle age had experienced both material success and personal sorrow. While the acting company for which he wrote and acted and in which he was part owner was prospering, his only son died. Later his eldest daughter was accused of adultery.[3] Especially important is Shakespeare's wide literary knowledge, gained from both academic and popular reading and also literary conversation, all working to expand his imaginative world.

MLA

¹ April 23, 1616, is the date of Shake-speare's death. The specific date of his birth is uncertain but was evidently April 21, 22, or 23 of 1564. The date in the parish register given for his baptism is April 26, 1564. It is traditionally held and altogether quite possible that Shake-speare was born and died on the same calendar day.

² See Jaques' speech on the "seven ages of man" in <u>As You Like It</u> (2.7.136-66) for a cynical view of life that is contradicted in the play and often mistaken for Shakespeare's own.

³ Shakespeare had three children: Susanna (1583-1649) and the twins, Hamnet and Judith (b.1585). Hamnet died in 1596 at the age of eleven and a half. Judith died in 1662, outliving her twin by sixty-six years. In 1613 Susanna sued to clear her name of slander, and the case was closed in her favor.

CMS

1. April 23, 1616, is the date of Shake-speare's death. The specific date of his birth is uncertain but was evidently April 21, 22, or 23 of 1564. The date in the parish register given for his baptism is April 26, 1564. It is traditionally held and altogether quite possible that Shake-speare was born and died on the same calendar day.

2. See Jaques' speech on the "seven ages of man" in <u>As You Like It</u> (2.7.136-66) for a cynical view of life that is contradicted in the play and often mistaken for Shakespeare's own.

3. Shakespeare had three children: Susanna (1583-1649) and the twins, Hamnet and Judith (b.1585). Hamnet died in 1596 at the age of eleven and a half. Judith died in 1662, outliving her twin by sixty-six years. In 1613 Susanna sued to clear her name of slander, and the case was closed in her favor.

APA

1. April 23, 1616, is the date of Shakespeare's death. The specific date of his birth is uncertain but was evidently April 21, 22, or 23 of 1564. The date in the parish register given for his baptism is April 26, 1564. It is traditionally held and altogether quite possible that Shakespeare was born and died on the same calendar day.

2. See Jaques' speech on the "seven ages of man" in <u>As You Like It</u> (2.7.136-66) for a cynical view of life that is contradicted in the play and often mistaken for Shakespeare's own.

3. Shakespeare had three children: Susanna (1583-1649) and the twins, Hamnet and Judith (b.1585). Hamnet died in 1596 at the age of eleven and a half. Judith died in 1662, outliving her twin by sixty-six years. In 1613 Susanna sued to clear her name of slander, and the case was closed in her favor.

CBE Author-Year

1. April 23, 1616, is the date of Shakespeare's death. The specific date of his birth is uncertain but was evidently April 21, 22, or 23 of 1564. The date in the parish register given for his baptism is April 26, 1564. It is traditionally held and altogether quite possible that Shakespeare was born and died on the same calendar day.

2. See Jaques' speech on the "seven ages of man" in <u>As You Like It</u> (2.7.136-66) for a cynical view of life that is contradicted in the play and often mistaken for Shakespeare's own.

3. Shakespeare had three children: Susanna (1583-1649) and the twins, Hamnet and Judith (b.1585). Hamnet died in 1596 at the age of eleven and a half. Judith died in 1662, outliving her twin by sixty-six years. In 1613 Susanna sued to clear her name of slander, and the case was closed in her favor.

CBE Alphabetical and Consecutive Notation

Let us consider Shakespeare's scope of life in relation to that of his plays. First, it is interesting that his dates span an exact, or nearly exact, fifty-two years.[a] This figure, rendered as weeks, reminds us of Shakespeare's interest in all

the seasons of earthly life—its generation, flourishing, and decline.[b] More important is the fact
that Shakespeare by middle age had experienced
both material success and personal sorrow. While
the acting company for which he wrote and acted
and in which he was part owner was prospering, his
only son died. Later his eldest daughter was
accused of adultery.[c] Especially important is
Shakespeare's wide literary knowledge, gained from
both academic and popular reading and also literary conversation, all working to expand his imaginative world.

a. April 23, 1616, is the date of Shakespeare's
   death. The specific date of his birth is uncertain but was evidently April 21, 22, or 23 of
   1564. The date in the parish register given for
   his baptism is April 26, 1564. It is traditionally held and altogether quite possible that
   Shakespeare was born and died on the same calendar day.

b. See Jaques' speech on the "seven ages of man"
   in As You Like It (2.7.136-66) for a cynical
   view of life that is contradicted in the play
   and often mistaken for Shakespeare's own.

c. Shakespeare had three children: Susanna (1583-
   1649) and the twins, Hamnet and Judith

(b.1585). Hamnet died in 1596 at the age of
eleven and a half. Judith died in 1662, outliving her twin by sixty-six years. In 1613
Susanna sued to clear her name of slander, and
the case was closed in her favor.

ONLINE AND ELECTRONIC SOURCES

Frequently, documenting online resources poses a problem to the writer because such resources are not always compatible with the documentation paradigms commonly used in academic writing. Furthermore, many online resources are not well documented, lacking such standard pieces of information as the author's name or the publication date. Although most of the major documentation styles offer guidelines for online sources, much of the information that they require or recommend is not available for many online sources. Because of the continual change in electronic media, it may be some time before a comprehensive, flexible standard emerges. In the interim the writer should use a system that addresses the majority of the available resources, one that is flexible enough to accommodate the many variations that occur in the online world.

Probably the most effective standard currently available is the Columbia Online System (COS) developed by Columbia University. Philosophically similar to the MLA standard, the COS system is simple and very flexible. Furthermore, it is easily adaptable to special or unusual situations.

The COS documentation standard takes a pragmatic approach to documenting online sources. It defines a list of *possible* elements that may be used in a bibliographic entry, and it specifies the correct order and format for those elements. It recognizes, however, that many of those elements may be unavailable in particular instances. Absent elements may be omitted as long as the available ones are kept in the correct order and format. The writer should therefore obtain as many of the suggested elements as possible and list them in the order and format that the standard specifies. COS entries should be alphabetized and double-spaced with a one-half inch hanging indent. There should be one space between each major element. COS entries follow this formula:

```
Name of Author. "Document Title." Site Title.

    Version Number. Date of Publication or

    Revision. URL (Date of Access).
```

If the source has a single author, list it in the Last, First order common to most other documentation systems. If the source has multiple authors, list the first author in Last, First order followed by the other authors in normal order. If the website's author is a corporation or organization, list the corporation's or organization's full name.

The Document Title section should contain the page name, which can be determined by looking at the web browser's title bar when it is displaying the page in question. Always enclose the title in quotation marks.

The Site Title section contains the name displayed on the website's homepage. Italicize the title rather than underlining it, since underlining has other associations in electronic sources.

If the page has a version number (usually found at the bottom of the page), place it in the Version Number location. Most websites, however, do not include version numbers, so this item rarely appears.

The Date of Publication or Revision often appears at the bottom of the page. If this information is not listed on individual pages, use the date listed at the bottom of the home page. Unfortunately, many sources are undated. If the date is available, list it in Day Month Year format.

List the URL (Universal Resource Locator) in its entirety, even if it is very long and complex. Do *not* enclose the URL in angle brackets as some other documentation systems specify. Always include the protocol identifier (e.g., http://, ftp://, or telnet://) at the beginning of the URL.

The Date of Access is the date on which the researcher accessed the site. Enclose it in parentheses in Day Month Year format.

A minimal website entry should include either the Document Title or the Site Title, the URL, and the Date of Access. Anything less is too minimal to be useful as a bibliographic entry.

Typical website entry

Losch, John C. "Lacquering Brass." *Articles on Clockmaking*. http://home.att.net/~jclosch/articles.htm#brass (14 Dec. 2001).

Reynolds, James D. "Corneal Transplants." *Hawaii Lyons Eye Bank*. 30 Jul. 2001. http://www.eyebank.com/corneal.html (14 Dec. 2001).

Typical "minimal" website entry

"Biography." *The Edmund Spenser Home Page.* 17 Feb.

2000. http://www.english.cam.ac.uk/

Spenser/biography.htm (2 Aug. 2001).

"Neon Tetra." *Petfish.* http://www.petfish.net/

neon.htm (14 Dec. 2001).

Corporate website

ABIOMED, Inc. "AbioCor Clinical Trial Informa-

tion." *ABIOMED: Focus on the Heart.* 13 Dec.

2001. http://www.abiomed.com/Fabiocor.html

(14 Dec. 2001).

Organizational website

American Cancer Society. "Learn About Cancer."

American Cancer Society Homepage. http://www

.cancer.org/eprise/main/docroot/lrn/lrn_0 (14

Dec. 2001).

Government website

U.S. Treasury. "U.S. Treasury Bureaus." *U.S.*

Treasury. http://www.treasury.gov/bureaus

.html (14 Dec. 2001).

Online journal or periodical

Online journals and periodicals follow the same basic format as do "ordinary" webpages, but they impose a few additional requirements. Many online publications are actually nothing more than electronic copies of printed publications. Others are true electronic publications available only in online form. Several publishers of major printed journals offer electronic journals that are completely different from their regular printed versions. Other organizations publish only in electronic format. In both cases, document the source using whatever information is available.

Electronic publications may or may not follow the dating and pagination conventions of their printed counterparts. If the online publication is arranged in volumes and issues, indicate the volume and issue number as a pair of Arabic numerals separated by a period. If the publication date is available, enclose it in parentheses and place it after the volume and issue numbers in Day Month Year format. If the volume and issue numbers are not available, use the publication date alone. The following formula and examples show the proper form for documenting an online publication.

Name of Author. "Article Title." *Publication Title*

Volume.Issue (Date of Publication). URL (Date

of Access).

Matthews, Betsy. "Mara and Galadriel: MacDonald's

and Tolkien's Vehicles for Spiritual Truth."

Premise 5.3 (1998). http://capo.org/premise/

98/july/p980718.html (14 Dec. 2001).

Powrie, Don. "Jump on the Bus: Taking a Look at

the USB." *Circuit Cellar Online* (Dec. 2001).

http://www.chipcenter.com/circuitcellar/

december01/c1201dp1.htm;$sessionid$1G3CXUAAMP

HDJ4Y5XDCFEQ (14 Dec. 2001).

Electronic book or text

Document electronic texts (e-books and e-texts) using the same basic rules as other online sources. Unfortunately, they may be difficult to document properly because of their somewhat informal nature. Most electronic texts are simply scanned versions of a printed text that is no longer under copyright. A small number of electronic texts are actually original works published directly into an online form. In the case of both derived and original electronic texts, the source and URL of the electronic text may be unknown if the researcher obtained the file indirectly. Again, the writer should include whatever information is available in order to make his bibliographic entry as useful as possible.

The more reputable electronic texts come with a revision number or letter or a date of electronic publication or both. If this information is available, include it in the entry. The following formula and examples show the proper form for documenting an electronic text:

```
Name of Author. Title of Text. Rev. xx. Date of

    Electronic Publication. URL (Date of Access).

Dickens, Charles. A Child's History of England.

    http://www.memoware.com/b/childshistory.zip

    (14 Dec. 2001).

Hope, Anthony. Rupert of Hentzau. Rev. 10. Dec.

    1997. ftp://ibiblio.org/pub/docs/books/

    gutenberg/etext97/rprhn10.txt (14 Dec. 2001).
```

If the standard publication facts of the original printed version are supplied (they rarely are), insert them immediately after the title in MLA format: place (city) of publication: publisher, year of publication.

Online encyclopedia article

Online encyclopedia articles follow the same basic form as other online sources. Since they almost always have a clear publisher, however, include this piece of information along with the date of publication in the entry. If the article has an author, include his name as well. The following formula and example show the general format for an online encyclopedia article:

Name of Author. "Article Title." Name of Encyclo-

    pedia. Publisher, Date of Publication. URL

    (Date of Access).

"Edison, Thomas Alva." Microsoft Encarta Online

    Encyclopedia 2001. Microsoft Corporation,

    2001. http://encarta.msn.com/find/Concise

    .asp?z=1&pg=2&ti=761563582 (14 Dec. 2001).

Online news article

    Online news services can be very tricky to document since they usually do not actually publish the articles that they make available. The writer must therefore determine the true publisher of the article and include it in the entry along with the article title, the name of the news service, the date of the article, the URL, and the date of access. The following formula and example show the correct format for an online news article:

Article Publisher. "Article Title." *Name of News*

    Service. Date of Article. URL (Date of Ac-

    cess).

AP. "Bush Pledges Anew to Get bin Laden."

    Yahoo!News. 14 Dec. 2001. http://dailynews

    .yahoo.com/h/ap/20011214/us/afghan_us_

    military_9.html (14 Dec. 2001).

E-mail

    Document an e-mail by specifying the originator's name in Last, First order, the e-mail's subject line enclosed in quotation marks, the words *Personal e-mail,* and the date upon which the e-mail was received. E-mail entries should contain no references to the originator's or recipient's e-mail address. The following formula and example show the correct format for an e-mail:

Name of originator. "Subject." Personal e-mail.

(Date of Receipt).

Raymond, Walter. "Question about sailboats."

Personal e-mail. (28 Apr. 2001).

Online graphic, audio, or multimedia file

Online graphic, audio, or multimedia files may be difficult to document because very little may be known of them other than their source. At the minimum, document a file by specifying its filename, the URL from which it came, and its date of access. If the file has an author, include the name in Last, First order. If the file has a title (other than the filename), italicize it, and include it after the author's name. The following formula and example show the correct format for a file:

Name of Author. *Title*. filename. URL (Date of

Access).

Corbis. *Frenchman Weeping in Marseille*.

WW20004jpg. http://www.corbisimages.com/

search/ReadyToBuyEvents/InfoPageOnLoad.asp?Id

=11411296&SearchHistoryID=1&AppTag=EP&OldId=W

W2004&LastUrl=ThumbsPageOnTBClick.asp?QuerySo

urce=7|Query=162|TotalRows=100|StartHit=0|

Action=0 (15 Dec. 2001).

CD-ROM

Document a CD-ROM source using a format as close as possible to the format used for the print source that it represents. CD-ROM entries are therefore very close in form to regular MLA-style entries. An entry for a CD-ROM should contain the author of the work, the title (either italicized or in quotation marks as the work requires), the word *CD-ROM*, the name of the CD-ROM itself (italicized), the location and name of the publisher, and the publication date. If the original printed publication information is available, include it before the CD-ROM publication information. The following formula and examples show the correct format for a CD-ROM entry:

```
Name of Author. Title of Work. CD-ROM. CD-ROM

    Title. Place of publication: CD-ROM Pub-

    lisher, Year of Publication.
```

```
Pearlman, E. William Shakespeare: The History

    Plays. CD-ROM. Twayne's English Authors on

    CD-ROM. New York: G. K. Hall, 1997.
```

```
Thomas, Dylan. "Do Not Go Gentle into That Good

    Night." CD-ROM. The Columbia Granger's World

    of Poetry. New York: Columbia UP, 1999.
```

When in doubt as to the proper form, follow the general philosophy embodied in the examples presented here. Supply as much information as is available in order to make the entry as useful as possible. An increasing number of online and electronic sources include guidelines as to how to cite their contents. Although their example citations may not be in COS form, they will at least provide you with the basic information necessary to construct the correct COS-type entry. Finally, for more information about the COS system, consult *The Columbia Guide to Online Style* by Janice R. Walker and Todd Taylor (New York: Columbia UP, 1998).

CAUTIONS FOR ONLINE USERS

With the rapid proliferation of online and other electronic sources, it is no wonder that students, researchers, and writers are eager to take advantage of the easy accessibility and wide variety of such sources. At the same time, however, the wise writer recognizes that online and electronic materials carry with them a number of problems and potential risks. Although no one disputes the advantage of having a large number of sources instantly available, serious scholars recognize that online and electronic sources do not yet have the same credibility as traditional printed materials. While these sources have a definite

place in academic writing, they must be used with care and intelligence to prevent the writer from making serious mistakes.

When performing research, remember first of all that most online sources do not receive the same level of editorial evaluation as high-quality printed materials. Anyone with a few dollars and a modicum of technical skill can author and publish a website. While some online sources are as good as their printed counterparts, many are little more than venues for cranks to air their ideas to an uncritical audience. Since no one exercises control over the Internet and its content, the writer must develop a sense of judgment and discernment when using online sources in academic research and writing. The following guidelines offer a few suggestions to help develop this sense of perspective and judgment.

First, determine whether you are looking for facts or information from the site. For example, a website promoting an inventor's ideas about a perpetual motion machine is probably not a good source of factual information since its author has a flawed understanding of basic physics. On the other hand, such a website is invaluable as a source of information about the kinds of things such inventors believe.

Second, be on the alert for obvious biases and prejudices in a particular direction. Just as strong biases in printed material should raise intellectual red flags, so too should strong biases in online sources. Admittedly, biased sources are still potentially valuable as information even though their so-called facts are highly suspect. For example, an extremist militia website is probably not the best place to gather facts about the government and its activities since extremist groups are highly biased. On the other hand, such a site is an ideal source of information about the beliefs and attitudes that such groups hold.

Third, recognize that some online resources are identical to their printed counterparts and are therefore of equal quality. Many major newspapers, magazines, and journals now offer online versions of their printed material. Since the material is identical to the original printed material, it has essentially the same quality as the original. When dealing with these sources, evaluate their quality and credibility using the same rules that apply to their printed counterparts. It is a fact that some online sources do undergo careful screening and are as reliable as the same material would be in printed form. For example, a corporation's website that includes figures, statistics, and corporate data is probably as accurate as any printed material that the corporation releases to the general public since such accuracy is in the company's best interest.

Fourth, the writer should always examine the online source itself for signs of quality. Unreliable websites often look amateurish in design. Many show poor grammar, spelling and mechanical mistakes, and a weak writing style. Although these flaws do not necessarily tell against the site's factuality, they do throw its credibility into doubt. Unless the site itself is known to be authoritative in its particular area, it should be avoided.

In this regard, the writer should be cautious when dealing with online resources produced by mass volunteer efforts. For example, the content found on electronic text (e-text) websites is often the result of volunteer efforts. Although the sites themselves are often managed by universities and other scholarly organizations, the quality of the texts tends to be rather low since their production is often unsupervised. E-texts frequently contain numerous typographical errors and usually are not produced from authoritative texts. Indeed, many e-texts are actually composites of several texts. In general, use a quality printed edition of a text whenever possible rather than using e-texts. Use an e-text only when a printed text is unobtainable.

Basic Sentence Analysis

Sentence analysis begins with the classification of words into what are called parts of speech. It is important to master the parts of speech, for the lessons that follow depend on them.

Multiple Identities

Our task would be simpler if every word in every situation acted as one part of speech and no more. But words have a way of jumping categories as they serve different uses. Notice how the word *home* acts differently in each of the following sentences.

> We bought a *home* on the south side. (noun)
>
> I prefer *home* cooking to restaurant meals. (adjective)
>
> He went *home* for lunch. (adverb)
>
> These heat-seeking missiles *home* on other missiles. (verb)

A desk dictionary with detailed definitions will help you identify word uses according to the standard parts of speech.

Nouns

Nouns are namers. Nouns designate a person, place, or thing, or a group or category of these. They are "something" words or "someone" words. *City, telephone, fact, Susan, friend, question, circumstance*—all are nouns in their normal function.

Tests of function

Words that can follow the articles *a, an,* and *the* or the demonstratives *this, that, these,* and *those* to form simple statements are nouns.

Words that can act as agents or topics to form simple statements are nouns.

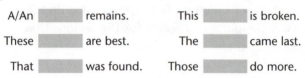

Clues from form

Words that can form plurals by adding *-s* or *-es* or in some other way are nouns.

Singular	Plural
idea	ideas
glass	glasses
ox	oxen

Words that can add an apostrophe and an *-s* (or just an apostrophe) to show possession are nouns.

Simple	Possessive
father	father's
fathers	fathers'

Form is secondary to function in our analysis, however. Not all nouns form plurals. Also, a noun in its possessive form usually leaves its noun function behind. But words that have these capacities are nouns in their original state.

Kinds of nouns

Nouns are divided in several ways. Knowing the divisions will give you a sense of what is included in the concept *noun*.

Proper nouns, as distinct from *common* nouns, name particular persons, places, or things and are capitalized.

Common Nouns	Proper Nouns
city	Chicago
orchestra	New York Philharmonic
team	Houston Astros
restaurant	Mabel's Tables

Common nouns divide into concrete nouns and abstract nouns. *Concrete* nouns refer to objects that can be seen, heard, touched, tasted, or smelled. *Abstract* nouns refer to entities that cannot be known directly through the senses.

Concrete Nouns	Abstract Nouns
soldier	courage
tablecloth	manners
cloud	climate
brain	mind

Common nouns divide also into count and noncount nouns. *Count* nouns refer to items that can be counted; they can form plurals. *Noncount* nouns refer to what cannot normally be counted, and they remain singular. Most count nouns are concrete; most noncount nouns are abstract.

Count Nouns	Noncount Nouns
cow	milk
goal	progress
treaty	peace
pencil	accuracy

Collective nouns are singular in form but plural in meaning, designating a group: *committee, team, audience.* Grammatically we treat them as singular unless their context requires otherwise.

Pronouns

Pronouns are noun substitutes. Speaking and writing would be tedious if we had to repeat a noun each time we referred to the thing it named. Standing in for nouns, pronouns not only prevent monotony, but they also promote efficiency and strengthen coherence.

The word for which a pronoun substitutes and to which it points is its *antecedent*. The antecedent normally precedes the pronoun (*ante-*, before + *cede*, go) but can follow it when the distance is short and the connection is obvious.

> Before *he* could stop *himself,* Bill blurted out the ugly truth.

Kinds of pronouns

As with nouns, so with pronouns: becoming aware of their types can help us recognize them better.

Personal pronouns refer to definite persons, places, or things. Notice in the chart below that the pronouns show differences in person. First person is the speaker or writer; second person, the person spoken or written to; third person, the person or thing spoken or written about. Notice also that third-person singular distinguishes gender, with forms for masculine *(he, him, his),* feminine *(she, her, hers),* and neuter *(it, its).*

	Singular	Plural
First person	I, me, my, mine	we, us, our, ours
Second person	you, your, yours	you, your, yours
Third person	he, him, his	they, them, their, theirs
	she, her, hers	
	it, its	

Indefinite pronouns refer to undetermined persons, places, or things and do not therefore have an antecedent. The following are some common ones.

someone	somebody	some	none	most
anyone	anybody	any	few	least
everyone	everybody	each	all	many

Demonstrative pronouns specify which among several or many is being referred to.

this	these
that	those

Relative pronouns introduce lesser statements in a sentence and connect (relate) them to the main statement. (He is the man + *who* sold me the car.)

who	whoever
whom	whomever
which	whichever
what	whatever
that	whose

Interrogative pronouns appear at the beginning of questions. They can also be relative pronouns.

who	which
whom	what
whoever	whose

Reflexive and *intensive* pronouns end in *-self* or *-selves*.

myself	ourselves
yourself	yourselves
himself	themselves
herself	
itself	

Reflexive pronouns "reflect" the sentence action back on the actor.

Kara adores *herself.*

Kara gave *herself* a party.

Intensive pronouns intensify the force of the noun to which they refer.

Kara made the cake *herself.*

Kara *herself* made the cake.

Notice that the intensive pronouns, unlike the reflexive, are optional and movable. They can drop out or shift position without changing sentence meaning.

Reciprocal pronouns express a mutual or common relationship between or among individuals.

> The elderly couple helped *each other* down the steps.

> The family members entertained *one another* with old stories.

Pronominal adjectives

Be aware that pronoun possessives (*his, their, whose, everybody's, each other's*, etc.) and demonstratives (*this, that, these, those*) when immediately followed by nouns are not pronouns in function but adjectives. Because they retain the characteristics of pronouns while acting as adjectives, they are sometimes called *pronominal adjectives*. You should identify them as adjectives in your sentence analysis.

Adjectives

Adjectives *modify* noun elements. That is, an adjective expands or restricts the meaning of its associated noun or pronoun. It joins with the noun element to fill out the noun idea or to specify which among several or many the noun idea is referring to. Consider these examples.

> Highway 11, *picturesque* and *historical,* is chosen by many travelers.

> Many travelers choose *picturesque* and *historical* routes.

In the first sentence the italicized adjectives enlarge the bare idea of Highway 11 by relating to it the ideas of picturesqueness and historical interest. The noun idea expands. In the second sentence the same adjectives limit the noun meaning from the routes in general to a specific type of routes: those that are picturesque and historical. They supply a necessary focus to the statement. So whereas the adjectives' function in the first sentence is purely *descriptive* and therefore nonessential, in the second sentence their function is logically *restrictive* and essential.

Tests of function

Adjectives usually occur immediately before the noun element they modify to form a noun phrase.

> The *magnificent* music continued.

Adjectives can also follow the noun element they modify.

> The music was *magnificent.*

> The music, *magnificent,* lifted the heavy hearts.

Test for adjectives by trying words in these locations.

the ▒▒▒▒ man   The man is ▒▒▒▒ .

the ▒▒▒▒ idea   The idea is ▒▒▒▒ .

the ▒▒▒▒ situation   The situation is ▒▒▒▒ .

Clues from form

Most adjectives form degrees of comparison.

Positive	Comparative	Superlative
early	earlier	earliest
athletic	more athletic	most athletic

Many adjectives are formed by adding a suffix to a noun base.

peaceful	foolish	angelic
blameless	joyous	cloudy

Types of adjectives

In addition to words whose primary function is adjectival, we must be prepared to recognize as adjectives words not normally adjectival when they are functioning as adjectives.

Nouns, as well as certain pronoun and verb forms, can function as adjectives, at which times we identify them as adjectives.

> He crouched behind the *stone* wall.

> *Yesterday's* performance went well.

> David did *his* best.

> *Everybody's* tickets were free.

> I prefer *these* oranges to the others.

> *Any* news is good news.

> He repaired the *ruined* wall.

> The *visiting* team won.

> It was a day *to remember.*

The indefinite articles *a* and *an* and the definite article *the* are restricting adjectives with the special function of indicating that a noun is following. They are noun signifiers. Noun and pronoun possessives are restricting adjectives with this function (*Justin's* mother, *his* friend). So also are indefinite and demonstrative pronouns that occur immediately before a noun (*all* students, *this* page). Words of this sort are known as determiners.

Adjectives join nouns to form noun phrases such as the following:

classical music	a difficult question	this hunting season
dark nail polish	the final score	your last birthday

Verbs

Verbs are words that express action or condition. Verbs turn a topic into a statement. *Weather* is a topic, a popular one. Add a verb and the topic becomes a statement.

> Weather *changes.*

The verb *changes* declares something about the topic *weather.*

Notice that the statement can become a question.

> Weather *changes? Does* weather *change?*

The topic of the verb, *weather,* is called its *subject.* It is a noun.

The verb's subject can also be a pronoun, since pronouns are noun substitutes.

> *He* changes with the weather.

Verbs then join with nouns and pronouns to form statements or questions. However long a sentence may be, you will find a verb at its core.

> Often after a pleasant Indian summer, the weather *changes* abruptly into winter with gusts of freezing rain.

Tests of function

Since verbs are words that can combine with noun elements to form simple statements, you can test for verbs with these frames.

> He/It/They _____ .
> He/It/They _____ him/it/them.

The second test frame provides for verbs that require a completing element to form a full statement.

Test frames will help you distinguish verbs from verb forms used as other parts of speech, which are known as *verbals.* In the example on the previous page, *freezing,* a form of the verb *freeze,* is an adjective modifying *rain.* Inserted in a test frame, it forms a phrase of sorts but fails to form a statement: *It freezing.* Verbals function as adjectives, adverbs, or nouns.

Clues from form

Verbs are words that can change form to show changes in time (I change; I changed), person (I change; he changes), number (it changes; they change), voice (I change; I am changed), tone (I change; I do change; I am changing), and mood (I am changing; if I were changing).

Verbs can occur as single words or as phrases. Identifying the verb of a sentence requires identifying all the parts of the verb.

A verb phrase is made up of auxiliaries, or helping verbs, as well as the verb base. Compare the following.

> The weather *changes.*
>
> The weather *will change.*
>
> The weather *does change.*
>
> The weather *is changing.*
>
> The weather *is changed.*
>
> The weather *has been changed.*
>
> The weather *will have been changed.*
>
> The weather *will have been being changed.*

Though the last example is improbable, the tense, voice, and tone of a verb can require as many as five verb parts to express a shade of meaning. Be alert then for forms of the auxiliaries *will* (future tense), *have* (perfect tenses), *do* (emphatic tone), and *be* (passive voice, progressive tone) acting in combination with the verb base to create the full verb.

Auxiliaries combine with the verb base to form the complete verb in the following ways.

Tenses		Auxiliaries			Principal Parts			Progressive
		will	have	be	1st	2nd	3rd	
SIMPLE								
Active								
Present	They				choose			
Past	They					chose		
Future	They	will			choose			
Present perfect	They		have				chosen	
Past perfect	They		had				chosen	
Future perfect	They	will	have				chosen	
Passive								
Present	They			are			chosen	
Past	They			were			chosen	
Future	They	will		be			chosen	
Present perfect	They		have	been			chosen	
Past perfect	They		had	been			chosen	
Future perfect	They	will	have	been			chosen	
PROGRESSIVE								
Active								
Present	They			are				choosing
Past	They			were				choosing
Future	They	will		be				choosing
Present perfect	They		have	been				choosing
Past perfect	They		had	been				choosing
Future perfect	They	will	have	been				choosing
Passive								
Present	They			are being			chosen	
Past	They			were being			chosen	
Future	They	will		be being			chosen	
Present perfect	They		have	been being			chosen	
Past perfect	They		had	been being			chosen	
Future perfect	They	will	have	been being			chosen	

Be aware also of the modal auxiliaries that occur in verb phrases.

The weather *can change.*

The weather *could change.*

The weather *may change.*

The weather *might change.*

The weather *must change.*

The weather *should change.*

The weather *would* not *change.*

The adverb *not* is not considered part of the verb.

Another kind of phrasal verb combines a verb with a trailing adverb known as a particle. Together verb and particle produce a meaning different from the sum of their individual meanings.

The batter *struck out* for the third time in the game.

Patrick and Emily *broke off* their engagement.

In one month the company *made up* last year's losses.

The performance *came off* well in spite of the delay.

Adverbs

Adverbs modify verbs, adjectives, or other adverbs. They also can modify verbals used as nouns. Surprisingly (as in this sentence) some adverbs seem to modify whole statements. Because adverbs have such varied functions and include certain specialized subclasses, they are of all the parts of speech the most difficult to visualize as a single category.

Adverbs that modify verbs typically tell when, where, how, or how much. They are often movable within the sentence.

Rachel exercises *often.* Rachel *often* exercises. *Often* Rachel exercises.

The bus stops *here.*

The plan worked *well.*

The injured shoulder hurts *terribly.*

Adverbs that modify only adjectives and other adverbs tell how much. They are known as qualifiers.

The table was *very* dusty.

A *really* beautiful poem is a treasure.

The team played *rather* poorly.

The game is *almost* over.

Just then the rain began.

The paved road lasts for *only* three miles.

Other types of adverbs are the negators *not* and *never;* conjunctive adverbs such as *therefore* and *however,* which join equal statements; and the relative adverbs *when, where, how,* and *why,* which join (relate) unequal statements.

The speech will *not* offend anyone.

I believe; *therefore,* I understand.

This is the place *where* we stopped before.

The suspect explained *why* he fled the crime scene.

Clues from form

Many adverbs are formed from adjectives by the addition of the suffix *-ly.*

wrongly	surely	nicely	helpfully	definitely
quickly	pleasantly	actually	joyously	consciously

Be aware, however, that *-ly* forms an adjective, not an adverb, when added to a noun base: *friendly, timely, manly, shapely.*

Most adverbs, like most adjectives, can form degrees of comparison.

Positive	Comparative	Superlative
soon	sooner	soonest
easily	more easily	most easily

Prepositions

Prepositions show a relationship between a noun or pronoun and another word in the sentence. This relationship can be of time, place, or other condition such as possession.

Prepositions begin prepositional phrases.

after the game	*on* the shelf	*of* the people
until noon	*over* the hill	*from* a friend
within an hour	*through* the cloud	*with* effort

At the end of a prepositional phrase is a noun or pronoun known as its *object.* Between the preposition and its object may be modifiers of the object.

after *the hard-fought championship football* game

Prepositional phrases act as adjectives and adverbs.

The lamp *on the piano* is an heirloom. (adjective)

The visitor performed *on the piano* brilliantly. (adverb)

A few prepositions consist of more than one word.

Because of the delay, we arrived late.

According to the map, we are nearly there.

He volunteered *together with* his friends.

Women *as well as* men are actively recruited.

As for me and my house, we will serve the Lord.

Conjunctions

Conjunctions join two or more words or groups of words. *Coordinating* conjunctions *(and, but, for, or, nor, yet, so)* join equal or similar elements.

The game is postponed until Friday *or* Saturday.

Cucumbers, yellow squash, *and* okra should be picked small.

Correlative conjunctions also join equal or similar elements but only as pairs.

> Access to the village is by *either* boat *or* helicopter.
>
> *Neither* blizzards *nor* floods stopped the mail delivery.
>
> *Both* Hannah *and* Andrea have entered the contest.
>
> *Not only* the mayor *but also* the city council favors the plan.

Subordinating conjunctions (like relative pronouns and relative adverbs) join unequal elements, subordinating one statement to another. Some common ones are *if, although, unless, because, since, when, where, while, whereas, after, before,* and *until.*

> We will come *unless* we are providentially hindered.
>
> *Where* there is smoke, there is usually fire.

Interjections

Interjections are expressions of emotional reaction that are inserted—interjected—into a sentence. They have no specific grammatical relation to the rest of the sentence. When expressing surprise or strong feeling, they commonly are followed by an exclamation point. Most often they appear in writing that has a spoken quality.

> *Well!* Now you tell me.
>
> *Oh,* bill me later.
>
> *Yes,* we all agree.

Expletives

The adverb *there* and the pronoun *it* can take the place of a delayed subject of a sentence. When they do, they are known as expletives. The delayed subject is often a clause.

> *There* are only two injured players on the team roster.
>
> *It* is likely that the strike will end soon.
>
> *It* is the child in us that wonders. (That [which] wonders is the child in us.)

Verbs, nouns, pronouns, and adjectives provide the sentence core. Their definitions and functions must be thoroughly understood before basic sentence analysis is possible. If these are unclear, study the explanations in Parts of Speech.

Finding the Verb

The first step in sentence analysis is locating the verb. Verbs declare, question, demand, or affirm, making a sentence out of what otherwise would be a mere topic or loose limb of a statement.

If the verb is a phrase, be sure to find all parts of it. (The verb chart on page 240 shows the many forms a verb may take.) Also be sure not to confuse verbs with verbals (verb forms used as other parts of speech).

The package *came* yesterday.

August weather *is* unpleasant.

Computers *have replaced* typewriters in businesses and even homes.

Songbirds *make* him nervous.

Songbirds *give* him fits.

Who *ate* the candy?

Where *did* the newspaper *go?*

Call an attorney.

Nearly frozen, he *tried* to build a fire in the gathering darkness.

Finding the Subject

The second step is identifying the subject of the verb. The subject is the person or thing that acts, is acted upon, or is described. It can be a noun or pronoun or, as we shall see later, a group of words acting as a noun. In a command or request, the subject may be an implied *you.*

Use this formula to identify the subject of a sentence after you have located the verb.

Who?/What? + VERB → SUBJECT

In the sentence "The package came yesterday," the question "Who or what came?" is answered with "package." So the noun "package" is the subject of the verb "came."

Recognizing Compound Subjects and Predicates

The part of the sentence associated with the verb (the verb with its completing and modifying elements) is known as the *predicate*. The part of the sentence associated with the subject is sometimes called the *complete subject*. Be aware that a sentence can have a compound subject or a compound predicate or both.

Morgan and Michelle came earliest to team practice.

Morgan came earliest to team practice and left last.

Morgan and Michelle came earliest to team practice and left last.

A sentence can itself be compound, uniting two or more subject-predicate sets as yoked statements.

Morgan came earliest to team practice, and Michelle left last.

Finding the Verb Complement

The third step in sentence analysis is finding any verb complements. (The word *complement* means "completer"; a complement *completes* the declaration of the verb.) For finding the verb complement, we also have a formula.

SUBJECT + VERB + Who?/What? → COMPLEMENT(S)

In the sentence "The package came yesterday," the formula yields no sensible answer to the questions "Who?" or "What?" The verb has no complement. In the sentences "Computers have replaced typewriters" and "August weather is unpleasant," the formula yields the answers "typewriters" and "unpleasant." In the sentence "Songbirds make him nervous," the formula yields two complements of the verb "make": "him" and "nervous." A verb then can have one complement, two complements, or none.

Identifying the Verb Complement

The fourth step in sentence analysis is identifying the verb complement. This step requires first determining the kind of verb the complement follows. For this purpose we classify verbs as intransitive, transitive, or linking.

Intransitive verbs have no complement. The action expressed by the verb is complete without a completing noun or adjective.

Sarah laughed.

Do not mistake an adverb modifying an intransitive verb for a complement.

Sarah laughed quietly.

Transitive verbs have a receiver of the verb action. (The grammatical term *action* refers not only to physical action; it designates also mental or logical action such as knowing or possessing or containing.) The receiver is a noun element toward which the verb action is directed.

Computers have replaced typewriters in businesses and even homes.

The transitive verb "have replaced" requires the noun "typewriters" to complete the core meaning of the sentence. This noun element is called the *object* of the verb (or *direct object* [DO] for reasons that will appear shortly).

A third type of verb, sometimes included within intransitives, is the verb that links its subject with a related idea in the predicate. Accordingly, it is called a *linking* verb.

August weather is a burden. (weather ↔ burden)

August weather is burdensome. (weather ↔ burdensome)

The words "burden" and "burdensome" are coupled with the subject "weather" by the linking verb "is." They are called *subject complements* (SC).

Linking verbs are only a handful in number. The common ones can be easily remembered.

be (is, are, was, were, etc.)	seems	becomes
	appears	remains

Another group is the verbs of sensation (when followed by adjectives).

looks	tastes	feels
sounds	smells	

Subject complements are further divided by part of speech into *predicate nouns* (PN) and *predicate adjectives* (PA), nouns or adjectives in the predicate that either rename or describe the subject. In the preceding examples, the noun "burden" is a predicate noun that renames "weather"; the adjective "burdensome" is a predicate adjective that describes "weather." In these sentences there is no *action across* (the literal meaning of *transitive*) from subject to receiver of the verb action. The verb equates or associates ideas, declaring a relationship.

Notice then the possibilities when a verb has a single complement. If the verb is transitive and targets a receiver of the action, the complement is a direct object. If the verb does not express action but simply connects its subject to an idea in the predicate, the complement will be a subject complement—more specifically a predicate noun or adjective, depending upon its part of speech.

The formula for finding complements, when applied to transitive-verb sentences, sometimes yields two complements rather than one. One of these complements (the one that answers more logically to SUBJECT + VERB + Who?/What?) is the direct object. The other will be either an *indirect object* (IO) telling *to* or *for whom* or an *object complement* (OC) renaming or describing the direct object.

> She made him a pie.
>
> The pie made him sick.
>
> The pie made him a pie hater.

In the first example "pie" is the direct object and "him" the indirect object. In the second example "him" is the direct object and "sick," which describes "him," the object complement. In the third example the object complement is a noun, "hater," rather than an adjective.

Indirect objects precede direct objects; object complements follow direct objects. Indirect objects and object complements never occur in the same sentence statement; they belong to different sentence patterns.

The options for identifying complements can be easily charted.

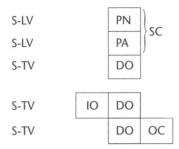

Notice the symmetry between subject complements, which either rename (PN) or describe (PA) the verb subject, and the object complement, which either renames (noun) or describes (adjective) the verb object. Noun and adjective object complements are not, like subject complements, distinguished in named categories.

When identifying verb subjects and complements, you can make your task easier by mentally bracketing out all prepositional phrases in the sentence. The object of a preposition cannot be the subject or complement of a verb. In the following sentence, the subject is "five" rather than "children," and the direct object is "all" rather than "money."

Five *of the children* spent all *of their money on snacks.*

Finally, be aware that whether certain verbs are transitive, intransitive, or linking depends upon the sentences in which they appear.

He felt anxiously for the wall in the dark. (intransitive)

He felt the wall in the dark. (transitive)

He felt anxious in the dark. (linking)

Identifying Sentence Patterns

Sentences are classified according to their subject-verb-complement structure. A final step in basic sentence analysis is to identify a sentence according to the patterns you have learned.

The hit went into the record books.	S-IV
The hit was a home run.	S-LV-PN
The hit was timely.	S-LV-PA
The hit won the game.	S-TV-DO
The hit won Babe Ruth fame.	S-TV-IO-DO
The hit made Babe Ruth a hero.	S-TV-DO-OC
The hit made Babe Ruth famous.	S-TV-DO-OC

Word Groups as Parts of Speech

Groups of words often function as nouns and adjectives in the sentence skeleton.

Word groups fill **noun** slots in these sentences.

Subject

Sean's *memory* saved us an extra trip.

Sean's *remembering the lock combination* saved us an extra trip.

What Sean remembered saved us an extra trip.

Predicate noun

Sean's hobby is *astronomy.*

Sean's hobby is *tracking the stars.*

Sean's hobby is *what you would never expect.*

Direct object

Sean tried our *solution.*

Sean tried *to solve the puzzle our way.*

Sean tried *what we had suggested.*

Indirect object

Sean gives a *task* his best effort.

Sean gives *working crossword puzzles* his best effort.

Sean gives *whatever task he undertakes* his best effort.

Object complement

Sean considers his hobby *astronomy.*

Sean considers his hobby *tracking the stars.*

Sean considers his hobby *what you would never expect.*

Object of preposition

Sean returned sunburned from *vacation.*

Sean returned sunburned from *sailing in the Bahamas.*

Sean returned sunburned from *where he had been sailing last month.*

Appositive

Sean's greatest temptation, *television,* is mine also.

Sean's greatest temptation, *watching too much television,* is mine also.

Sean's greatest temptation, *whatever television program may presently be airing,* is mine also.

Word groups fill **adjective** slots in these sentences.

Adjacent adjective

The *winning* team will receive a large trophy.

The team *winning the tournament* will receive a large trophy.

The team *that wins the tournament* will receive a large trophy.

Adrift, the pack ice endangered shipping.

Having broken free, the pack ice endangered shipping.

The pack ice, *which had broken free,* endangered shipping.

Predicate adjective

The project seemed *foredoomed.*

The project seemed *too poorly planned to succeed.*

The project seemed *as if it were designed to fail.*

The light switch is *hidden.*

The light switch is *behind the tapestry.*

The light switch is *where you will never find it.*

Notice in addition how word groups can serve as **adverbs.**

Verb modifier

> *Afterward* he regretted his decision.
>
> *After changing his major,* he regretted his decision.
>
> *After he had changed his major,* he regretted his decision.
>
> The rookie fireman tested the ladder *nervously.*
>
> The rookie fireman tested the ladder *with anxious hesitation.*
>
> The rookie fireman tested the ladder, *slowly committing his full weight.*
>
> The rookie fireman tested the ladder *as though it might not carry his full weight.*

Adjective modifier

> The speech was *unusually* long.
>
> The speech was longer *than usual.*
>
> The speech was longer *than what the audience usually hears.*

Adverb modifier

> The first lap was run *very* slowly.
>
> The first lap was run more slowly *than usual.*
>
> The first lap was run so slowly *that the crowd grew restless.*

Phrase or Clause

Groups of words forming sentence units are either phrases or clauses. Clauses have subjects and verbs, whereas phrases do not. A phrase may contain and even be built upon a verb form, but without a subject and a true verb it cannot be a clause.

In the sets of examples on the previous page, notice the difference between the italicized phrases and clauses: the clauses (in the last sentences of the sets) have subjects and verbs, whereas the phrases do not.

Independent or Dependent Clause

Clauses divide into two types: independent and dependent. An independent clause forms a complete sentence by itself. It may be a statement, a question, or a command. (The subject of a command is an implied *you*.)

> Rookies arrive early.
>
> Do rookies arrive early?
>
> Arrive early!

Dependent clauses branch off from, or are contained by, independent clauses or other structures. They do not form sentences by themselves.

> We learned *that the rookies arrive early.*
>
> The time *when the rookies arrive* has not been determined.
>
> The veterans *who arrive with the rookies* will be paid extra.
>
> *Though the rookies arrive early,* they must work doubly hard.

A clause is made dependent by a head word that relates it to the rest of the sentence. This head word may be a relative pronoun *(who, whom, which, whose,* or *that)*, a relative adverb *(when, where,* or *why)*, or a subordinating conjunction *(that, though, if, unless, because, when, where, whenever, wherever,* or *whereas)*. There are many subordinating conjunctions, including phrasal ones (such as *so that, as if*).

Distinguish subordinating conjunctions, which always begin dependent clauses, from conjunctive adverbs, which can begin independent clauses.

> The losing candidate called for a recount of the ballots, *whereas* the vote margin was not even close.
>
> The losing candidate called for a recount of the ballots. *However,* the vote margin was not even close.

Notice the difference in punctuation.

Types of Sentences

Sentences are classified according to the number and kind of clauses they contain. *Simple* sentences contain one independent clause and no dependent clauses. *Compound* sentences contain two or more independent clauses and no dependent clauses. *Complex* sentences contain one independent clause and one or more dependent clauses. *Compound-complex* clauses contain two or more independent clauses and one or more dependent clauses.

	Ind	Dep	
S	1	0	The banks close Monday.
CP	2+	0	The banks close Monday, but they will be open Tuesday.
CX	1	1+	Though the banks close Monday, they will be open Tuesday.
CP-CX	2+	1+	Though the banks close Monday, they will be open Tuesday, and they will remain open Tuesday until six o'clock.

Distinguish between the compound sentence and a simple sentence with a compound predicate.

Compound: The banks close Monday, but they will be open Tuesday.

Simple: The banks close Monday but will be open Tuesday.

This distinction is important for punctuation. The joining point of a compound sentence requires punctuation, whereas the branching point of a dual compound predicate should have none.

Types of Dependent Clauses

Dependent clauses are classified by function as noun, adjective, or adverb. Adjective and adverb clauses are usually detachable from the sentence. Noun clauses usually are not.

Adjective clauses, like all adjectives, modify nouns or pronouns.

> A truly desirable car is a debt-free car *that runs.*
>
> The stadium, *which seats eighty-five thousand,* was already packed.
>
> The president *who reopened trade with China* was Richard Nixon.
>
> I am he *of whom you speak.*
>
> Your proposal is an idea *whose time has come.*
>
> Return the merchandise to the store *where you bought it.*
>
> She was gone during that afternoon *when you called.*
>
> The money *that you sent* was more than enough.
>
> The rock formation looked *as though it might topple at any moment.*
>
> The blood of Christ can make a sinner *as if he had never sinned.*

Adverb clauses modify verbs, adjectives, or other adverbs. When they modify a verb, they may seem to modify the entire idea of the sentence. They can begin with a wide array of subordinating conjunctions. They can be elliptical, leaving a part unexpressed. Often they are movable within the sentence.

> *When the curtain rose,* the auditorium became quiet.
>
> *Where the sun never rises in midwinter,* it never sets in midsummer.
>
> The china was not broken, *though it was poorly packed.*
>
> *If the water rises another foot,* it will overflow the levee.
>
> The program began late *because the soloist was caught in traffic.*
>
> They opened the main gate *so that the bus could enter.*
>
> The gate is so wide *that a truck can enter.*
>
> You may choose *as you wish* among the gift items.
>
> Joseph did *according as he was told by the angel.*
>
> You may stay *as* long *as you wish.*
>
> He is *as* tall *as his older brother.*
>
> He is taller *than his twin brother.*

Noun clauses act as subjects and complements of verbs, as appositives, and as objects of prepositions. Removing them usually breaks
the structure of the sentence.

> *What he told me* is the truth.
>
> The truth is *what he told me.*
>
> I believe *what he told me.*
>
> I understood only half of *what he told me.*
>
> You may tell *whoever comes* the reason for my absence.
>
> They found the truth *what they had dreaded.*
>
> The truth, *what they had dreaded,* was kept secret.

Types of Phrases

Phrases, like dependent clauses, function as nouns, adjectives, or
adverbs. They divide into two sets: the verbal and the nonverbal.

Nonverbal phrases

The nonverbal phrases are of three types: the prepositional, the
absolute, and the appositive.

Prepositional phrases consist of a preposition, its object, and any
modifiers of the object. They act as adjectives or adverbs (see Parts
of Speech).

The ability to recognize prepositional phrases in a sentence is important in sentence analysis and in certain usage situations. Learning to
ignore the prepositional phrases in a sentence will help you see its
skeletal structure and avoid such errors as mistaking the
object of a preposition for the verb subject.

> No: A rash of highway accidents are raising insurance rates.
>
> Yes: A rash of highway accidents is raising insurance rates.

Absolute phrases are structurally independent of ("absolute" with
regard to) the rest of the sentence. They may be said to modify the rest
of the sentence as a whole, providing a context for it.

The typical absolute phrase combines a noun with a participial phrase.

> *Darkness having settled,* the hikers built a fire.
>
> The crowd stared at the trophy buck, *its antlers spreading four feet.*
>
> *All things considered,* the program went well enough.

But absolute phrases can have other forms.

> *The interview over,* Brice returned to the lobby.
>
> It was, *to be sure,* a dull performance.
>
> *To begin with,* the writing was almost illegible.
>
> *Generally speaking,* the marketing plan was a success.

Appositive phrases are noun phrases that follow other noun elements and rename them, extending their meanings. They can be essential, specifying a certain item within a class of items, or nonessential, supplying extra information.

> The American novelist *Stephen Crane* wrote highly regarded poetry.
>
> Stephen Crane, *an American novelist,* wrote highly regarded poetry.

Verbal phrases

Verbal phrases are built on verb forms used as other parts of speech: noun, adjective, or adverb. Like the nonverbal phrases, they are of three types: gerund, participial, and infinitive.

Gerund phrases are noun phrases built on verb forms ending in *-ing* (or whose first auxiliary ends in *-ing*).

> *Planting crops* was impossible during the rainy March.
>
> The wet weather made *planting crops* impossible.
>
> He had a fear of *having planted too early.*

Participial phrases are adjective phrases built on verb forms ending in *-ing* (present participles) or in *-ed, -d, -t, -en,* or *-n* (past, passive, and perfect participles). Present and present perfect participial phrases are identical in form with gerund phrases; they are distinguishable only by function.

> The contestant *performing now* is the likely winner.
>
> The piece *performed yesterday* was moderately easy.
>
> The piece *being performed now* is very difficult.
>
> *Having adjusted the piano bench,* the pianist nodded to the conductor.

Infinitive phrases are usually easy to identify by their form. They typically begin with *to,* known as the sign of the infinitive. They can function as nouns, adjectives, or adverbs.

His purpose in coming to New York was *to visit art museums.*

The best time *to visit art museums* is the early afternoon.

He was always ready *to visit art museums.*

Infinitive phrases can occur without the sign of the infinitive and can also be in the perfect or passive form.

We can go *visit art museums* this afternoon.

He hoped by Friday *to have visited ten art museums.*

The National Gallery expects *to be visited heavily today.*

The National Gallery expects *to have been visited more heavily than usual today.*

Let's *go to the museum* before noon.

Because of the dual identity of a verbal phrase, it may, like a verb, have a subject or complement or both while acting as a noun, adjective, or adverb.

They wanted *the winner to be Joshua.*

Gerunds, being verbal nouns, can be modified by both adjectives and adverbs.

Their acting quickly saved them from embarrassment.

Note that gerunds may not have noun or pronoun subjects. They are preceded instead by possessive adjectives.

No: We appreciate them giving so generously of their time.

Yes: We appreciate their giving so generously of their time.

The forms and functions of verbals can be charted as follows:

	n	adj	adv	
Gerund	X			-ing
Participle		X		-ing; -ed, -d, -t, -en, -n
Infinitive	X	X	X	to + verb form

Word Groups Within Other Word Groups

Expect to encounter phrases within phrases, clauses within clauses, phrases within clauses, and even clauses within phrases. In the following examples phrases are enclosed in parentheses, dependent clauses in brackets.

[If the name [with which you were born] does not suit you,] you can always take a nickname.

John, (the apostle (of love,)) had an undesirable nickname, [which he shared (with his brother)].

Simon, (the disciple [who seemed the least stable,]) received a nickname (signifying a strength [that was not yet apparent]).

Glossary of Grammatical Terms

Consult the index to locate fuller treatment of a topic in the main text. **Bold terms** in definitions occur as separate entries in this glossary.

absolute phrase.   A **phrase** structurally unconnected with the **sentence** and modifying the sentence as a whole. It typically consists of a noun followed by a participial phrase. (*The sky growing dark,* we ran for shelter.)

active voice.   See **voice.**

adjective.   A word that modifies a **noun** or **pronoun.**

Descriptive adjectives have three forms of comparison: positive (good, tall, beautiful), comparative (better, taller, more beautiful), superlative (best, tallest, most beautiful).

Adjectives typically are but need not be positioned immediately before the nouns they modify. (Their *brave* action was *brave* in every way. The *purple* flowers looked especially *purple* in the rosy dawn.) Adjectives in the predicate that modify the subject of the verb are called predicate adjectives.

Most noun and some pronoun and verb forms can also function as adjectives. (*This customized exercise* program from *Robert's* trainer is responsible for *his improving* scores.)

The articles *a* and *the* may be considered a subclass of adjective. See **determiner.**

adjective clause.   See **clause.**

adverb.   A word that modifies a **verb,** an **adjective,** or another adverb.

Many adverbs are formed from adjectives by the addition of the suffix *ly* (really, badly, tightly, suddenly).

Adverbs that modify verbs typically tell *when, where, how,* or *how much.* (The ruling came *later.* The word spread *far.* The engine ran *smoothly.* They finished *completely.*) They are often movable in their sentence. (*Often* they are movable.

They *often* are movable. They are *often* movable. They are movable *often.*)

Adverbs that modify only adjectives and other adverbs tell *how much.* They are known as qualifiers. (On *very* cold days he jogged *less* vigorously or *only* inside.)

Other types of adverbs include the negators *not* and *never;* conjunctive adverbs such as *therefore* and *however,* which act as transitional expressions before or within independent clauses; and the relative adverbs *when, where, how,* and *why,* which introduce dependent clauses.

adverb clause.   See **clause.**

agreement.   Grammatical correspondence in number, person, and gender. **Verbs** must agree with (match in form) their **subjects** in number and **person.** Disagreement in person alone ("I is tired," "I says the truth," "You does me wrong") occurs mostly in spoken dialectal English and does not require addressing here. Disagreement in number occurs because third-person-singular present-tense verb forms end in *s* or *es*), whereas third-person-plural forms do not. Avoiding errors in verb agreement requires locating the true subject of the verb, recognizing its number (whether it is singular or plural), and matching it with the verb form of its number (singular or plural). (The *camera* with its accessories *costs* five hundred dollars.)

A pronoun or pronominal adjective must agree with its antecedent (the noun or pronoun to which it refers) in person, gender, and number. Disagreement in person and gender is uncommon among native speakers of English. Disagreement in number usually occurs when a singular pronoun refers to a plural antecedent. (*Each* of the men plays *his* best tennis on a clay surface.)

antecedent.   The **noun** or **pronoun** for which a pronoun substitutes and to which it refers. (Where the *river* bends, *it* flows slowly.)

appositive.   A **noun** that follows another noun to re-express it. An appositive can be either a word or a group of words used as a noun. (The political columnist *David Broder* is a well-respected moderate. David Broder, *a political columnist,* is a well-respected moderate.)

article.   The indefinite article *a* (or *an*) and the definite article *the* indicate that a noun is following, either immediately (the house) or after intervening modifiers (the old, dilapidated house).

auxiliary verb.   A **verb** that precedes the main verb or verb base in a verb phrase. (She *has* slept two hours. We *are* stopping for lunch. There *must have* been a power outage last night.) These include the helping verbs that form the perfect tenses and passive voice as well as the modal auxiliaries *can, could, may, might, must, should,* and *would.*

case. The form of a **noun** or **pronoun** indicating how it is used in its **sentence.** Nouns have only one case form, the *possessive* (the *house's* location). Pronouns (personal, relative, and interrogative) have in addition to the *possessive* case the *subjective* and *objective* cases. The subjective case forms (I, he, she, we, they, who, whoever) are used for subjects of verbs, for predicate nouns, and for appositives of these. The objective case forms (me, him, her, us, them, whom, whomever) are used for objects of verbs, of verbals, of prepositions, and of appositives of these. See **pronoun, appositive,** and **predicate noun.**

clause. A group of words forming a **sentence** unit that contains a **subject** and **verb.** *Independent clauses* form complete statements. (The storm drew near.) *Dependent clauses* form parts of statements. (*When the storm drew near,* we ran for cover. No one knew *that the storm drew near.*) Dependent clauses may act as nouns (subjects, direct objects, etc.), adjectives, or adverbs.

collective noun. A **noun** singular in form though denoting a group (committee, team, jury). It is considered grammatically singular if the members are acting as a unit, plural if they are acting as individuals. (The team is leaving for the ballpark. The team are taking their seats on the bus.) Prefer the singular when uncertain of plurality. See **agreement.**

comma splice. The error of using a comma alone (without a coordinating conjunction) to join a pair of independent clauses in a **compound sentence.**

comparative form of comparison. See **adjective.**

complement. A **noun** or **adjective** that follows the **subject** and **verb** and finishes the core meaning of the **sentence.** Types of complements are direct object (She made a *cake*), indirect object (She made *him* a cake), object complement (She made him her *friend*), subject complement (He is her *friend;* he is *friendly*). The subject complement, if a noun, is a predicate noun; if an adjective, a predicate adjective. The object complement also can be either a noun or an adjective. (We thought him a *hero;* we thought him *heroic.*)

complex sentence. A **sentence** containing one independent **clause** and at least one dependent clause. See **clause.**

compound-complex sentence. A **sentence** containing at least two independent **clauses** and at least one dependent clause. See **clause.**

compound sentence. A **sentence** containing at least two independent **clauses** and no dependent clauses. See **clause.**

conjunction. A word that joins other words, **phrases,** or **clauses.** *Coordinating conjunctions* (and, but, for, or, nor, yet, so) join sentence elements of equal grammatical status. (Proteins *and* carbohydrates are both important, *but* carbohydrates are especially needed before high exertion.) *Subordinating conjunctions* (when, where, how, if, although, because, since, while, etc.) join sentence elements of unequal grammatical status: independent and dependent clauses. (*Although* proteins and carbohydrates are both important, carbohydrates are especially needed before high exertion.) See **phrase** and **clause.**

conjunctive adverb. Words such as *therefore, however,* and *thus* that relate (either as introducers or interrupters) independent clauses. (The rain came; *therefore,* the party ended suddenly. The food, *however,* was saved.)

coordinating conjunction. See **conjunction.**

coordination. The arrangement of ideas as logical pairs or sets using similar grammatical structures. Compare **subordination.**

correlative conjunction. **Conjunctions** consisting of a pair of words or **phrases** (both . . . and, either . . . or, neither . . . nor, not only . . . but also). See **conjunction.**

dangling modifier. A participial **phrase** or elliptical **clause** whose implied subject is not identical with the grammatical subject of the main statement.

demonstrative pronoun. A kind of **pronoun** that points to and specifies certain persons or things among several or many (this, that, these, those).

dependent clause. See **clause.**

determiner. A word that signifies a **noun** is soon to follow. Determiners include articles, possessive nouns and pronouns, demonstrative adjectives, cardinal numbers, and words such as *each, every, all, many,* and *another.* See **adjective.**

direct object. A **noun** or **pronoun** that receives the **verb** action. See **complement.**

ellipsis. A mark consisting of three *spaced* dots indicating an omission in a quotation. If the omission concludes a sentence or occurs between sentences, a fourth dot is needed for the period ending the sentence.

essential and nonessential dependent clause or phrase.   Modifying elements distinguished as either nonessential (supplying extra information) or essential (specifying identity). This distinction is crucial in punctuation. Nonessential modifying word groups are set off in pairs of commas or other marks to indicate their noncrucial relation to the main statement. (Pastor Jones, who has a farm background, organized the food relief.) Essential modifying word groups are not set off, for they have a necessary identifying function. (The pastor who has a farm background organized the food relief.)

Because of this principle, the presence or absence of enclosing commas can determine meaning. "Dickens's novel, *Great Expectations,*" is mispunctuated, for the commas indicate that Dickens wrote only a single novel when in fact he wrote many. The novel title is an essential appositive phrase, specifying a certain novel among others. Write, "Dickens's novel *Great Expectations.*"

fragment.   A **sentence** part punctuated as if it were a grammatically complete sentence.

fused sentence.   The error of combining two independent clauses in a **compound sentence** without either a semicolon or a comma with coordinating conjunction at the joining point. See also **comma splice.**

gerund.   A **verb** form ending in *ing* and used as a **noun.** See **verbal.**

imperative mood.   See **mood.**

indefinite pronoun.   Pronouns (someone, everybody, each, any, etc.) that refer to undetermined persons, places, or things. They therefore do not have antecedents. See **pronoun.**

independent clause.   See **clause.**

indirect object.   See **complement.**

infinitive.   A **verb** form normally consisting of *to* plus the present tense of the verb and acting as a **noun, adjective,** or **adverb.** See **verbal.**

intensive pronoun.   Pronouns ending in *self* or *selves* that intensify the force of the **noun** or **pronoun** to which they refer. (Bill did it *himself.* He *himself* did it.) See **pronoun.**

interjection.   Words of emotional reaction inserted—interjected—into a **sentence.** (*Well,* it might work. *Oh,* the job might take a week.)

interrogative pronoun.   Pronouns that appear at the beginning of questions. (*Who* came last? *What* was his reason?) See **pronoun.**

intransitive verb.   A **verb** that has no **complement.** The action it expresses is complete without a completing noun or adjective. (He *wandered.* He indeed *wandered* far.)

linking verb.   A type of **verb** that links its **subject** with a related idea in the **predicate.** The related idea may be expressed in a noun (as a *predicate noun*) or in an adjective (as a *predicate adjective*). These related ideas in the predicate are known as *subject complements.*

misplaced modifier.   A modifying word, **phrase,** or **clause** that is situated in such a way as to allow misreading. (He *only* forgot three of his lines.) Place limiting adverbs such as *almost, only,* and *hardly* immediately before the words they modify. (He forgot *only* three of his lines.)

modal verb.   Helping verbs that indicate **mood.** See **auxiliary verb.**

modifier.   A word or group of words that connects with and modifies (expands or limits or otherwise affects) the meaning of another word or group of words. Types of modifiers are adjectives, adverbs, and, by some accounts, appositives.

mood.   A form of statement indicating speaker intent. The *indicative* mood comprises statements and questions. (He left the room.) The *imperative* comprises commands and requests. (Leave the room. Please leave the room.) The *subjunctive* comprises expressions of uncertainty or unreality. (Though he leave the room, he will be listening.)

nonessential clause or phrase.   See **essential and nonessential dependent clause or phrase.**

noun.   A word or group of words that names or designates a person, place, or thing or a category of these. Words that can form plurals by adding *s* or *es* or that can add an apostrophe and an *s* to show possession are nouns. Nouns are *something* words or *someone* words. *Proper nouns* name particular persons, places, or things and are capitalized. *Common nouns,* which are not capitalized, divide into *concrete nouns,* which refer to objects that can be sensed, and *abstract nouns,* which refer to entities that cannot be known directly through the senses.

noun clause.   See **clause.**

noun phrase.   See **phrase.**

object.   See **complement.**

objective case.   See **case.**

object of the preposition.   A **noun** or **pronoun** that follows the **preposition** in a prepositional phrase and completes the **phrase.**

parallelism.   Similarity of grammatical form required for structuring ideas as pairs or in sets. Errors in parallelism occur when similarity of form is not maintained throughout a series. Compare "with a purpose of serving the people and to serve himself as well" and "with a purpose to serve the people and to serve himself as well." See **coordination.**

parenthetical elements.   Interruptive words, **phrases,** or **clauses** set off by commas, dashes, or parentheses.

participles.   **Verb** forms other than **infinitives** used as **adjectives.** Those ending in *ing* are *present participles.* Those ending in *ed, d, t, en,* or *n* are *past participles.* See **verb** and **verbal.**

part of speech.   One of the kinds of words **(verb, noun, pronoun, adjective, adverb, preposition, conjunction,** and **interjection)** that we use to make up sentences. The common eight-part classification, though satisfactory for the present purpose, is modified in modern technical studies of language.

passive voice.   See **voice.**

past participle.   See **participles.**

perfect tenses.   The forms of the **verb** that indicate completed action, whether in the present *(present perfect),* in the past *(past perfect),* or in the future *(future perfect).* The perfect tenses use the auxiliary verb *have.* (He *has* now *finished* his homework. He *had finished* his homework by then. He *will have finished* his homework by then.)

person.   A grammatical term differentiating the person speaking or writing *(first person),* the person spoken or written to *(second person),* and the person or thing spoken or written about *(third person).* English in the third-person-singular distinguishes gender, with forms for masculine (he), feminine (she), and neuter (it).

personal pronoun.   Pronouns referring to definite persons, places, or things. They include *I, me, my, mine; we, us, our, ours; you, your, yours; he, him, his; she, her, hers; it, its; they, them, their, theirs.* The possessives (e.g., *my, our, your,* and *their*) that are followed by nouns actually function as adjectives and should be regarded as adjectives in sentence analysis. See **pronoun.**

phrase.   A **sentence** unit of two or more words not containing a **subject** and **verb.** Types of phrases include prepositional, appositive, absolute, gerund, participial, and infinitive. The latter three are known as **verbal** phrases because they are built on verb forms used as other parts of speech.

possessive pronoun.   The **pronouns** that indicate ownership (my, mine, your, yours, his, her, hers, its, our, ours, their, theirs, whose). See **personal pronoun.**

predicate.   The part of a **sentence** stemming from the **verb.** Sentence structure divides into the subject and its associated structures and the predicate.

predicate adjective.   An **adjective** in the **predicate** describing the **subject** of the **sentence.** Predicate adjectives, like *predicate nouns,* follow linking verbs. (The action was *bold.*)

predicate noun.   A **noun** in the **predicate** renaming or re-expressing the **subject** of the sentence. Predicate nouns, like *predicate adjectives,* follow linking verbs. (The action was a *success.*)

predication.   The elements of a **sentence** core (**subject, verb,** and **complements,** if any) and their relations. Strong predication is logical unity and grammatical connectivity in the subject-verb-object sentence core.

preposition.   A word that stands at the head of a **phrase** showing a relationship between a **noun** or **pronoun** that follows it (its object) and another word in the **sentence.** The relationship can be one of time (*after* the warning), space (*inside* the mansion), or other condition such as intention, means, or possession (*for* this purpose, *with* our help, *of* the people). Prepositional phrases typically begin with a preposition, end with its object, and contain modifying elements between (*around* the grassy field, *within* two weeks, *from* his latest best-selling novel). They often occur in linked series (*in* hope *of* a quick return *from* his investment *in* oil stocks). Some prepositions are phrasal (*according to* report, *because of* her effort, *together with* better personnel). Prepositional phrases act as adjectives (the town *near the river*) or adverbs (left *after midnight,* succeeded *by hard work*).

pronoun.   A noun substitute, a word that stands *for* (pro-) a **noun.** Kinds are *personal* (I, me, you, he, she, we, us, they, them, etc.), *indefinite* (someone, everybody, each, few, etc.), *demonstrative* (this, that, these, those), *relative* (who, whom, which, what, that, whose, whoever, etc.), *interrogative* (who, whom, which, what, whose, whoever), and *reflexive* and *intensive* (myself, yourself, yourselves, himself, herself, ourselves, etc.). See **case.**

pronoun case.   See **case.**

proper noun.   See **noun.**

reflexive pronoun.   Pronouns ending in *self* or *selves* that return, "reflect," the action back on the **subject.** (She served *herself.*) Reflexive pronouns function as objects (direct objects, indirect objects, or objects of the preposition) and occasionally as predicate nouns. See **pronoun.**

relative clause. A **clause** that begins with a **relative pronoun.**

relative pronoun. A **pronoun** that begins a dependent clause, connecting it to the main **clause** of the sentence while also performing a **noun** function (**subject, direct object,** etc.) within the dependent clause. (The surgeon *who operated on your father* is the best in the state.) Relative pronouns can begin noun and adjective clauses.

restrictive and nonrestrictive clause or phrase. See **essential and nonessential dependent clause or phrase.**

retained object. A **complement** in a passive **voice** construction that would be also a complement in the active voice form of the same statement. It occurs in a passive-voice statement whose verb in the active voice would have two complements: a direct object and an indirect object or a direct object and an object complement. In the passive voice, one of the two objects will become the subject and the other the *retained* object. Compare "Bill gave Sue a book" (active voice), in which *book* is the direct object and *Sue* the indirect object, with (1) "A book was given Sue by Bill" (passive voice), in which *book* has become the subject and *Sue* retained as an object (a retained indirect object), and with (2) "Sue was given a book by Bill" (passive voice), in which *Sue* has become the subject and *book* retained as an object (a retained direct object). Compare also "They voted Bill treasurer" (active voice), in which *Bill* is the direct object and *treasurer* the object complement, with "Bill was voted treasurer," in which *Bill* has become the subject and *treasurer* retained as an object (a retained object complement). Think of retained object complements as grammatical hybrids. Though following transitive verbs, they act as subject complements (which can follow only intransitive linking verbs), re-expressing or describing the subject. Treat them as subject complements in your analysis. In formal English, the subjective case is preferred for the retained objective complement in such improbable statements as "We were considered they."

sentence. A group of words containing at least one independent **clause.** Sentences are classified according to the number and kind of clauses they contain as *simple, compound, complex* and *compound-complex.* They are also classified according to whether the main clause appears in completeness at the beginning of the sentence (loose sentence) or follows subordinate elements and is not complete until the end (periodic). See **clause.**

sentence fragment. See **fragment.**

split infinitive. An **infinitive** with modifying elements between *to* and the **verb.** Avoid splitting infinitives unless not splitting creates more awkwardness than splitting. Compare "to sometimes go" and the preferred "sometimes to go."

subject. The word or words for the person or thing that acts, is acted upon, or is renamed or described in a **clause.** It can be a noun or pronoun or a group of words acting as a noun. The subject, the verb, and any complements form the core statement.

subject complement. A **predicate noun** or **predicate adjective** that follows a **linking verb** and renames, re-expresses, or modifies the **subject.** See **complement.**

subjective case. See **case.**

subjunctive mood. See **mood.**

subordinating conjunction. See **conjunction.**

subordination. The relating of logically unequal ideas hierarchically in unequal grammatical structures. Compare **coordination.**

superlative form of comparison. See **adjective.**

syntax. The grammatical relations of words in a **sentence.**

tense. The time expressed by a **verb** and the form of the verb expressing it.

transitive verb. A **verb** that has a receiver of the action it expresses. In the active voice the receiver is a direct object. In the passive voice the receiver is the subject, which is passive to the verb action.

verb. A word or **phrase** that expresses an action or a condition. Verbs combine with noun elements (their subjects) to form clauses. Verbs occur as single words (run) and as verb phrases (has run, is running, will run, etc.). They have tense, forms that indicate present, past, and future time. Verbs must agree with their subjects in person and number. See **agreement.**

verbal. A **verb** form used as another **part of speech.** Types are *gerund* (a verbal noun ending in *ing*), *participle* (a verbal adjective ending in *ing* if a present participle or in *ed, d, t, en,* or *n* if a past participle), and *infinitive* (a verbal phrase formed by *to* plus the verb and functioning as noun, adjective, or adverb).

voice. A form of the **verb** indicating a relation between the **subject** and the action expressed by the verb. In the *active voice* the subject acts (*She mailed* the letter yesterday). In the *passive voice* the subject is acted upon (The letter was mailed by her yesterday).

Glossary of Usage

Just as we choose our clothes carefully for different occasions, so we instinctively choose our language to fit different circumstances. We do not go to a banquet in tennis shoes and a tuxedo nor to a soccer match in a formal evening dress. Accordingly, we do not use slang in introducing the president of our university or in writing a letter of application. Nor do we use formal language when giving directions for picking up a pizza or showing someone how to change a tire. By adapting our level of language to the audience, the subject, and the situation, we illustrate the biblical ideal of "a word fitly spoken" (Proverbs 25:11).

On the pages that follow appear two lists of expressions that you should avoid in writing. They vary in seriousness, ranging from the **barbarisms,** which should be avoided in both writing and speaking, to the **colloquialisms,** which are passable in at least lighter conversation but problematic in writing. *Barbarism,* a term originating with the ancient Greeks, is used today for words and forms considered by educated writers and speakers to be incorrect or nonstandard. Such expressions are always wrong and should therefore be "unlearned" by those who already use them and never learned by those unfamiliar with the expressions. Undoubtedly, many of them you already avoid. They appear in color in the list that follows.

The term *colloquialism* refers to expressions that are of questionable value in writing. Some of them are regionally acceptable and still others are allowable in casual conversation, which generally requires less stringent standards of accuracy and precision than conscientious writing. In writing, colloquialisms are questionable because many readers, especially among the better educated, regard them as outright errors or at best imprecise expressions. Although you may not see anything wrong with some of them, they are best avoided in your writing. As Yogi Berra might say, "It is always right to be right."

according to Webster   Cite the specific dictionary. Write, "According to the *Merriam-Webster Collegiate Dictionary,* tenth edition, to plagiarize is 'to steal and pass off (the ideas or words of another) as one's own.'"

aggravate   Do not use *aggravate* ("to make worse") as a synonym for *irritate* ("to annoy") in such sentences as "The shrill barking of my neighbor's dog aggravates me." Rather, use the word in its proper context as in the sentence "The shortage of supplies *aggravated* the distress of the soldiers."

a half a   Expressions such as "Bring me a half a cup of coffee" are redundant. Only one *a* is necessary. Write either "*a half* cup" or "*half a* cup."

all the farther, all the faster   Do not use these phrases as substitutes for *as far as* or *as fast as* in sentences such as "A mile is *as far as* [not *all the farther*] I can run" and "A mile a minute is *as fast as* [not *all the faster*] the jalopy can go."

a lot   An informal expression meaning *many* or *a good deal of,* commonly misspelled *alot*. Do not confuse *a lot* with the word *allot*, "to distribute or assign."

alumni   This plural form of *alumnus* should not be used in place of the singular forms: *alumnus* (male), *alumna* (female—the plural of *alumna* is *alumnae). Alumni* may refer to a mixed group as well as to a male group.

and etc.   *Etc.* is an abbreviation for the Latin *et cetera* (*et,* "and" + *cetera,* "other things"). To use *and* before this abbreviation is redundant. Write simply *etc.* Do not use *etc.* as a catchall expression after a list beginning with an expression like *such as,* which already indicates that more is referred to than what is listed: "I avoid leafy vegetables *such as* lettuce, turnip greens, broccoli, spinach, etc." Instead write, "I avoid leafy vegetables *such as* lettuce, turnip greens, broccoli, and spinach."

anxious   Do not use *anxious* (adjective form of the noun *anxiety*) as a synonym for *eager* in such sentences as "I am anxious to try jogging after seeing how it helped my brother lose weight." Write instead, "I am *eager* to try jogging . . ."

anyone, everyone   Distinguish the pronouns *anyone* and *everyone* from the forms *any one* and *every one,* which refer to individual persons out of a group: "*Anyone* may participate"; "*Any one* of the club members may participate"; "*Every one* of the passengers was on time."

anyways, anywheres, nowheres, somewheres   Write *anyway, anywhere, nowhere, somewhere.*

appraise   Do not confuse the verbs *appraise* ("estimate the value of") and *apprise* ("inform"). Write and say, "I was sure to *apprise* my fiancée of the dollar amount at which her engagement ring was *appraised*."

apt, liable   Do not use *apt* ("suitable") or *liable* ("legally obligated" or "susceptible") as synonyms for *likely* in such expressions as "He is *likely* to lose the race if he does not train properly." The acceptable uses of *apt* and *liable* are illustrated in the following sentences: "His comment was well timed and *apt*"; "Careless record keeping makes one *liable* for investigation by the IRS."

as   Do not use *as* in place of *that* or *whether* in sentences such as "I am not so sure *that* [not *as*] I agree with you" and "I do not know *whether* [not *as*] I will have the courage to begin again." Do not use *as* ambiguously by employing it as a substitute for *since* or *while*. Write, "*Since* the team was playing badly, the crowd grew nervous"; "*While* the team was playing badly . . ."

as . . . if not . . . than   Do not omit the second *as* in such sentences as "He is as tall *as*, if not taller than, his older brother." It is also correct to write "He is as tall as his older brother, if not taller."

as to   A weak substitute for *about* or *of* in such sentences as "He informed me as to his plans." Write instead, "He informed me *about* his plans" or "*of* his plans."

at about   A mixed expression used in reference to the time of day. If you are referring to the exact time, use *at:* "We arrived *at* five o'clock." If you are referring to an approximate time, use *about:* "We arrived *about* five o'clock."

awful, awfully   Do not use these words as synonyms for *very* in such sentences as "I was awfully glad you came." Write instead, "I am *very* glad you came." Cf. *aweful,* "full of awe."

bad, badly   Use the adjective *bad* after intransitive linking verbs (verbs such as *is* or *feel* requiring a predicate adjective), as in the sentence "I feel *bad* about Mrs. Brown's cat's death." Use the adverb *badly* after transitive verbs (such as *do),* as "He did his drawing *badly* on the final project."

behalf   Distinguish *"in behalf"* (in support of) from *"on behalf"* (as an agent for) in such a sentence as "He spoke *on behalf* of the absent chairman *in behalf* of the proposed zoning change."

being as   Do not use *being as* in place of *since* in sentences such as "*Since* we had already discussed the plan, he did not send me a memorandum."

beside, besides   *Beside* ("by the side of") is interchangeable with the preposition *besides* ("in addition to") *only* when the prepositions are to mean "except." Write, "William has interests *besides* his job and family" not "beside his job and family."

best, worst   Do not use the superlative forms *(best, worst)* when comparing only two persons or things; instead use the comparative forms *(better, worse):* "He is the *better* player of the two," "Sally is the *taller* of the twins," and "This leg hurts *worse*." The superlative forms are reserved for comparing three or more items: "Sam is the *best* player on the basketball team," and "This is the *worst* winter in years."

better   Do not use *better* without *had* in such sentences as "You *had better* start now if you wish to finish on time."

between   Do not use *between* (referring to two items) in place of *among* (referring to three or more items) in such sentences as "Distribute the cookies evenly between the four children." Instead write, "Distribute the cookies evenly *among* the four children." If specific individuals are named, *between* is acceptable no matter what the number: "Distribute the cookies evenly *between* Mary, Sally, and Joan."

between you and I   A common error in pronoun case. Use the objective-case pronouns *(me, us, him, her, them, whom)* as objects of prepositions and verbs: "*Between* you and *me*, I think Charles is the better candidate of the two"; "He helped Bill and *me*." A compound object does not affect the pronoun's objective case form.

blatant   Do not confuse the word *blatant* ("offensively noisy") with *flagrant* ("conspicuously bad") in such sentences as "His membership was canceled because of his *flagrant* violation of club rules."

bust, busted, bursted   Nonstandard forms of *burst,* whose principal parts are *burst, burst, burst:* "Today I *burst* a balloon"; "Yesterday I *burst* a balloon"; and "I have *burst* many balloons in my lifetime."

but what   Do not use *but what* for *that* in negative expressions such as "He had no doubt *that* the kindergarten mountain-climbing club would reach the summit."

can, may   Use *can* to denote ability: "*Can* you carry this bag for me?" Use *may* to denote permission: "You *may* borrow the car for your date tonight."

cannot help but   A mixed expression. Write *cannot help* with a gerund, as in the sentence "I *cannot help* wondering whether he is sincere"; write *cannot but* with an infinitive (minus *to*) in such sentences as "I *cannot but* wonder whether he is sincere."

can't hardly   A mixed expression or a kind of double negative. Write and say *can hardly.*

center around   An illogical expression. Write *center in, center on,* or *center upon.*

come   Do not confuse the first and third principal parts of *come* (*come, come*—"He *comes* to visit me every day"; "He has *come* to visit me every day for a month") with the second principal part (*came*—"I *came* to see you yesterday, but you were gone").

comprise, constitute, include   Do not use these words as synonyms. *Comprise* means "to be made up of," *constitute* means "to make up," and *include* means "to contain": "A county *comprises* townships, *includes* towns, and *constitutes* an electoral administrative district."

considerable, reasonable   Use the adverbs *considerably* and *reasonably,* not the adjectives *considerable* and *reasonable,* to modify verbs or adverbs: "He tried *considerably* harder this semester"; "He improved *considerably* with the new diet"; "He performed *reasonably* well after surgery"; "He has a *reasonably* happy home life."

continual, continuous   Distinguish between *continual* ("recurring at intervals") and *continuous* ("continuing without interruption"): "The *continual* breaking of the waves fascinated those on the shore"; "The *continuous* drifting of the ship with the current was soon remedied by the captain."

convince, persuade   Do not use these verbs interchangeably. *Convince* means "to compel assent or belief by argument"; *persuade* means "to influence to a decision or course of action." Write, "I *persuaded* him to go fishing after I had *convinced* him of the value of a vacation."

correspond with   When one uses *correspond* to mean "bear a resemblance," it should be followed by the preposition *to* as in the sentence "This scene *corresponds to* the description in the tour booklet." The phrase *correspond with* means "to communicate by an exchange of letters."

data, strata, criteria, phenomena   Do not confuse these plurals with their singular forms: *datum, stratum, criterion,* and *phenomenon.* In the United States *data* is becoming increasingly accepted, though, as a singular noun.

different than   In formal American usage, *different* must be followed by a prepositional phrase beginning with *from*, not the conjunction *than* (except when *than* is followed by a clause). Do not write, "The result was different than the intention," but rather write, "The result was *different from* the intention."

differ from, differ with   These phrases are not interchangeable. *Differ from* means "to be dissimilar to," and *differ with* means "to disagree with."

disinterested   Distinguish between *disinterested* ("impartial") and *uninterested* ("without curiosity, care, concern"). A judge should be *disinterested* but not *uninterested.*

done   Do not use *done* (the past participle of *do*) for *did* (past tense form) as in "I done the work yesterday"; do not use *done* for emphasis as in "I done told you all I know." Write (and say), "I *did* the work yesterday" and "I *already* told you all I know."

don't   Correctly used, *don't* is a contraction of *do not* ("I *don't* think I will go skiing today"), but it is not a contraction for *does not* ("It don't seem fair"). Most academic and all formal writing avoids the use of contractions altogether.

due to   Do not use *due to* for *because of* in such sentences as "The picnic was postponed *because of* the weather." The phrase is properly used when *due* is a predicate adjective and *to* is a preposition: "The postponement was *due to* the weather."

each and every   A redundant expression intended for emphasis. It is a poor substitute for other types of emphasis in writing. (Another similarly redundant expression is "lead, guide, and direct.") Write *each* or *every,* not both.

each of . . . are . . . their   Pronouns such as *each, everybody, somebody, anyone, everyone, either,* and *neither* are singular. Use verbs and pronouns that match the singular nature of these pronouns: "*Each* of the boys *has* a shirt with the logo of his soccer team" and "*Everyone* remembered to bring *his* books."

either . . . or . . . are   When *either . . . or* or *neither . . . nor* joins singular subjects, the verb must be singular: "*Either* paint *or* wallpaper *is* needed." If the sentence has multiple subjects, one of which is singular and one plural, the one nearer to the verb determines whether the verb is singular or plural: "*Either* rugs *or* carpet *is* needed"; "*Either* carpet *or* rugs *are* needed."

enthuse, enthused   Write "show *enthusiasm*" or "be *enthusiastic*."

equally as . . . as   A mixed expression. Make the comparison using the pattern *equally . . . with* ("Training is *equally* important *with* natural ability") or the pattern *as . . . as* ("Training is *as* important *as* natural ability"). Or you can write, "Training and natural ability are equally important."

ever so often   Do not use *ever so often* for *every so often* in sentences such as "He visits me only *every so often.*"

expect   Do not use *expect* as a synonym for *presume* or *suppose* in such sentences as "I *presume* [not *expect*] he gave his usual excuse." The error derives from the confusion of *'spect,* a contraction which orally stands for both *suspect* and *expect.*

farther, further   Use *farther* to express literal distance ("*farther* from Milwaukee") and *further* to express figurative distance or extent ("*further* from the truth").

feel   Do not use *feel* loosely for *think* or *believe* in such sentences as "I *feel* that mercy to the criminal is cruelty to society." Write rather, "I *believe* that mercy to the criminal is cruelty to society." Restrict *feel* to nonrational perceptions or impressions: "I *feel* lonely today"; "I *feel* the mist of the sea upon my face as I walk along the shore."

fewer, less   Both words refer to measurement. *Fewer,* however, refers to number (the countable)—"Students generally spend *fewer* hours on courses they dislike"; *less* refers to amount (mass or bulk), degree, and value— "Students generally spend *less* time on courses they dislike."

flout   Do not confuse the verb *flout* ("scoff at") with *flaunt* ("show off") in such sentences as "She *flaunts* her superiority in Greek among the male ministerial students."

former, latter   When referring to one of two persons or things mentioned previously, use *former* to designate the first item and *latter* to designate the second item.

fun   Do not use *fun* as an adjective in such sentences as "We had an enjoyable [not *a fun*] time at the beach."

good, well   Use the adjective *good* after intransitive linking verbs as in the sentence "The car looks *good.*" Use the adverb *well* after transitive verbs or as a modifier of other adverbs, as in the sentences "He played the game *well*" and "It is a *well-paying* job." The adjectival use of *well* is acceptable only with reference to health: "The patient is *well* today."

got, have got   Do not use as present-tense substitutes for *have* (possess). "At present I *have* [not *got* or *have got*] only three dollars in my billfold." Use them only as past and present perfect tenses of *get* (receive): "Yesterday, I *got* three dollars for mowing the lawn"; "So far this week, I *have got* only three dollars for my work." (American usage prefers *have gotten* over *have got* for the meaning "acquired.")

had of   Omit the *of* in such sentences as "If we had of only known about the sale, we would have come here sooner."

had ought   Drop the *had* in sentences such as "You had ought to have learned that by now" and "You hadn't ought to have gone." Write, "You *ought* to have learned that by now" and "You *ought* not to have gone."

hanged   Distinguish between the principal parts of *hang* ("to fasten or suspend"—*hang, hung, hung*) and *hang* ("to execute by hanging"—*hang, hanged, hanged*). "I *hung* the picture on the wall in the bedroom"; "The posse found the rustler during the night, and he was *hanged* in the morning."

healthy, healthful   Distinguish *healthy,* "having health," from *healthful,* "giving health."

how, how that   Do not use *how* or *how that* as substitutes for *that* or *how much* in sentences such as "She realized how that he loved her" or "She realized how he loved her." Write instead, "She realized *that* he loved her" or "She realized *how much* he loved her."

if In formal writing do not use *if* as a substitute for *whether* or *that* in sentences such as "We do not know *whether* [not *if*] she will come" or "It is doubtful *that* [not *if*] she will come."

imminent, immanent, eminent, emanate Do not use these three adjectives and one verb as synonyms. Though often confused because of the similarity of their pronunciations, they are quite distinct in meaning: *imminent* ("impending or threatening")—"Christ's return to earth is *imminent*"; *immanent* ("existing within; inherent")—"Her true beauty is *immanent*"; *eminent* ("standing out; prominent")—"George is an *eminent* member of our community"; and *emanate* ("come out or give out, as from or by a source")—"A blinding light *emanated* from the warehouse ceiling."

imply, infer Both words relate to passing and receiving meanings indirectly. The writer or speaker *implies* ("suggests" or "indicates indirectly"), but the reader or listener *infers* ("draws a conclusion"). An *implication* is a suggestion or hint; an *inference* is a conclusion.

individual, people Not to be loosely used for *person* and *persons*. Use *individual* as a designation of a person only when emphasizing the person's individuality: "To follow Christ in this world, one must be willing to be an *individual*." Use *people* to designate a group of significant size and homogeneity (such as a nationality, a constituency, or an audience): "The evangelist addressed the *people* with great fervency."

inferior than A mixed expression. When expressing comparison, *inferior* should be followed by the preposition *to,* not the conjunction *than.* Write either "*inferior to* him" or "less capable *than* he."

ingenious, ingenuous Do not confuse *ingenious* ("clever") with *ingenuous* ("innocent, without guile").

in, into Distinguish *in,* "location within," from *into,* "motion or direction to a point within." Write, "The ball is *in* the water" or "The ball fell *into* the water."

inside of, outside of Do not use these phrases as replacements for *within* and *except* in such sentences as "Dinner will be ready inside of half an hour," or "She has no ambitions outside of being a good wife and mother." Write instead, "Dinner will be ready *within* a half hour" and "She has no ambitions *except* being a good wife and mother."

instance, incident, incidence These words are not synonymous or interchangeable. *Instance* ("case or example") should not be used for *incident* ("a happening or a narrative scene or situation"): "Carol's test scores are an *instance* of the invalid measurement of intelligence by standardized tests"; "Sam was embarrassed by the whole *incident.*" Do not use *incidents* (plural of *incident,* above) for *incidence* ("rate of occurrence; prevalence"): "The highway patrol keeps a tally of the *incidence* of accidents involving drunk drivers."

in the worst way   A wordy, vague phrase when used to express the concept *very much, exceedingly,* etc. Write simply, "He wanted to win *very much.*"

irregardless   A nonword and double negative. The prefix *ir- (in-)* and the suffix *-less* both mean "without." Use the correct word: *regardless.*

is, was   Use the subjunctive *be* and *were* (not *is* or *was*) to express volition, resolution, recommendation, command, or request; to express conditions contrary to fact; and in certain idiomatic expressions. Write, "I recommend that he *be* admitted into the society today"; "If I *were* [not *was*] you, I would come early"; "I wish he *were* [not *was*] coming." The present-tense subjunctive form of other verbs is the *s*-less third-person singular: "I recommend that he *see* [not *sees*] the doctor at once."

is when, is where   After the linking verb *is*, formal usage requires an adjective or a noun element, rather than an adverbial clause, to define the subject. Do not write, "Satire is when a writer ridicules something in order to correct it" or "Sarcasm is where a person ridicules someone by pretended praise." This problem often occurs because of the writer's imprecision. Write instead, "Satire is corrective ridicule in literature" and "Sarcasm is mock praise."

it is me   Formal written usage requires that pronouns used as predicate nouns take the subjective case *(I, he, she, we, they, who)*. Write, "It is *I.*"

it says   Do not use the pronoun *it* without an antecedent in such expressions as "In the Bible *it* says . . ." Write instead, "The Bible says . . ."

Jone's, Jones'es   Do not insert the apostrophe of possession into the non-possessive base of the word. Add the apostrophe and (except in instances of plural nouns ending in *-s*) an *-s* to the word as it would appear were it not indicating possession. The book of Bill Jones is Bill *Jones's* book; the house of the Joneses is the *Joneses'* house; clothes for children are *children's* clothes; clothes for boys are *boys'* clothes; the purse of a certain lady is that *lady's* purse; hats for ladies are *ladies'* hats. Neither personal pronouns nor the relative/interrogative pronoun *who* uses the apostrophe to form the possessive case *(his, hers, its, theirs, yours, whose)*. Moreover, the apostrophe and *-s* are not used to form plurals except for letters, figures, and words for words' sake: "You added too many *a*'s, *3*'s, and *and*'s." Make proper nouns plural by adding *-s* or *-es* without making any other spelling changes: two *Bobs,* two *Nancys,* the *Browns,* the *Kennedys,* and the *Davises.* Never add an apostrophe to make the plural of a proper noun. Finally, never use a singular as if it were a plural: Todd and Sally Jones (and their children) are not the Jones but the *Joneses.*

just because . . . does not mean   A mixed expression. Do not make the adverb clause ("Just because a man is a peasant") the subject of a verb ("does not mean"). Write either "The fact that a man is a peasant does not mean he is a tramp" or "Being a peasant is not the same thing as being a tramp."

kind of a(n)   In speech omit the *a(n)* of this expression. In writing avoid the use of *kind of* and *sort of* as adverbs meaning "rather" in such sentences as "That test was kind of hard." Write instead, "That test was *rather* hard."

lay, set, raise   These are transitive verbs (verbs that take direct objects, i.e., receivers of action), and their principal parts *(lay, laid, laid; set, set, set; raise, raised, raised)* are often confused with the intransitive verbs (verbs that do not take direct objects but show states of being) *lie, sit, rise* and their principal parts *(lie, lay, lain; sit, sat, sat; rise, rose, risen)*. Compare the following sentences: "I *lay* down for a nap yesterday"; "I *laid* the book on the table yesterday"; "He *sat* in the same seat yesterday"; "He *set* the planter on the windowsill"; "The prophets foretold that the Christ would *rise* from the dead"; "Tom *raises* corn in his garden."

leave   Do not use *leave* ("depart from") in place of *let* ("permit"). Write, "*Let* [not *Leave*] him do as he wishes." An exception is the idiomatic expression "*Leave* him alone."

let's us   A redundant expression. *Let's* is the contraction of *let us; us* thus repeats the *'s*. Write, "*Let us* go to the game" or "*Let's* go . . ."

like   Do not use the preposition *like* for the conjunction *as* or *as if* in sentences such as "He did it just *as* [not *like*] he intended to do it." Do not use *like* where *such as* is more precise. "A dramatist *such as* Shakespeare knows an audience's range of response." Avoid the archaic expressions *like as* and *in like manner* in general writing.

literally   Do not use *literally* ("in a manner that accords precisely with the words") so as to mean "figuratively." Do not write, "Her heart literally turned somersaults," for it did not unless she is a physical phenomenon worthy of national attention. Instead write, "Her heart seemed to turn somersaults" or "Her heart turned somersaults."

loan   Do not use the noun *loan* in place of the verb *lend*. Write, "His father would not *lend* [not *loan*] him the money."

mad, upset   Do not use *mad* ("insane") as a synonym for *angry* in such statements as "His unfairness made me *angry*." Neither should you use *upset* ("turned over") as a synonym for *angry* or *exasperated* in such sentences as

"He was *angry* with me for walking on his wet cement." (Use the preposition *with* when anger is directed toward people; use the preposition *at* when it is directed toward things. "She was angry *with* me for jilting her"; "She was angry *at* her typewriter for misspelling so many words.")

me, him   Use possessive case (*my, his, their, Bob's, women's,* etc.) before a gerund (*-ing* verbal noun): "Do you mind *my* asking why?"; "I disapprove of *his* leaving early."

might could, used to could   Do not use *could* as a substitute for *be able to* in sentences such as "I *might be able to* [not *might could*] come after supper"; "I *used to be able to* [not *used to could*] work an eighteen-hour day."

mighty, pretty, plenty   In writing do not use *mighty, pretty,* and *plenty* as adverbs meaning "very" in such sentences as "He was *very* tired after running a mile through a swamp."

more known   The adverbs of comparison *more, less, most, least* should be followed by an *-ly* adverb when modifying past participles. Write, "Bill was more widely known than Tom." However, *better* and *best* can precede a past participle directly without awkwardness. "He was better known than Tom."

most   Do not use *most* instead of *almost* in such expressions as "*almost* everybody."

most favorite   A redundant expression since both *most* and *favorite* are superlative expressions. Write just *favorite.*

most perfect, very parallel   Redundant, illogical expressions. Write simply *perfect* or *parallel,* since these are absolute qualities and do not possess degree. *Almost perfect* and *very nearly parallel* may be used to express superlative degree.

myself   The *-self* pronouns (*myself, yourself,* etc.) should be used either reflexively ("I hurt *myself* ") or intensively ("I did it *myself* "), not as supposedly polite substitutes for the personal pronouns *(me, you).* Write, "You may give your donation to either the pastor or *me* [not *myself*]"; "Between you and *me,* the offerings need to be larger."

nice   An overused and vague word expressing approval. Rather than "We had a nice time," write, "We had an *enjoyable* time."

nohow   Do not use for *anyhow, anyway, after all,* in such sentences as "He said he couldn't come *anyway.*"

not . . . no, not . . . nothing   A double negative frequently misused in such sentences as "We don't want no favors" and "We don't want nothing from strangers." Write instead, "We do *not* want *any* favors" and "We do *not* want *anything* from strangers."

not, only   Place *not* and adverbs like *only* immediately before the elements they modify. Write, "*Not* all are able to contribute" or "*Not* everybody is able to contribute" rather than "All are not able to contribute" or "Everybody is not able to contribute" (both of which imply that *no one* could contribute). Write, "He said *only* three words" rather than "He only said three words" (which implies he should have communicated in some other way). In speech, oral emphasis on the word modified often prevents ambiguity.

of   Do not use the preposition *of* for the auxiliary verb *have* in verb phrases such as *could have* or *would have. Of* is a misspelling of the con-tracted *have: 've.*

off of, out of   Omit the redundant *of* in such sentences as "Keep off of the grass" and "He jumped out of the window." Write instead, "Keep *off* the grass" and "He jumped *out* the window."

Old English of the KJV   A poorly informed description. Old English (also called Anglo-Saxon) is the term used for the English language from the fifth century to the beginning of the twelfth. It is not decipherable except by someone trained in that language. The King James Version (KJV) of the Bible was published in 1611, a date that places it in the period called early modern English. The language of the KJV is the language of Shakespeare's day (he died in 1616).

on   Do not use *on* in place of *for* in sentences such as "We planned on three guests"; "We waited on the mail all day"; "The defendant blamed the crime on his upbringing." *Wait on* means "serve," "give attendance upon," as a valet, waiter, or waitress. Write instead, "We planned *for* three guests"; "We waited *for* the mail all day." "The defendant blamed his upbringing *for* the crime." The object of *blamed* is the cause of the action incurring blame (i.e., the crime) rather than the action itself.

one of . . . who is   In the construction *one of . . . who,* the pronoun *who* refers not to *one* but to the object of the preposition *of.* Therefore, the num-ber of the verb following *who* and the number of the pronouns and pronom-inal adjectives referring to *who* is usually plural rather than singular: "Bill is *one of* the students *who are* always trying *their* hardest." There are three use-ful tests to help determine the correct construction: (1) Start the sentence with *of* and place the main clause ("Bill is one") at the end of the sentence. Your ear will help you hear the correct verb form. (2) Sort out the logic of the sentence: is Bill being excluded from the students or included within the stu-dents? (3) Look for the word *only:* if *only* appears in this pattern, then the verb in question will be singular; if *only* does not appear, the verb will be plu-ral: cf. "Bill is *the only one of* the students *who is* always trying hard."

ourself, themself, theirself, theirselves, hisself   Use the correct forms: *ourselves, themselves, himself.*

plus   Do not use *plus* as a substitute for *and* or *besides* to join main clauses or to begin a sentence: "Labor unions want a four-day work week; plus they want a six-hour day." Write instead, "Labor unions want a four-day work week *and* a six-hour day" or "Labor unions want a four-day work week. *Besides*, they want a six-hour day."

practical, practically   Distinguish *practical* ("useful, nontheoretical") from *practicable* ("feasible, capable of being done") in such sentences as "We bought a *practical* economy car" and "He devised a *practicable* plan of escape." Distinguish *practically* ("in a way that is practical") from *virtually* in such expressions as "*virtually* extinct" and from *almost* in such expressions as "*almost* finished."

proven   Adjectival form of *prove*. Do not use *proven* in place of the second or third principal part, *proved:* "It was *proved* [not *proven*] that the keys were mine." Use *proven* only as an adjective: "a *proven* recipe."

proving that, as seen when   These phrases create dangling constructions when one moves from example to generalization or from generalization to example: "She finally married Jim, proving that truth is stranger than fiction"; "Truth is stranger than fiction, as seen when she finally married Jim." Modifying clauses and phrases "dangle" when their implied or logical subject is not the same as the grammatical subject of the sentence. Write rather, "Her marrying Jim after all the delay proves that truth is stranger than fiction" or "That truth is stranger than fiction became obvious when she finally married Jim." Better yet, "She finally married Jim. Indeed, truth is stranger than fiction." The link between the generalization does not necessarily need to be stated.

real   Use the adjective *real* to modify nouns and pronouns ("This jewel is a *real* diamond"). Use the adverb *really* to modify adjectives or other adverbs ("He was *really* happy"; "The pizza smells *really* good").

reason is because   An expression mixing two ways of presenting explanatory material: "The reason I was late was because I had a long-distance telephone call." Write either, "The *reason* I was late was *that* I had a long-distance telephone call," or "*Because* I had a long-distance telephone call, I was late," or "I was late *because* I had a long-distance telephone call."

reason why   A redundant expression. Instead of "the reason why I called," write either, "the *reason that* I called" or "the *reason* I called."

respectfully   Do not confuse *respectfully* ("in a respectful manner") with *respectively* ("in the order given") in such sentences as "He spoke *respectfully* to his elders" and "Bill and Jim were the pilot and copilot *respectively.*"

Reverend   An adjective expressing honor (like *Honorable*). Do not use as a noun. Rather than "the Reverend Johnson," "Reverend Johnson,"

"Reverend Bill," or "the Reverend," write "the *Reverend* Mr. Johnson" or "the *Reverend* William Johnson."

says, etc. Do not shift tenses in reporting an incident. Write (or say), "When the fish began to nibble at the lure, my friend *said* [not *says*] to me, 'You've got a bite!' " Be consistent with tenses rather than shifting arbitrarily from past to present to past. It is usually better to adopt the present tense as the norm when you are summarizing or paraphrasing what someone has written: "Next the apostle Paul *reminds* Timothy . . ."; "Edward Taylor *declares* in 'The Preface' . . ."

seldom ever, seldom or ever Do not use these phrases in such sentences as "I seldom ever see him" or "I seldom or ever see him." Use the proper expressions *seldom if ever* or *seldom or never:* "I *seldom if ever* see him"; "I *seldom or never* see him."

some Do not use *some* instead of the adverb *somewhat* in sentences such as "He feels *somewhat* [not *some*] better this morning."

so, such, too Do not use *so, such,* or *too* without a completing clause or phrase: "The reception was so disappointing"; "The reception was such a disappointment"; and "The reception was too disappointing for words." Write, "The reception was *so* disappointing *that* I left early." Do not omit *that* after *such* when *such* is followed by a result clause: "His appearance was *such that* they refused him entrance."

suppose, use, ask The second and third principal parts of these verbs end in *-d,* a sound which is sometimes "swallowed" in speech. Do not forget to write the *-d* in such sentences as "I *used* to do what I was *asked* to do, not necessarily what I was *supposed* to do."

sure Use the adverb *surely* instead of the adjective *sure* to modify verbs: "The food *surely* looks good"; "He was *surely* relieved to learn he had passed the course."

that Avoid the redundant *that* in sentences such as "So you can see *that* if Wolsey had been elected Pope by Charles *that* Luther's doctrine at the university might have been squelched." Replace the second *that* with a comma: "So you can see *that* if Wolsey had been elected Pope by Charles, Luther's doctrine at the university might have been squelched."

thee, thou, thy, thine Either use archaic pronouns (with the appropriate verb forms) consistently in public prayer or use modern pronouns exclusively. Avoid mixing archaic and modern references to the Deity: "We believe You [modern] will send a revival to Thy [archaic] people if they obey Thee [archaic]." Write or say either, "We believe *Thou wilt* send a revival to *Thy* people if they obey *Thee*" (all archaic pronouns), or "We believe *You* will send a revival to *Your* people if they obey *You*" (all modern pronouns).

Be aware that the use of *thou* as a grammatical subject requires an *-est* verb ending (e.g., "Thou knowest").

them   Do not use the pronoun *them* for the adjective *those* in a phrase like "them culprits." Write or say instead "*those* culprits."

the most . . . of any   A mixed expression. Write either, "He has the *most* grace of *all* the losers in the election" or "He has *more* grace than *any other* loser in the election." Do not omit *other* in the second of these constructions if the person or thing is being compared to other members of its own group.

these kinds, those kinds   Do not use the plural forms *these* and *those* to modify singular nouns like *kind* or *sort*. Write "*this* [or *that*] *kind* of story," "*these* [or *those*] *kinds* of stories." Historically, *kind* (like *fold*) is both singular and plural.

thusly   A nonstandard adverb. *Thus* is already an adverb without the suffix *-ly*. Use the correct word: *thus*.

too   Do not use *too* as a substitute for *very* in sentences such as "Obviously you did not try *very* hard to remember."

try and, be sure and   Do not use *and* in place of the infinitive *to* after the verb *try* or the verb phrase *be sure*. Write, "Try *to* [not *and*] do better next time"; "Be sure *to* [not *and*] pay attention next time."

type   Do not omit the *of* in such phrases as "that *type of* product."

us   Use pronouns according to their proper cases. Do not use the objective case for the subjective case in such sentences as "Us boys are not afraid." or "Me and Jill went shopping." Write or say instead, "*We* boys are not afraid"; "Jill and *I* went shopping."

very, rather, too   Use these words as intensives cautiously. Write, "The patient was *very much* improved [not *very* improved]"; "He was *rather seriously* inconvenienced [not *rather* inconvenienced] by your coming late"; "He was *too badly* weakened [not *too* weakened] by the disease to sit up"; "a *very highly* respected [not *very* respected] leader"; "a *rather well-*prepared [not *rather* prepared] class"; "a *too strictly* disciplined [not *too* disciplined] behavior."

very unique   An illogical construction. Since *unique* means the only one of its kind, it is not a synonym for *strange* or *unusual,* nor can it be modified by words like *very.* Instead write *very unusual, incredibly strange, almost unique,* or *nearly unique.*

want in, etc.   Do not omit the infinitive *to come* (or *to get*) in such expressions as *want to come* (or *to get*) *in, into, out, down, up, off, through.* Instead of "She wanted in the club very much" or "I want off this bus right now," write, "She *wanted to get into* the club very much" and "I *want to get off* this bus right now."

want that   Drop the *that* in such sentences as "I want that you be more careful next time." Write, "I *want* you to be more careful next time." The object of *want* should be an infinitive phrase (with a subject) rather than a noun clause beginning with *that*.

ways   Do not use *ways* (which refers to various methods of doing something) for *way* (which refers to a direction or distance) in such sentences as "It is a long *way* to Alabama" or "We are still a long *way* from perfection."

we, us, our, ours   When referring to yourself alone, always use the singular pronouns *I, me, my, mine.* Plural personal reference *(we, us, our, ours)* when used by a single person is reserved exclusively for royalty or for persons representing a large group (as in a minister leading a congregation in prayer). Rather than "We are glad to be with you tonight," write and say, "*I* am glad to be with you tonight."

where   Do not use *where* as a substitute for *in which* or *that* in sentences such as "I like the incident where she realizes he loves her" or "I saw in the paper where the game had been postponed." Write instead, "I like the incident *in which* she realizes he loves her" or "I saw in the paper *that* the game had been postponed."

whereas   The subordinating conjunction *whereas* may not be used as though it were the conjunctive adverb *however* to begin an independent clause: "He prefers ice cream for dessert. Whereas I prefer yogurt"; "He prefers ice cream for dessert; whereas I prefer yogurt." The result of the above constructions is either a sentence fragment or a semicolon fragment. Write instead, "He prefers ice cream for dessert, *whereas* I prefer yogurt."

where . . . at?   A problem usually occurring in contracted expressions such as "Where's he at?" The problem is partially a rhythmic one in speech caused by the contraction. "Where is he?" is the correct expression.

which   Use the relative pronoun *which* to refer to nonpersonal antecedents and to introduce nonessential adjective clauses: "The package came by the most reliable delivery service, *which* is UPS." When the antecedent is personal, use *who, whom,* or *that:* "The package came with my best friend, *who* is Terry." When the antecedent is nonpersonal, use *that* if the adjective clause is essential ("The package came by the delivery service *that* is most reliable: UPS.") and *which* if the clause is nonessential (see first sentence above).

which, this, that   Avoid the vague reference of these pronouns in such sentences as "He always tries hard, and this is why he usually succeeds"; "He tried hard, and that is why he succeeded"; "He tried hard, which is why he succeeded." Write instead, "*Since* he always tries hard, he usually succeeds"; "By trying hard, he succeeded"; "His trying hard caused him to succeed."

while   Avoid ambiguity by distinguishing *while,* which expresses the idea of simultaneous actions, from *whereas* and *although,* which express contrast and concession: "*While* George was arriving from New York, Carol was leaving Los Angeles"; "*Although* I disagree with you, I want to be your friend."

without   Do not use the preposition *without* as a substitute for the conjunction *unless* in sentences such as "I cannot fix your car by five o'clock *unless* [not *without*] you help me."

would   Avoid using *would* as compensation for insecurity in such sentences as "The albatross in *The Rime of the Ancient Mariner* would be a symbol of Christ." Be sure of your position, and then assert it by writing, "The albatross in *The Rime of the Ancient Mariner* is a symbol of Christ."

would have   Do not use for *had* in such sentences as "If you *had* [not *would have*] come in time, you might have been chosen."

you, they   Do not use *you* or *they* as indefinite pronouns in such sentences as "In order to succeed in some fields, you must be willing to multiply your failures" or "In England they drive on the left side of the road." Write instead, "In order to succeed in some fields, *a person* must be willing to multiply his failures" and "In England *the people* drive on the left side of the road."

interjections, 86, 89, 244, 265
    defined, 244, 265
internal punctuation, 85–98, 200, 222
    brackets, 95, 222
    colon, 93–94
    comma, 85–92
    dash, 94
    discretionary, 95–96
    italics, 96–98
    parentheses, 85, 94–95, 200
    quotation marks, 96–98
    semicolon, 92–93
Internet. *See* online and electronic sources, Internet
interrogative pronouns. *See* pronouns, interrogative
intervening modifiers. *See* agreement, of subject and verb, intervening modifiers
in-text citation. *See* citation, in-text
intransitive verbs. *See* verb use, intransitive verbs
introductory paragraph. *See* paragraphs, introductory
inverted order. *See* agreement, of subject and verb, inverted order
irregular verbs. *See* verb use, principal parts, irregular verbs
italics, 96–98, 153, 155, 222

J
journals, 17

L
layout (of paper), 153–56
    See also format; standard form
length (of paper), 9–10
library, use of, 17–18
lie, lay, 146–47
linking verbs. *See* agreement, of subject and verb, linking verbs; pronoun use, pronoun case, linking verbs; verb use, linking verbs
literary present tense, 129
logic. *See* arrangement of ideas, logical order; sentence logic

M
major heading. *See* outline, headings
manuscript, 19, 155
    neatness of, 155
margins. *See* format, margins
may, use of. *See* verb use, modal auxiliaries, *may* and *can*
mechanics, 75–101
    abbreviations and numbers, 77–79, 80, 95, 97
    apostrophes, 79–81
    capitals, 75–76
    end punctuation, 82–85
    hyphens, 76–77
    internal punctuation, 85–98
    punctuation of compound sentences, 99–100
    sentence fragments, 100–101
    See also entries under specific marks of punctuation; plurals; possessives
metadiscourse, 41
misconduct in the use of sources. *See* plagiarism
misplaced and dangling modifiers, 119–23, 152, 264, 266, 270
    acceptable dangling elements, 123
    awkward splitting of other grammatical unities, 121
    defined, 264, 266
    introductory dangling elements, 121–22
    only and similar words, 119
    other confusing misplacements, 120
    split infinitives, 120, 270
        defined, 270
    squinting modifiers, 119–20

(continued ↓)